Demetrius C. Boulger

England and Russia in Central Asia

Demetrius C. Boulger

England and Russia in Central Asia

ISBN/EAN: 9783743407251

Manufactured in Europe, USA, Canada, Australia, Japa

Cover: Foto ©ninafisch / pixelio.de

Manufactured and distributed by brebook publishing software (www.brebook.com)

Demetrius C. Boulger

England and Russia in Central Asia

ENGLAND AND RUSSIA

IN

CENTRAL ASIA.

ENGLAND AND RUSSIA

IN

CENTRAL ASIA.

BY

DEMETRIUS CHARLES BOULGER,
MEMBER OF THE ROYAL ASIATIC SOCIETY,
AUTHOR OF "THE LIFE OF YAKOOB BEG OF KASHGAR."

WITH TWO MAPS AND APPENDICES.
(One Map being the latest Russian Official Map of Central Asia.)

VOL. I.

LONDON:
W. H. ALLEN & CO., 13 WATERLOO PLACE,
PALL MALL, S.W.
PUBLISHERS TO THE INDIA OFFICE.

1879.

(All rights reserved.)

LONDON:
PRINTED BY W. H. ALLEN AND CO., 13 WATERLOO PLACE, PALL MALL, S.W.

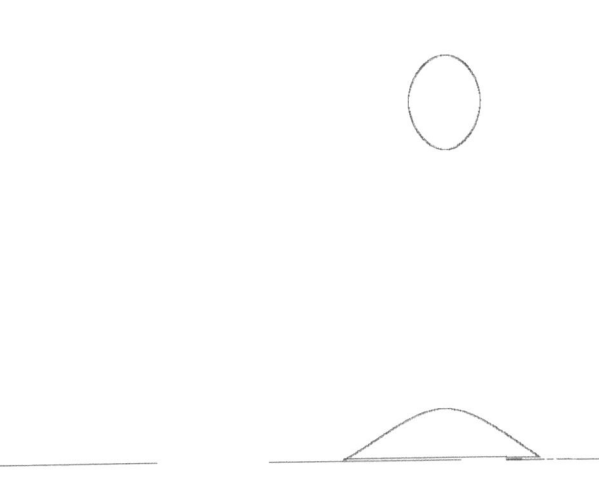

THE FOLLOWING PAGES ARE INSCRIBED

BY PERMISSION

TO

MAJOR-GENERAL
SIR HENRY CRESWICKE RAWLINSON, K.C.B.,
ETC., ETC.

IN TOKEN OF

THE AUTHOR'S SINCERE ADMIRATION

FOR

THE FAR-SEEING AND STATESMAN-LIKE POLICY HE HAS

CONSISTENTLY ADVOCATED IN REGARD TO

CENTRAL ASIA, AND THE CONFLICT OF ENGLISH AND RUSSIAN

INTERESTS THEREIN.

PREFACE.

The following pages were commenced at a time when it appeared as if the final stage of the rivalry between England and Russia in Central Asia had been reached. War between the two countries was held to be imminent. A Russian officer had come as ambassador to Cabul, in contravention of distinct pledges to the effect that no Russian ambassador should be sent. An English representative had been refused permission to proceed to Cabul. The Ameer was employed in fêting his Russian friends, and in dictating discourteous and semi-hostile letters to his English. The preparations for war were being pressed on with all possible speed in the Punjab and Bengal. There were bustle and activity perceptible on all sides, and rumour magnified the scope of the war and the intentions of the Home and Indian Governments.

They are brought to a close when a widely different condition of affairs obtains. We have concluded a successful campaign. Our foe has expiated his folly with his life. The Russian Embassy, which was the original cause of the war, has been withdrawn. The credit of Russia has been lowered. The reputation of England has been exalted. Fortune has been on our side in every respect, and the machinations of our foes, secret and proclaimed, have been thwarted. The mission of General Stoletoff has been proved to be what the more skilled observers of Central Asian affairs at the time pronounced it to be, "a huge mistake." Yet none the less for this happy conclusion of an involved and dangerous business is it incontestable that the rivalry of England and Russia is as keen as ever, possibly more keen, because of the failure of the Russian scheme. For that reason the following pages, which claim to be based upon permanent truths, relate to as active a force as if they had been produced last November, when the want for information on the subject first made itself perceptible. The conclusions at which the writer has arrived are expressed without hesitation, and while they point to a very bold line of policy, it is in the full conviction that there is an absolute necessity for such plain speaking that they have been stated in these volumes. The time must come when the words used here will be proved true, and the only effectual remedies against the evil are those bold measures from which timid spirits would shrink. The pith of the whole argument is to be found in the fact that we are now strong enough to solve the Central Asian Question wholly in our own favour. Are we to put off action until the tables are turned and Russia is more prepared than she is at present, while we may have grown less strong? or shall we finish the business out of hand?

Sir Henry Rawlinson has permitted the work to be dedicated to him, and the author is only too sensible of its deficiencies to make him feel confident of its having deserved the honour. But it will perhaps be conceded to the writer that, while endeavouring to throw as much light as possible upon the Central Asian Question, he has had the courage to define a line of political action, which, however open to criticism as aiming at too much, is consistent, and calculated to secure the object towards which it points. Much that is contained in these volumes has been told before, and the writer does not claim merit for originality in information. But the arrangement and mode of treatment are wholly different to those adopted in any other work on the subject, even to Von Helwald's, to whose it bears most affinity. The book seeks above all to apply the lesson to be derived from history and the record of travellers to the burning political questions of the age. If the reader derives from the perusal of these pages a clearer insight into the causes of the conflict between English and Russian interests in Central Asia, and also rises with the conviction that the policy of Russia is such that it is worth a bold effort to paralyse its effects, the author will have been more than repaid for the three months' labour of writing them. The Central Asian Question should not be the monopoly of a few specialists, or even of the Anglo-Indian world. It is a matter of vital consequence—daily increasing—to every Englishman, and as such it should be studied and gravely considered.

NOTE ON THE MAP.

THE map of Central Asia which these volumes have the privilege of containing may certainly be considered to be the most remarkable that has accompanied any work upon this subject, or probably any other. I may say this without fear of being considered egotistical, as my share in its production has been very small. The credit belongs exclusively to Messrs. W. H. Allen and Co., who with rare enterprise have, at very great expense, placed at the disposal of the English reader and student a *fac-simile* of the latest issue of the map of Central Asia compiled by the Russian War Department. The names of all the principal places are marked upon it. The original map is contained in twelve sheets, and there are probably not a dozen copies of it in this country. The *fac-simile* is in half-scale—that is, one fourth the size of the original—and even thus reduced its bulk is considerable. I would beg to be permitted to point out that the great value of the map is that it discloses what the Russians believe to be the true geographical configuration of Central Asia. By reference to Walker's Turkestan, or other English maps, it will be found that in many points their information differs from ours. It may certainly be accepted as the highest authority on all the region north of the Oxus, including more particularly the Pamir and the adjoining khanates. While offering my acknowledgments to the publishers for the great assistance they have given my pages by the production of this, I believe, unequalled map, I indulge in the hope that their enterprise will be duly appreciated.

D. C. BOULGER.

CONTENTS.

CHAPTER I.

Recent Russian Explorations in Central Asia - - 1

CHAPTER II.

The Amou Darya - - - - - - 36

CHAPTER III.

The Russian Government of Turkestan - - - 60

CHAPTER IV.

Russia's Military Strength in Central Asia - - - 85

CHAPTER V.

The principal Routes from the Russian Frontier to India - 119

CHAPTER VI.

Russia's Relations with Khiva and Khokand - - 144

CHAPTER VII.

Russia's Relations with Bokhara - - - - 172

CHAPTER VIII.

Russia and Persia - - - - - - 192

CHAPTER IX.

The Turcomans - - - - - - 210

CHAPTER X.

The Merv Question - - - - - - 258

CHAPTER XI.

Balkh, Kundus, and Badakshan - - - - 297

APPENDIX A.

The Ukase for the Formation of the Province of Turkestan - 315

APPENDIX B.

Russia's Programme in Central Asia - - - - 318

APPENDIX C.

Russia and Khiva - - - - - - 326

APPENDIX D.

Russia and Bokhara - - - - - - 333

APPENDIX E.

First Treaty between England and Dost Mahomed of Cabul 339

APPENDIX F.

Second Treaty between England and Dost Mahomed of
Cabul - - - - - - - 341

APPENDIX G.

Treaty between Heraclius, Prince of Georgia, and the Empress Catherine of Russia - - - - 345

ENGLAND AND RUSSIA

IN

CENTRAL ASIA.

CHAPTER I.

RECENT RUSSIAN EXPLORATIONS IN CENTRAL ASIA.

In commencing a work of this character, which aspires above everything to place the intricate phases of the Central Asian Question in a clear light before the English reader, it is necessary to state concisely what meaning we attach to the definition Central Asia. No term has been more abused in its use than that of Central Asia, for, geographically speaking, it has never been applied with accuracy; and those events which have attracted so much notice in Turkestan, and have become known as the Central Asian Question, have really taken place in Western Asia. Yet it would be perfectly useless for anyone to attempt to revolutionise the phraseology of the subject by seeking to apply to that burning Central Asian topic any new title. It only remains to fix some limit, some precise signification to the term, and this is by no means easy. For we may give it too wide a significance or too narrow; and as the term is convenient rather than correct, we should seek to confine it to those limits which are required by convenience alone. Therefore it would seem that Central Asia is an elastic phrase that must yet be defined before we proceed any further, both for the sake of perspicuity and for the assistance of the ordinary reader.

The simplest definition we take to be the following: Central Asia is that portion of Asia which intervenes between the English and Russian frontiers wherever they now are, or wherever they in the future may be. It is consequently a variable tract of country in accordance as those frontiers advance or recede. Khokand and the districts Amou Darya and Trans-Caspiania are by this definition no longer in Central Asia; but Bokhara, Khiva, the Turcoman country, and Afghanistan remain included in it, and these countries, with Persia and the Pamir Khanates, actually constitute the whole of what may be called Central Asia. Beloochistan and Cashmere, which now extends to Baroghil, are within the practical limits of our Indian Empire, and Central Asia is consequently restricted to those countries and regions before mentioned. In this sense, therefore, Eastern Turkestan, which has passed once more into the possession of China, the third great power in Asia, is outside the sphere we have defined as Central Asia; but as some most interesting explorations have recently been made in the Tian Shan regions, it is proposed to include them in this chapter, which summarises the results, so far as they are yet known, of the discoveries of the last three years on the part of Russian explorers. To shut out the highly important journeys of Potanin, Prjevalsky, and Kuropatkine from our retrospect, would be to give a very partial description of what has been done by the Russian Government and its subordinates. But in treating of political events Central Asia has, for convenience sake, been assumed only to embrace all those minor countries which lie between the frontiers of England and Russia in Asia. The Central Asian Question really is, What is to be the destiny of those countries? Are they to remain independent, or to become portions of the dominions either of Russia or of England? Regarded in this light its complexity would not appear to be great.

In 1874 the Czar, acting upon his own authority, sanctioned the scheme which had been proposed by the Grand Duke Michael, Lieutenant of the Caucasus, for the formation of the country east of the Caspian Sea into a district under the immediate control of the Tiflis authorities. The extent of this district was held to be from a place known as Mertvii Kultuk on the north to the river Atrek on the south, and from the Caspian on the west to the Khivan frontier on the east. The Turcomans were practically ignored. It is scarcely necessary to say that over a considerable portion of this extensive region the authority of Russia was, and still is, vague, and that even geographical information about it is not as complete or as accurate as could be desired. Yet, despite these weak points in the Russian administration over the Trans-Caspian district, it is the law that every Turcoman and every Kirghiz within that zone shall pay an annual tax to the Russian Government. The district or governorship is divided into two sections, that of Mangishlak and that of Krasnovodsk. The latter is the more important, and under the immediate supervision of the governor of the whole region. In the Mangishlak sub-division the Kirghiz element greatly preponderates, and we may suppose that their taxes are paid with a certain amount of regularity. The wells that the Russians have sunk in two directions across the Ust Urt plateau as far as the Aral Sea, and Khiva, place in the hands of their officers the means of acting with promptitude against any turbulent Kirghiz. Moreover, since the days of that daring leader, Kutebar, the Kirghiz appear to have lost all their former courage, and have never dared to resist in any form the demands, just or unjust, of the Russian officials. We may assume that the *Kibitka* tax of three roubles for each tent is paid without murmuring, and at the stipulated season. But it has been far different in the Krasnovodsk district, where the people are not Kirghiz, but Turcomans. It will be more to the purpose to defer any remarks upon these people until a later chapter, but we may say here that the reconnoissances of General Lomakine have resulted in the acquisition of precise information concerning the river Atrek to a distance of one hundred miles from its mouth, that is to say, to its junction with the river Sunbur, as well as of the country between Krasnovodsk and Beurma, a

village beyond the strong position of Kizil Arvat. The
results of those investigations have not been made
known, but we can judge of the importance of the latter
by the fact that General Lomakine has recently advanced
to Kizil Arvat and Kizil Tchesme, still further on, at
the head of a considerable army, and that he is supposed to be meditating a *coup* against Merv from those
posts of vantage. Notwithstanding these results, which
have however been obtained entirely within the Russian frontier, it may be said that Russia has not done
much towards exploring the country held by the Turcomans, and that the great sandy expanse of Kara
Kum, with its oasis of Merv, and the fertile strip of
country from Sarakhs to Abiverd is still a *terra incognita* to Russia as well as to ourselves. Of course
it is just possible that great diligence may have been
shown by the Russian officials in collecting information
concerning these places from native sources in Khiva
and at Charjui; but if there has been this diligence it
has apparently borne little fruit. The Russian official
map of Central Asia, which is to be obtained only with
great difficulty outside Russia, and which the author
has been so far privileged as to have secured for these
volumes, throws no more light on the Kara Kum
desert than Petermann's or Walker's Turkestan.
Russia, with great opportunities, has done scarcely
anything for the advancement of geographical knowledge in this quarter, and this apathy has been the
more surprising because political and military advantages were here the sure rewards of success. It
should, however, be remembered by those who may

reckon upon a prolonged continuance of apathy in this direction, that the advantages of action are so obvious that sooner or later they must induce Russian governors to sanction operations upon a large scale, and that once they are sanctioned the results must be certain and immediate. Elsewhere in Central Asia the result of geographical research, and of individual courage and labour, can only be reaped after years of patient and persistent toil; but here the prize can be secured in a few months.

And what has been said with regard to Kara Kum applies with equal force to Kizil Kum. Although the latter desert is mostly within the Russian frontier, it is so barren that the Russian Government has never been at any pains to explore it, nor has it made any attempts at improving it. The few routes which are marked across it, or which skirt its edges, are traversed by few travellers or caravans; and so long as Russians strain the resources of their country in efforts to press forward in all directions towards India, so long must the Kizil Kum expanse remain the waste which it has been since the alteration in the course of the Jaxartes. It is within the strict limits of accuracy to assert that, since the annexation of the Amou Darya district, nothing has been done in the way of exploring Kizil Kum, and that, with the securing of a waterway from Kazala to Khiva and the Oxus, even the old caravan route through Kalenderhana has been to some extent neglected by the Russian authorities. In olden days the highly prosperous and thickly populated kingdom of Khwaresm stretched on both sides of the Oxus far into Kizil Kum and Kara Kum. The aqueducts and canals can still be traced in the sand, which were constructed by beneficent khans of the Chaghtai and other dynasties; but the civilised rule of Russia has not conceived it to be necessary to imitate those laudable and prudent measures.

During the campaigns which resulted in the capture of Samarcand and the virtual subjection of Bokhara, the Russians acquired copious information concerning the roads leading to Charjui and Kerkhi from Bokhara. Charjui is exactly one hundred and ten miles distant from Bokhara. The road passes through Bugudjan, Kara Kul, and Ardan to Ustik, on the Oxus, whence the route lies south-east to Charjui, which is on the left bank of the Oxus one hundred and fifty miles from Merv. From Bokhara to Kerkhi there is a road through the desert for a portion of the journey, passing through Hosh Robat and Shaha to Karalindai, which is opposite to Kerkhi. The distance is one hundred and thirty miles, but there is a want of water and an absence of cultivation that greatly increase the difficulties an army would have to encounter. Recent explorations along the Karshi-Kilif road tend to show that there are practicable roads to Kerkhi from the east. But after all, the Kerkhi road, and Kerkhi itself, are of far less importance than Charjui. But Charjui itself is only the half-way house to Merv, and recently events have moved so fast that if Russia should now if ever resolve to play the bigger of the two games which always lie ready to her choice, Merv, important as it is and must ever be, sinks for the moment into a secondary place. The Russians in Tashkent have never ceased to hope and to believe that they could advance upon India through Balkh and from the Pamir; and they have indulged in those hopes and beliefs chiefly for the reason that if they are not founded on fact they must give up all claim to the foremost part in any proposed invasion of Hindostan. Given the requisite number of troops, and the due amount of roubles, and Russia can always advance against India from Khorasan and the Atrek; but that would be an expedition under the immediate control of the authorities at Tiflis and St. Petersburg. Neither in its dangers nor its glory could the Tashkent army or Governor General claim the first place. It is unnecessary to point out that to such a deprivation the Tashkent army, which has conquered "Central Asia," will not willingly submit. Therefore it is that during the past few summers explorations have been so persistently carried on in Kulab, Hissar, Karategin, and on the Pamir, and it is of those investigations that we must now speak.

When Russia annexed Samarcand, Bokhara was in a state of disunion, and its vassals, the Beks of Kulab and Hissar, were in reality independent princes in the close vicinity of the new Russian frontier. Russia at once interested herself in this domestic quarrel, and General Kaufmann had the satisfaction of settling the matter on the basis that these Beks were to be the vassals of Bokhara. Still more to the content of Mozaffur Eddin, a Bokharan garrison was placed in possession of Shahr-i-sebz, and thus the nominal dominions of the Ameer of Bokhara were carried to the foot of the Pamir. Karategin passed at the same time under the influence of Khudayar Khan of Khokand, and when that potentate was deposed, partly by his own people and partly by Russia, in 1875, it is to be conjectured, although nothing definite has been said upon the subject, that Karategin passed under the controlling influence of Russia. In the summer of 1875 a Russian mission visited Hissar, and proceeded through that province to Kulab on the borders of Badakshan and Darwaz. That mission was composed of Messrs. Vishniefski, Maieff, and Captain Schwartz, and their object was to throw light on the little-known province of Hissar and the country lying east of that district in the direction of the Pamir. Our chief information of those places was derived from the Chinese, and to a great extent we are in a no better position now, as the results of the Russian explorations have been only partially divulged.* The journey of the Indian explorer, Faiz Baksh, which will be referred to in a later chapter, alone to some degree makes us independent of Russian sources of knowledge. It is known, in a general way, that this mission acquired some very useful and important information concerning Hissar and Kulab, and more especially of the Guzar and Shirabad oases. At the place called Baisun, close to the road to Shirabad, there is a range of mountains through which there passes a gorge that these Russian explorers pronounced to be impregnable. The importance of Baisun is to be found in the fact that it is on

* See "Geographical Magazine," November, 1875.

the road from Karshi, the chief town of eastern Bokhara, to Hissar and Kilif on the Oxus. The rivers Surkhan and Surkhab were crossed in several places, and considerable fresh information was also acquired of those little-known states Shignan, Darwaz, and Roshan, which lie immediately beyond the Afghan frontier in the direction of the Alai Tau. A map was drawn of the region by Captain Schwartz, which showed the results that had been attained, but what these precisely were we as yet only vaguely know. Such as have been divulged are to be found upon the map. It acquires fresh importance from the later journeys of M. Maieff and Captain Schwartz.

From that period to last year little or nothing was done in this direction, but the warlike preparations that were made last spring gave a fresh impulse to general explorations south of the Russian frontier. In fact it was absolutely necessary for the staff to know what sort of country it was between Karshi and Kilif before the army could advance to the Oxus. For the primary object at which Kaufmann intended that the corps concentrated at Djam should strike was Balkh, and to reach Balkh could only be accomplished by a direct march from Karshi either upon Khoja Salih or Kilif. Therefore it was that M. Maieff, editor of the "Tashkent Gazette," was sent upon those two expeditions which enabled him to describe the nature of the road to Shirabad, and its branches which led to Hissar and Khoja Salih. The information he acquired during these journeys was of great practical value, but it was confined to the roads leading to the Oxus fords. He found that the best road was the direct one by Derbend and Shirabad to Kilif, but that the mountain road through Guzar was more practicable than had been supposed. On that road Baisun may be said to be the half-way post to Kilif. In August M. Maieff set out upon a second journey in Hissar, and on this occasion his discoveries were more important than on the former. He accompanied M. Weinberg's mission to Bokhara as far as Karshi, but at that town he turned in a south-easterly direction to Guzar. He explored the road leading from Tengi Khoram to the thickly-populated district of Koristan, passing through Akbatch and the valley of the Kerchak river, the existence of which was previously unknown. Another road, leading from Koristan eastwards through the Tengi pass to Shirabad, was found to be passable at all times, and constantly used by the inhabitants. From Shirabad the traveller turned in a north-easterly direction, crossing the Surkhan near Kakaity, and proceeded along the river to Regar and Sarijui. He then by a circular route reached Shahr-i-sebz, passing through the kishlaks of Sengri-dagh, Batch, Tashkurgan, and Yakobak. During this exploratory tour he acquired an immense amount of geographical and political information, that is stored away in the archives of Tashkent. It speaks well, however, for Russian influence that a traveller should have been able to pass in safety through that wild and semi-independent country which lies between Karabagh and Shahr-i-sebz. With regard to this journey the following information as to the southern parts of the

khanate of Bokhara has oozed out in the proceedings of
the Russian Geographical Society. The khanate is, as
is known, subdivided into several bekdoms, which remained very imperfectly known until M. Maieff explored
them. Three of these bekdoms—Chirakcha, Guzar,
and Shirabad—are on the route from the town of Guzar
to Kilif, on the 'Amou Darya. That of Chirakcha
occupies the mountains of Djam, and the neighbouring
steppe, which last reaches the Kashka Darya river.
Both mountains and steppe are but scantily watered,
and therefore but poorly peopled with Usbegs of the
Saray-kipchak branch, who are engaged in agriculture
and cattle-breeding. Grain is raised on the steppe and
exported to Samarcand and Katty-kurgan; the crop
is estimated to produce annually six thousand four
hundred hundredweights of wheat, and three thousand
two hundred hundredweights of barley; rice is not cultivated, because of want of water. The bekdom of Guzar
also is rich in wheat, and especially in cattle, which is
bred on the hilly part of the bekdom. More than
four thousand head of cattle may be seen at once in
the weekly fairs of Guzar. The bekdom of Shirabad
is rather poor, the export of grain being difficult;
owing to the great distances from the larger centres
of Karshi and Bokhara, agriculture cannot be profitable; and the trade in grain is in the hands of the
tuachi, or travelling merchants, who purchase the
grain at very low prices. The bekdom of Kobadgan
lives on silkworm culture. The inhabitants of Kilif
town, on the Amou Darya, live mostly by the salt
trade, rock-salt being raised on the mountains, Kuityn-

tan, and exported to Afghanistan, where it is exchanged for wheat, barley, and rice. There are, however, settlements engaged in agriculture in the valleys around the bekdom of Kilif. The bekdom of Baisun numbers a good many nomad Usbegs and a few settled Tajiks; both live by cattle-breeding. On the contrary, the bekdoms of Denau, Yurchi, and Ghissar, which occupy the upper parts of the Surkhan and Kafirganan rivers, as well as the Shahisabs (bekdoms of Shaar and Kitab), are very fertile; much rice, wheat, millet,¦barley, oats, and various fruits, are raised in the well-watered steppe-like valleys at the foot of the mountains, while the bekdom of Karshi is an important centre for trade with the steppe of the Amou Darya, and for the transit trade between India and Bokhara. The nomad Turcomans and Usbegs bring here the varied produce of their domestic manufactures—carpets, rough cloths, and saddles, and large flocks of horses—which are met by the caravans for the transport of merchandise. The *krokesh* from Karshi (men engaged in the transport of wares on horseback) are met with everywhere in the khanate of Bokhara, and the prices of transport are invariably one *tena* for the *tash* (about sixpence for 5·3 miles). As to the routes which lead from Guzar to the Amou Darya, and the exploration of which was the chief aim of M. Maieff's journey, there are two—one of them, one hundred and forty-six miles long, passes by Tengakhoram and through the cleft of Shirabad, while the other, ninety-seven miles long, leads through Takashur and Kuitan. Both offer several difficulties in the mountainous region; but the former is preferable to the second, which crosses uninhabited regions without sweet water and wood. Both led to passages across the Amou Darya river to those of Shur-oba and of Kilif. The former is most important, as it is on the route to Balkh, Mazar-i-sherif, and to the great highway of Cabul; but it is rather difficult, the Amou Darya having here a width of about two thousand yards. The crossing at Kilif is far better, the river being only four hundred yards wide, steamers going as far up the river as that town, and the environs of Kilif affording very favourable conditions for a larger settlement. The distance from Kilif to the next Afghan town, Akche, is estimated to be only five *tashes* (twenty-seven miles) long; twenty-seven miles more would lead them to Shiborgan; and a further eighty-five miles to Maimene, from which there remains only a ten-days' travel to Herat. M. Maieff observes, however, that all these distances must be estimated somewhat greater than the true ones. The results of M. Maieff's tour have been supplemented by another Russian traveller, M. Otshanin. This gentleman may be said to have explored Karategin more completely than any-one else, visiting the capital, Gharm, and the winter settlement of Zaiglan, between which places he found an admirable road. The distance is sixty-five miles. Zaiglan is situated close to the junction of the Muksu and Surkhab rivers. The mountains here are very elevated, and M. Otshanin had to abandon his intention of proceeding through the Muksu Valley, and follow the better-known route through the Zirsagar pass to the Pamir. His journey confirmed the general accuracy of the maps, and presents many features of interest. The results of this later journey were so striking that it was at once resolved to despatch another and a larger expedition from Samarcand. It was to follow the same route as that by which M. Maieff returned, and to turn off at Deh-i-nau on the Surkhan, whence it would proceed to Hissar, Khawaling, and Gharm, on the road to Ushkurghan in Ferghana. From Gharm it was to visit the Pamir. The scientific officer attached to this expedition, M. Muschketoff, has lately published some of the geographical results of that journey. His observations apply exclusively to the northern part of the Pamir, known by the name of Chargosch. The geological examination of the strata proved that the structure of the Pamir is mainly granite, metamorphic clay, and mica slate, and that the granite outcrops are generally the same in their direction as those of the Tian Shan, viz., east-north-east. The highest summit in this part of the Pamir is that peak called after General Kaufmann, which towers for twenty-five thousand feet into the air. M. Muschketoff's examinations of the region go to show that Humboldt was wrong in supposing that the Pamir represented a meridional mountain system, to which the name of Bolor was given. M. Muschketoff explains the misconception which the appearance of the Pamir had given rise to, in the following manner :—" On the ground both of the geological structure of the Pamir and Alai, as well as on the basis of the geological *data* collected by Stoliczka, I find no support for the assumption of a regular meridional mountain system. The aspect of these mountains, which has caused the erroneous belief, I should explain by the fact that eastward from the Kara Kul the Trans-Alai diorite mountains (which run from east to west) and the south Khokand syenite mountains (which run east-north-east) meet with the Ferghana diabase mountains (which have a north-west direction), whereby a colossal aggregation of mountain masses takes place, which is increased by the accession of the Pamir granite range (stretching east-north-east). The entire mass of this meeting point belongs to different mountain systems; but from a distance, from whatever side it be regarded, from east or west, the outline on the horizon of the several concurrent heights gives the impression of an entire meridional chain, which in reality does not exist." This is the latest opinion upon the structure of the Pamir, and in absence of other information M. Muschketoff's criticism must be accepted as correct. The Russian frontier has, as the result of these Pamir explorations, been pushed southward for a distance of eighty miles, thus including in the Czar's dominions both Karategin and the great Kara Kul lake.* In this direction Russia evidently expects to be able to work a way to Lake Victoria and the head-waters of the Oxus.

Of the almost inaccessible district of Karategin we know scarcely anything. Mr. Schuyler endeavoured to visit it, but the Khokandian officials refused to give

* This assertion is based on the new Russian map of Central Asia accompanying these volumes.

him the necessary permission. In 1869-70 a difficulty occurred between Bokhara and Khokand as to which state Karategin owed fealty, and Russia, under whose auspices the negotiations were carried on, solved the question by deciding that Karategin should be practically independent. Geographically speaking, Karategin should be Bokharan, but historically and politically it should have belonged, as it mostly has, to Khokand, which had always been in the habit of selecting the Beg or chief. When Russia annexed Khokand in 1876 Karategin virtually became a Russian possession. The inhabitants of this region are represented to be an exceedingly primitive people, and the following particulars have leaked out concerning their customs. They have no conception of measure or weight, no booths, caravanserais, or fairs, such as are common to all nations, and Eastern ones more especially. They possess no knowledge of public institutions, but live on in a state of primitive equality that is generally considered synonymous with Arcadian myths. They are principally cattle breeders, and with very few exceptions there are no agriculturists. The barrenness of their country is not redeemed by any feature of a brighter possibility such as is to be found in all the valleys of the Hindoo Koosh; but the total wealth of the district forms a common stock, out of which the necessities of the whole population are supplied. In times of dearth the suffering is often slight, as the whole community shares alike. The crime of theft is unknown, and the Karateginese are alike famed for their good humour and their sense of honour.

Mr. Schuyler, who saw some of these people in Khokand, describes them as "swarthy, thick-set, good-natured fellows."

From another source we learn that the mission sent to the Pamir consisted of Messrs. Severstof, Skassi, and Captain Schwartz, in addition to M. Muschketoff; and that its operations were carried on under considerable difficulties through the inclemency of the weather. The cold was often very great, the thermometer going as low as 25° below zero centigrade, but the actual cold was felt still more keenly through the bitter winds that swept across the barren wastes of the Pamir. On the Pamir there are no forests and hardly any herbage; and the expedition had to carry its own fuel with it. As the season was so advanced when the expedition left Tashkent in September, it is not at all fair to judge from the report of this expedition what the climate and condition of the Pamir are during the spring. No inhabitants were found either on the Pamir or in the Alai valleys, and the Russians assumed that they had taken shelter in the warmer valleys of Ferghana. They traversed the Shart Pass, which is the next to the Terek, on their road from the Alai to Pamir, then taking the same route as Scobelef's force in 1876. The river Kok-su was here reached and to some extent explored; but we have yet to learn accurately what is the true course of the Pamir rivers, which have been several times christened and re-christened. The natives assert that this particular stream flows eastward through Kashgar and into Lob-Nor, and is known as Tarimbal. If this be correct the Kok-su is merely the head-water of the Kashgar river, which eventually becomes the Tarim. The expedition did not get much beyond the Kok-su, on account of the snow, but returned viâ Osh to Tashkent, having acquired most valuable information on many points, and with a fine ornithological collection. Captain Schwartz revised the map he had previously prepared, but these new results are not of course shown on the official map to which we have already referred. Russia has thus stored up considerable information concerning the Pamir during the past twelve months, and the rapidity with which the missions succeed each other proves that the Tashkent authorities believe that explorations in the Pamir khanates, over which their influence is steadily increasing, may prove as advantageous in a political and a military sense as much as they are for scientific or geographical benefits.

In close connection with these Pamir explorations are the efforts that are being made to collect historical information concerning the Aryan races of the Upper Oxus, the Hindoo Koosh, and the Western Himalaya. The Russian Geographical Society has commissioned M. Minaieff to compile a systematic digest of whatever information has been acquired of those primitive peoples either by Russian, English, or native travellers. This work when completed should be most interesting, as much remains to be done in this respect. The people of the valleys of the Hindoo Koosh, the Kafirs, the Wakhis, the Chitralis, etc. etc., and also those of the Pamir, are of great sentimental interest; and their practical political importance may some day become very perceptible. M. Minaieff's region of observation includes the valleys of the Indus, the Cabul, and the Yarkand rivers.

Although M. de Ujfalvy is not a Russian subject, some record of his explorations in the country to the south and east of Ferghana may not be out of place at this point. M. de Ujfalvy was commissioned by the French Government to travel in Central Asia during the winter of 1877, and he returned to Paris in the summer of last year. The following description of his travels is taken from the narrative of the proceedings of the Paris Geographical Society. The real interest in his travels commences when he left Samarcand, and proceeding along the right bank of the Zarafshan river, passed through Paishambe to Penkajend, Urumitan, and Varsiminar. The result of that tour in the Zarafshan region was to convince M. de Ujfalvy that the Galtchas, Karateginese, and probably the people of the Pamir khanates and of Badakshan as well, represent the original inhabitants of Trans-Oxiania. He considers them to be an Iranian race distinct from the Tajiks. He devoted special attention to the customs of the Galtchas, who have been generally confused with the Tajiks. One great distinction is that the Galtchas only marry amongst themselves, while the Tajiks, as is well known, ally themselves with Usbeg or Kirghiz women, or vice versâ. The Galtchas are therefore a pure race. They are hyperbrachicephalic, tall in stature, with white skins, which are often bronzed from exposure to the sun and weather. Their hair varies in colour, but as a rule it is black, although fair and even red hair is often to be found amongst them. They have flowing beards, and their brown or blue eyes are close set in the head. The nose is well shaped and slightly arched, the face oval, the frame vigorous, and they are excellent horsemen and pedestrians, being of very active habits, and capable of enduring severe fatigue. Their language is a Persian dialect, which led to their being classed among the Tajiks, and their social habits are those of a contented and fairly prosperous community of agriculturists. The village assembly decides all matters of dispute, but there are degrees of station amongst them which are unknown in the more primitive regions lying to the south. Each village has a mayor or Aksakal—White-beard—who is as a rule the oldest man in that village. The greater number of the Galtchas are monogamists, but some of the more prosperous have two wives. The Galtchas say that their name signifies " The hungry raven which repairs to the mountains to find means of subsistence." M. de Ujfalvy returned to Samarcand after this interesting tour in the Zarafshan Valley.

But his later travels in Kuldja are still more important. From Samarcand he went to Khodjent, Margilan, Andijan, Osh, and Houlsha, or Gulsha, at the northern entrance to the Terek pass; and after a brief tour in the direction of the Pamir he went on to Kuldja. In this secluded quarter of the dominions of Russia M. de Ujfalvy found a temperate climate, not to be met with elsewhere in Central Asia in the same latitude. The winter, never very severe, lasts only for two months in the valleys of the Kash and the Ili, and the heat of summer is modified by the absence of those fierce dry winds which sweep across the steppes and sandy deserts of Turkestan. The inhabitants are mainly of Calmuck race, with the addition in the towns of the Tungani, descendants of Chinese military settlers, and of the Tarantchis, whose ancestors were natives of Kashgar. The country is extremely fertile, producing rice, sorgho, cotton, wheat, and fruits of all kinds in great abundance, and it is consequently a region eminently suitable for European colonisation. The Russians, during their seven years' rule, do not seem to have settled to any considerable degree in this favourable clime, and, according to the French traveller, they do not appear to have done as much for the country as had been supposed. Colonel Prjevalsky tells a different tale of the Kuldja administration; but this is what M. de Ujfalvy informs us: "Since the Russians came here more than a thousand persons have sought the favour of being allowed to settle in Kuldja, but the Russians refused, as they are said to count upon having to give the country up to China. Since the civil war which ravaged the country for several years, the valley of the Ili presents a sad spectacle. The traveller passes dozens of villages in ruins; the fields are covered with weeds; the numerous canals are dry; and even the fine forest of Karagatch, which the Chinese planted between Borohoudjie and Ak-kent over an extent of thirty miles, will perish for want of water if the remedy be not soon applied. Formerly the country contained more than 2,000,000 inhabitants, now there are scarcely 130,000. Flourishing towns, such as New Kuldja or Ili (300,000 inhabitants), Bazandai (100,000), and Tchimpansai (50,000), have disappeared; there remain only the ruins. The numerous industrial works which the country contained have been burnt, and the laborious inhabitants killed without distinction—men, women, and children."

This is the evidence of a traveller in Kuldja during last year, and it fully confirms what Mr. Schuyler saw six years ago. The Russians have done literally nothing for the advantage of Kuldja and its people during the seven years and a half that they have been there. The great works carried out by the Chinese, which were so ruthlessly destroyed by the Mahomedans in the great outbreak in 1863, still remain to testify by their ruins to the fact that the Chinese possessed administrative qualities which Russia has never evinced in any of her numerous annexations. If we are to judge between the merits of China and Russia as governing powers, is it a false test to apply to the question, to compare the state of Kuldja in 1860 with what it is now in 1879, after it has had the supposed benefit of seven years' administration by a Russian officer? In 1860 there were canals and roads, forests rising on the one hand, and fertile fields stretching on the other, tranquillity and order, a bustling trade, and a prosperous people; and in 1879 all those have disappeared or become useless, except the roads—which, like those of Rome, were indestructible—and the tranquillity which is only a military despotism. Under China, Kuldja contained two millions of people, and under Russia its population has not increased from the very small number to which Mahomedan violence had reduced it. China proved herself to be a thoughtful and considerate ruler; Russia can in this matter be only compared to a thoughtless and improvident one.

Before passing on to those other Russian explorers whose scene of activity lies still further to the east, we may summarise what M. de Ujfalvy has written upon the subject of Central Asia as a field for sportsmen. During his ethnological pursuits he was struck by the fact that the art, or rather the business, of hunting was closely interwoven with the daily life of the people of Central Asia, and he at once came to the conclusion that this was worthy of attention even from a scientific point of view. The causes for this devotion to sport vary with the particular people referred to. Some hunt as a means of subsistence, being naturally loth to, or ignorant of, sedentary pursuits; others because they are shepherds, and are obliged in self-defence to assume the offensive against the fierce beasts of the mountain or the plain. The former only engage with the combative animals when they interfere with the chase of those upon which these people, chiefly mountaineers, subsist; but the latter wage war against the combative animals alone. The people of the towns have long forgotten their old skill and eagerness in the chase; and M. de Ujfalvy's remarks apply exclusively to the Kirghiz, the Kipchaks, the Aryan people of Trans-Oxiania, and the Turcomans. Of these, perhaps, the Kirghiz are the most skilled hunters, and this can be explained by the fact that

they hold that mountainous and wild country which
stretches from the Jaxartes to Lake Balkash and
Semiretchinsk. Wolves, foxes, badgers, wild goats,
and grey hares are to be found in abundance in the
country specified, and in the province of Ferghana deer
are so numerous that he compares it to "an English
park." The large Maral stag is to be found in herds
of several hundreds. Water-fowl, herons, cranes,
ibises, wild geese, swans, and a bird resembling a
flamingo are also to be met with in immense quantities
round Issik Kul and along the Syr Darya and its
affluents. Bears are to be found in the rocky country,
and a tame kind of gazelle, which is, however, never to
be seen in greater numbers than five or six at a time.

The Zarafshan valley east of Samarcand is the haunt
of wolves, lynxes, foxes, etc. etc.; and eagles and
vultures are frequently to be seen. But on the whole
the wolves are of a cowardly race, and the Kirghiz
hunter does not hesitate to attack them single-handed
and armed only with a heavy riding-whip, which is
made of wire woven into the lash. With regard to
the Central Asian tiger, which M. de Ujfalvy states,
on what authority we know not, to be larger than the
Indian tiger, and particularly fierce, it seems to be an
animal which is gradually disappearing. Twenty-five
years ago, when the Russians were first advancing
along the Syr Darya, the marshes on the banks of
that river swarmed with them, but from this quarter
of the country they have been expelled by the encroachments of man. They are still found in limited
numbers along the banks of the Chu river and on the

shores of Lake Balkash. When Prince Dolgorouki was sent in 1876 to inspect the Central Asian forces, however, he was unable to discover a single specimen of this formidable animal; but the stories of its existence are too recent and too well authenticated to admit of any doubt as to its being a literal fact that there was such an animal, even if there is none still surviving, as the Central Asian tiger. Its size has, however, in all probability been exaggerated. The Russian authorities have offered a reward of ten roubles to the slayer of each tiger, and the skin generally fetches double that amount; so that it is probable that the tiger is gradually being exterminated.

The Kirghiz, who, as we have said, are the best hunters in Turkestan, are capital riders and possess horses which are not easily to be surpassed in the qualities of endurance and speed. The chiefs possess a very fine breed of Turcoman horse, which is believed to be an Arab breed with some English blood in its veins. It is longer-legged than the pure Arab, and is known as *argamak*. It comes from the Turcoman country. As this horse is very scarce and dear, it is not surprising to learn that it is only possessed by some of the wealthier of the Kirghiz chiefs. The indigenous Kirghiz horse is small and mean in its appearance; but it must not be condemned from appearance alone, for it is capable of enduring great and sustained fatigue, and can put up with the most meagre accommodation and the most irregular diet. The *karabair* is a cross of these two; but it possesses the virtues and good qualities of neither.

The Kirghiz dog, called *tazi*, is akin to a greyhound. It is intelligent, bold, and remarkably swift of foot. Among the Galtchas and the people of Pamir another dog, called *gurdja*, a species of basset with pointed ears, is to be met with. It is strong and intelligent, particularly in finding the track on mountains covered with snow or ice; but all attempts to take it out of its native haunts have failed, and even the short journey to Samarcand inspires it with an irresistible longing to return. M. de Ujfalvy has succeeded in bringing back to Paris three specimens of the *tazi*, which may be seen in the Jardin d'Acclimatation. It would have been as cruel as it would have been useless to have attempted the same task with the *gurdja*.

The journey of M. Gregor N. Potanin through the Altai mountains in the autumn of 1876 is too interesting to be passed over in silence. Travelling from the post of Zaissan in Kuldja he reached Bulun-tokhoi in seventeen days, travelling along a new carriage road that has been constructed leading to the valley north of the Saur mountains. Beyond the post of Bulun-tokhoi, which was held by a sotnia of cossacks, the traveller followed the eastern shore of Lake Ulyungur, crossing the deep and rapid Black Irtysh at Durbeljin in a ferry-boat. A month after he set out from Zaissan he arrived on the banks of the river Kran at a point about eight miles from the Chinese city of Tulta. The heat had been very intense during the march, and the annoyance from flies was extreme; but on reaching the Kran more temperate weather was encountered. In fact the nights were cold, as hoar frosts had set in; and most of the corn had already been harvested. The valley of the Kran is singularly fertile, and from the Phara-sumè monastery down to the town of Balbagai, a distance of about ten miles, the fields are in a high state of cultivation under the care of the native population, who are chiefly Eleuths and Kirghiz. It is the granary of the Eastern Ektag Altai, and the Kirghiz from as far away as Kobdo come hither to purchase their corn. Poppies are also sown to a great extent, and opium is exported to Kobdo and Buluntokhoi. While staying on the banks of the Kran, M. Potanin resolved to pay a visit to the lamasery of Phara-sumè, where a lama known as the Tsagangygen resided, and where he expected to obtain both a guide and general information concerning the country and the people. But the Chinese authorities were inimical to the advent of strangers here, as elsewhere, and they stirred up the people to acts of a semi-hostile nature. So that when M. Potanin appeared on the road leading to Phara-sumè he was on the first occasion met by a body of men who said it was too late that day to visit the Tsagan-gygen; and when M. Potanin returned the next day he was met by shouts of *arjur*, "be off!" from the townspeople. An excuse was then discovered for placing him under arrest, and during the one night of enforced residence in Phara-sumè he had to accept the hospitality of a lama.

Now, it is given on the authority of numerous travellers in all parts of China, and on the particular authority of one gentleman who has travelled across

North-west China, that the ordinary lama is a
thoroughly good fellow and boon companion. Not
free from much of that self-esteem which attaches to
the priestly office all the world over, he is yet far above
those prejudices and ignorances which make the mass
of Chinamen, in their unreasoning antipathy to everything that is foreign and unknown to them, the play-
things and the tools of an intriguing official class and
of a nervous, dominant caste. M. Potanin's host was
true to his cloth, and through his loquacity as well as by
his hospitality served to while away the time pleasantly
enough for the Russian traveller. The tea and mutton
with which he regaled his visitor were admirable in
their way, and although he declined to participate in
the meal, which he declared was provided at the expense of the Bogdo Khan (the Emperor of China),
he enlivened it with his presence and his bonhomie.
M. Potanin does not attempt to relieve the curiosity we
feel to be admitted into some of the mysteries of lama-
dom, nor does he in any way seek to throw light on the
manner in which the Chinese have succeeded in maintaining their authority for centuries in this far-off corner
of the empire. For a reply to these highly interesting
political questions we must still await the advent of some
gifted traveller. The next day M. Potanin was taken
before the governor, whom he found seated on a bench in
a small room, with four soldiers wearing yellow jackets
at his side. He was forthwith accused of having
entered a peaceable town with arms in his hands, and
of having committed sacrilege by approaching a temple.
After some delay, and an evident desire on the part of

the Chinese to hush the matter up, M. Potanin was permitted to depart; but the Chinese authorities declined all responsibility for his safety if he proceeded elsewhere than to Kobdo, and otherwise than by the line of the pickets. M. Potanin crossed the Altai range by the Urmogaity pass (nine thousand feet), which is near the sources of the Kran; the Jamaty pass, which is generally used, being impracticable at that time of the year. M. Potanin is one of the very few European travellers who have explored this portion of the Altai range, and that region which lies round Dannkul and Talnor. On the 16th of October, M. Potanin reached the town of Kobdo, where he passed the winter. M. Potanin's journey is, perhaps, the only one that has been undertaken at the instigation of the Russian Government in the interests of pure science and geographical research. It is well to do justice to this solitary instance of the Russian authorities showing that they have once recognised the wisdom of assisting an explorer whose explorations can bring them no political gain or military advantage.

Of the two recent Russian travellers in Eastern Turkestan, we have received very meagre records of the geographical information which Captain Kuropatkine placed at the disposal of the Tashkent authorities; and in the lecture that he delivered in that city he confined himself to the military and political aspect of affairs in Eastern Turkestan. At that moment attention was absorbed in the progress of events round Turfan, where Yakoob Beg and the Chinese were in close proximity to each other; and Captain

Kuropatkine was questioned rather as to the military preparations made by the Athalik Ghazi than as to the condition of the country itself and the accuracy of the extant geographical information. But during the course of his journey from Kashgar to Turfan, by the Aksu and Kucha road—a journey which, so far as we can ascertain, has never been performed by any other European within the present century—he must have acquired information that is still and will probably for some time remain unique. But as we possess no material for giving the details of his journey, we may pass on to the next and last of the Russian travellers, Colonel Prjevalsky.

Of all Asiatic travellers the Russian Colonel Prjevalsky is the most distinguished. More than any other does he appear to possess the qualities of Marco Polo. His travels in China, Mongolia, the Tangut country, and more recently in Eastern Turkestan, are all entitled to rank among the most brilliant of modern enterprises. At the present time Prjevalsky is preparing to set out from Kuldja on a journey across the deserts and mountain chains of the farther portion of Eastern Turkestan, in an attempt to reach Tibet and to visit the capital of the Dalai Lama. His last journey to Lob Nor was so remarkable, that, although a translation of his own narrative has just been published, it would be an omission not to give a brief sketch here of its salient features. *Colonel Prjevalsky

---

* See Mr. Delmar Morgan's translations of Colonel Prjevalsky's works.

set out from Kuldja on the 12th of August, 1876, and the task which he had put before himself was the discovery of the mysterious Lake Lob. He had also some intention of continuing his journey to Tibet, if he found the Calmuck route from Korla to be feasible. He was accompanied by six cossacks and a Kirghiz interpreter. His road lay along the banks of the Ili as far as its junction with the Kash, where the smaller river, the Tekes, marked his course, and proceeding by the valley of the lower Kunges and the Zanma river he approached the Kashgarian frontier. He then, after crossing several passes, reached the valley of the Yuldus. These valleys are singularly fertile, and abound in some parts with fruit trees, and in other parts with rich foliage and vegetation. In the wilder regions large game abound, and the Maral stag, of which we have already spoken, is to be found here in its largest dimensions. By the banks of the Balgantai-gol (river Haidu) the traveller reached Charimoti, to the north-west of Korla. While here Colonel Prjevalsky made inquiries concerning the lake known as Chaidu-gol, which is not marked on ordinary maps, but which, according to the information he received, was very deep, and eight or nine days' journey round. While staying in the town of Korla he did not learn much of its actual condition, although from subsequent evidence he heard that it contained six thousand inhabitants. But the country lying south of Korla was found to be very barren, and almost a desert. A mountain range, to which Prjevalsky gave the name of Turuk Tag, and a river, the Konche Darya, were crossed. After striking the Tarim at the village of Achtarma the aspect of the country improved. One hundred and forty miles south of Achtarma lies the town of Charchalyk, built about forty years ago by outlaws from Khoten, and two hundred miles across the desert to the south-west of Charchalyk is another town, called Cherchen, under the same administration as the former. There is a trade route across the desert from Charchalyk to Cherchen, Cherchen to Nai, Nai to Kiria, and Kiria to Khoten. The two lakes, Kara Koshun and Kara Bunar, the former of which Colonel Prjevalsky identifies with Lob Nor, lie to the north-east of Charchalyk on the route to Hamil. There is a great scarcity of water and in the supply of meat in the Charchalyk region, and the Russian traveller suffered much from both these wants; but from what he says of the country lying immediately to the north of the great Altyn Tag range, which he discovered, it would appear that there was a possibility of its becoming by judicious government and some outlay a very flourishing settlement. The people certainly possess many features of attraction to foreigners, and are harmless and industrious in the extreme. Of the vexed Lob Nor question we will say nothing here. The identity of that lake has not yet been decided beyond the shadow of a doubt, but Colonel Prjevalsky has so far obtained the best of the argument.

Herr von Helwald, in his interesting work, " Die Rüssen im Centralasien," says that everywhere do we see the progress of science and knowledge following in the rear of the victories of a civilised power. It is to be regretted that the English observer cannot but fail to perceive the accuracy of that assertion in the case of the subject of which Herr von Helwald was immediately treating. We find the progress of science and knowledge in the rear of Russia's conquests to be remarkably slow; we discover numerous undertakings of all kinds that should be promptly carried out neglected; and we look in vain for that enlightened administration which always follows, according to the German writer, in the rear of the triumphant armies of civilised nations. But we find, on the other hand, that remarkable enterprise is shown in Russian circles, military and scientific, in making science and exploration go before their armies. The territory that is already Russian is neglected; but that destined to become Russian is explored and mapped out with remarkable care. While Kizil Kum, Semiretchinsk, and Ust Urt, are, comparatively speaking, disregarded, Hissar, the Pamir, Kara Kum, and Kashgar are explored with the greatest possible diligence, and information bearing upon those places is snatched up with the most eager avidity. And this remarkable reversal of the natural order of things is one of the most unequivocal indications of the truth of the assertion that in her present Asiatic possessions Russia finds neither content nor satisfaction; and the result of her disappointment is that she looks beyond in her policy, just as her soldiers do in a mere spirit of *chauvinism*, to the prize that is to reward her for many years' expenditure in blood and treasure. Her reward can only be found in Persia, China, or India, and on the question of which it is to be hinges the whole Central Asian controversy. The problem is rendered more complicated by the fact that neither in Persia nor in China could England permit Russia to encroach any further. By encroachments in the first country our empire in India would be menaced more nearly than before; and by any change in the second, other interests, scarcely less important, would be seriously jeoparded. But it is evident that all recent Russian explorations tend to show that the Russian Government has sanctioned them only for the furtherance of its own selfish ends. Science owes nothing to them, for not only have they not been undertaken in its interests, but their principal results have also been concealed. Russian explorations are but the precursors of an advancing army; and those travellers whom we have mentioned are only the scouts of General Kaufmann's battalions. When Russia begins to perform her duty to the nationalities upon whom she has forced her rule, then we shall be more willing to do justice to the enterprise and courage of the by no means undistinguished band of Russian travellers. But until then we can only refuse to consider that they have conferred any service on mankind in general.

CHAPTER II.

THE AMOU DARYA.*

EVERY large river has a history of some kind or another; but few rivers have one so interesting as that of the Amou Darya, the Oxus of the ancients. There is none certainly in Central Asia that can vie with it either in point of historical associations or of present practical utility. In olden days it was the Oxus alone which made Khwaresm one of the most fertile countries in Western Asia, and which rendered the dynasty of the Chaghtai Khans respectable as well as formidable among its neighbours; and at the present time it is to the Oxus that some of the more prudent and foreseeing of Russians look for that prosperity which is as yet unknown to Khiva and Kara Kum. The Russian authorities have extended a benevolent patronage to the schemes of these persons, both because if they ever became realised they must materially facilitate military operations, and at the least, if those

* See Sir H. Rawlinson's monograph on the Oxus; and Major Wood's " Shores of Lake Aral."

military operations were considered undesirable or useless, they would bring an increased amount of prosperity to a region already Russian or about to become Russian. In fact, the schemes which have for many years been suggested with regard to the Oxus, of which we shall treat specifically by and by, must either enable Russian troops to be carried more easily to the Indian frontier, or must prove that the undertaking of invading India from Turkestan is an impossibility. In the latter case the diversion of the Oxus from its present course to one disemboguing into the Caspian, will at all events have fertilised a region that is now desert, and will have opened up an easy trade route between Russia and Bokhara, the central mart of Western Asia. Even as a *pis aller* the schemes* which we have referred to would have accomplished this much; so it is not to be wondered at that Prince Gortchakoff himself, and other responsible persons, should have patronised them in some special manner.

But although the history of the Oxus is so full of historical interest and of practical importance, it would be rash, however, to narrate it here after the very instructive account Major Wood has placed before the English reader in his "Shores of Lake Aral." A recent event, nothing less than a diversion, however slight, in the course of this river, gives a fresh aspect to the subject, and admits of some description in amplification of that for which we are indebted to the

---

* Consult operations of "The Company for encouraging Industry and Commerce," founded at St. Petersburg in 1870.

author just mentioned. The reader must understand that the credit for the historical portion of the narrative is mainly due to Major Wood, whose account is little more than condensed here. Since the year 1874 such information as has been published is given in further explanation of the bursting through of the dam at Bend, which had been constructed to block up the entrance to the Loudon canal.

We need not direct our attention on the present occasion to the information which Greek and Arabian geographers have afforded as to the old course of the Oxus, and of those other rivers which, known as the Amol and Arzass, flowed from the Oxus itself, or from the Aral, into the Caspian Sea. And our interest is also exclusively confined to those of its branches which appear to have been main channels in the olden time. Of these the Doudon and the Kunya-daryalik are the most important. Both of these branch off from the Oxus a short distance north of the town of Khiva, and they are each traceable to a common destination, the salt lake of Sarykamish. Beyond Sarykamish this channel becomes the Uzboi, which is marked across the Kara Kum desert to the Caspian Sea at the bay of Balkhan. Of each of these channels Major Wood says that their "dimensions are sufficiently large to allow of their having anciently been main courses of the river."

With regard to the Doudon, which is the Turcoman for "steep"—a name which Vambery and others apply to the Oghus, or Uzboi—it branches off from the Oxus at a point almost facing the Russian port of Petro-

Alexandrovsk, and immediately north of the town of Khiva. Following a north-west course, and then a due west one, it reaches Sarykamish in longitude $57\frac{1}{2}$; but of this channel we possess less authentic information than of the others. It is believed, however, that its further course has been choked up, and that the furrow in the soil is not perceptible much beyond the vicinity of Khiva itself. The term Oghus is applied by German writers to the Uzboi, which is generally accepted as the main channel from Sarykamish to the Caspian, whichever may have been the principal link between that lake and the river itself. The Kunya-darya-lik (the old little river) leaves the Oxus at a point fifteen miles lower down the river than the Doudon, and runs in a direct north-westerly course to the city of Kunya Urgendj, and it then passes under the base of the Tchink into the Sarykamish lake. This branch has generally been considered the main channel, and the term Uzboi has been extended so as to embrace that channel known as the Kunya-darya-lik. Major Wood expresses the opinion that the Uzboi was more probably "the channel of that other river into which the southerly overflow from Lake Aral finally resolved itself, and which is mentioned by Masudi in the tenth century;" but here we take it as the principal channel of the Oxus, because it is in all probability by means of it alone that the course of that river can be effectually diverted.

Whether the Kunya-darya-lik or the Doudon was the main course of the Oxus in olden days matters little at present; and the only practical problem that has to be considered is, which of them offers the easier and more satisfactory means of carrying the water of the Amou Darya in a perennial stream across the Khivan desert to the shores of Balkhan bay? The beds of both of those channels are now dried up save where the excess waters of a time of flood are diverted into various portions of them as a matter of safety; and along their course may be traced numerous dams which have been erected at several periods to keep out the main stream of the Oxus. It is important to note that these channels are a continuous low and level hollow in the Khivan plain; and at a glance there appears to be no other obstacle in the way of re-flooding them than the dams already referred to. These have certainly not been the only, or perhaps the chief, cause of the change in the course of the Oxus in the seventeenth century; but it is natural to suppose that they have contributed to that result, which has been of the most complete kind. With regard to the Uzboi itself, which extends in a southerly direction as far as the Igdy wells, and then in a westerly direction as far as Balkhan bay, it has been described as possessing the appearance of a "great ruined ravine," and in its bed are to be found lakes and wells, often of salt or brackish, but sometimes of fresh, water. The Uzboi forms the highway across the northern portion of the Kara Kum, and it has at times been suggested that it forms an admirable track for a railway from Krasnovodsk to Khiva. But the more hopeful plan, both in its prospects of success and utility, has been to make it a waterway to Central Asia. The Uzboi is also broken across by great mounds of sand, which, Vambery tells us, are of considerable altitude and great breadth.

There is, among other arms of the Oxus, the Loudon canal, which has recently been refilled, and of which something must here be said for the elucidation of the question under treatment. The Loudon canal used to flow from the vicinity of the fortified place of Bend into the lake of Aibughir. By means of that canal, which carried off a considerable portion of the waters of the Oxus, Aibughir was a lake, forming the south-west corner of the Aral sea. In that quarter of the Khivan state a section of the Yomult Turcomans resided and still reside; but between them and the Khan feuds were of frequent occurrence. In this quarter of Asia it has been, since the days of the sons of Genghis Khan, a common practice in warfare to supplement military strength and skill by manual labour; and whenever an enemy appeared too strong to be resisted in the field, the rivers and canals of the country have been dammed up, either to cause a flood to retard his advance, or for the purpose of removing the fertilising means which nature had placed at the disposal of the antagonistic people or tribe. It was with this latter object in view that the Khan of Khiva, in 1857, erected a dam across the upper end of the Loudon canal, near the fort of Bend, for in that year the Yomult chief, Atta Mourad Khan, declared war upon the Kkan, and the Khan retaliated in the manner described. Now, whether because that dam was imperfectly constructed, or that the force of the

Oxus was too great at this point to be restrained by any ordinary barrier, we know not; but for several years—Von Helwald refers to it—there had been symptoms that the dam erected at the entrance to the Loudon canal was insufficient to the strain that was daily brought against it. Observers said it was only a question of time when it would give way.

In the meanwhile, the Aibughir gulf, partly through the damming of the Loudon canal, and partly through the sinking of the Aral sea, had become dried up; and where there had once been a gulf, and in prehistoric times a mighty sea, there are now to be found the *kibitkas* and *aouls* of the Yomult Turcomans. For twenty years this has been the state of things with regard to Aibughir and the Loudon canal, and during that period the Yomults have been more subservient than theretofore to the Khan. It will be remembered that it was against these people that the Russians took those operations after the fall of Khiva, about which Mr. Schuyler gave us such remarkable revelations in his work on Turkestan. The damming up of the Loudon canal appears to have been attended with the one beneficent result that these Turcomans became more peaceably disposed than ever they had been before. The evil, however, of the act was also very apparent, for the waters of the Oxus, unable to find their usual outlet on the west, were forced to seek in those eastern ones—the Chertambye and Taldyk more particularly—the vent of which they had been deprived; and those branches, numerous as they are, were really incapable of performing what was required of them. The delta of the Oxus became more and more the almost useless swamp which it is at present; and the invaluable waters of the great river have been wasted on the Aral sea, which it would be far better disappeared altogether than to remain in its present useless state. The damming of the Loudon canal effected a temporary good, but at a serious price, for it aggravated evils which were already bad enough. It remains to be seen what its re-flooding signifies.

About the middle of October last the Russian papers announced that the Amou Darya had returned to its original bed. No details were vouchsafed to us, but with an air of triumph—as with reason they might have been triumphant had what they said been literally true—the Russian journalists proclaimed that it was only necessary to make this change definitive, and thus create a new route to India—the shortest and easiest—as well as secure the connection of the Russian possessions in Central Asia with the rest of the empire. Had that, which the Russians in their first glow of hope imagined had, occurred, there can be no doubt that even the wild suggestions of the Moscow and St. Petersburg press during the first week after the receipt of the news would not have been too far-fetched or exaggerated. To say that it would have been of great military and political importance is to treat with a light heart a circumstance that would have simply been a complete revolution in Central Asian affairs of the most momentous kind. But it is idle to speculate on what might have been, as the original news was entirely false and misleading. The

Amou Darya had not returned to its original bed or shown any disposition to do so. The dam erected twenty years ago in the Loudon channel had been burst through, as had been clearly foreseen that it would; and the Oxus was once more seeking its old outlet into the gulf of Aibughir. But as there is no desire to minimise the importance of any event connected with Central Asia in these pages, before we pass on to other subjects it is necessary to inquire, is there any importance at all in this fact, and if so, what is it?

It is highly improbable that the Loudon channel is still in a state of preservation as far as the Aibughir gulf. Probably it does not extend intact much to the west of Kunya Urgendj, which is upon its banks. In that case, the river, not having any proper vent, will flood the surrounding country, and continue to do so until the Khivans have taken some fresh step to regulate or check its encroachments. This step will most likely be the restoration of the dam at Bend, and a return to the *status quo ante*. There is just the possibility, however, that the Russians will have a voice in the matter, and it is conceivable that their attention having been turned to this subject, which has such historical claims upon them, they may devote more energy than they usually do to a matter that, if carried out, would make their advance on India a surer, if a slower, process than it can by any possibility be at present. And if such be the case, and the waters of the Oxus having presumably reached Kunya Urgendj, the country round which was flooded some time ago—

communications being maintained by boat alone—
an effort will be made not to carry the river into
its old channel beyond that town, but, by the construction of a canal—only three miles in length
—from it to the Kunya-darya-lik, to divert the
waters of the Loudon into that main channel which
eventually becomes the Uzboi. We say that the
Russians might attempt something of this sort, not
that we think it would be successful, but because the
tone of Russian official and scientific circles seems
to be that something should now be done in this
matter. Although the Loudon channel so far as
Kunya Urgendj may be in a good state of preservation
compared with the others, it is difficult to conceive
how the Oxus is to be turned by it into the Uzboi,
even if the Uzboi had been dug out and prepared for
its reception.

There is consequently a very slight prospect indeed
of the re-flooding of the Loudon canal being attended
by any permanent result in so far as the diversion of
the Oxus is concerned. Rather is it probable that the
Khivans may seek to stem at once this fresh inroad,
which threatens to flood a settled portion of the
khanate and also to again fill up that portion of
the country towards Aibughir which has become
inhabited and settled. If the Russians find that their
own design is futile they can scarcely forbid the repairing of the dam at Bend, which will be constructed on
a stronger basis than before. In the absence of specific
information of the state of things in Khiva it would
be hazardous to venture an opinion as to whether the

breaking-in of the Oxus has been regulated by human means or not; but its importance, save as an incentive to the Russians, is certainly very slight. *

There certainly appears to be no justification for the very jubilant views that prevailed at a meeting of the Russian Imperial Geographical Society, when the secretary, in his lengthy report, did not add much to what was already known of this inundation. He read a letter from the Khan of Khiva, however, which threw a ray of light upon the cause of the phenomenon. According to Seyyid Mahomed, the winter of 1877–78 was remarkably severe in Central Asia, and a mass of snow accumulated which in the spring caused floods more extensive than any that have taken place during the present century. All the way along the lower course of the Oxus the surface of the river rose to the top of the bank, and at length the waters broke through the barrier at three different points below Khiva, each about forty miles apart, and the inundation of the Kara Kum commenced. No opposition being encountered by the flood, the waters naturally swept towards the depression in the desert which originally held the Oxus, and forming a junction in this hollow, they filled up a number of stagnant lakes, including the spacious Sarykamish, and continued their west-

* The principal distances explaining the circumstances previously narrated are: from Bend to Kunya Urgendj, thirty-five miles; Kunya-Urgendj to the Kunya-darya-lik, two and a half miles; from the latter point to Sarykamish, one hundred and ten miles; Sarykamish to the Igdy wells, one hundred and eighty miles; and the Igdy wells to Balkhan bay, two hundred and fifty miles.

ward course in the direction of the Caspian, until the limit of their volume was reached. As soon as the spring floods began to subside, the Khan set labourers to work to repair the river bank, and by this time probably two of the rents have been closed. The third, however, on account of its size, will have to remain open until the Russians assist in the work of restoration, and, at any rate, will not be meddled with until it has been examined by the engineers despatched by General Possiet to view the effects of the inundation. In all likelihood the breach will be kept open altogether, the floods having occasioned a material benefit to Khiva in covering the contiguous desert with a convenient waterway (?), which may be ultimately extended to the Caspian. Without any effort on the part of Russia the four hundred and fifty miles of burning desert, treeless and waterless, intervening between Krasnovodsk and Khiva have been reduced to one hundred and sixty, and at a stroke the Oxus has opened up a highway which bids fair to change the fate of Central Asia.

Is the task, then, of bringing the Oxus back to its old Caspian outlet impossible? Must the design be given up as unattainable? Are all the aspirations that have been formed, on the supposition that it could be effected, to be abandoned? Herr Kiepert declares that it is impossible, and that this prospect is a mere delusion and a dream of Slav credulity.* He goes on to say that the only reasonable project would be to construct

* See "National Zeitung," 28th November, 1878.

a railway from the Caspian to the Aral. It should here be stated that if the bed of the Uzboi is to be utilised as the road for this line it will require to be levelled almost as carefully as if it were to receive the Oxus; and consequently the expense in this particular would not be much greater for either project. But is not Herr Kiepert a little rash in making this sweeping assertion, or rather, which is more to the point, do Russian authorities take the same gloomy view of its feasibility? Whoever knows anything of Russian official and scientific circles will at once say that they do not, as witness the absurdly over-sanguine meeting of the Imperial Geographical Society just quoted. The principal points of Herr Kiepert's criticism are the following. He begins by calling attention to the "re-appearance of the great Central Asian sea-serpent, that 'dream of Slav credulity,' the restoration of the Amou Darya, or Oxus, to its ancient bed; and he considers that General Stebnitzki's report of his explorations in 1873-5 brings down to its real proportions a 'warmed-up myth' which has at times dazzled Russian ambition and ignorance, from Peter the Great's days to ours, with the extravagant idea of the possession of an uninterrupted waterway from Moscow to Khulm or Kundus—that is, to within about one hundred miles from the Hindoo Koosh. It has been conclusively shown by Von Gojen and Lerch that the statements and traditions of the ancient Arabs and others, which describe the Oxus as once flowing, not, as now, into the Aral, but into the Caspian, were mere speculative combinations exclusively based on the fact of the existence of an abandoned river-bed at certain points of the plateau or isthmus of Ust Urt, which lies between the two great inland seas. Professor Kiepert alludes to Peter the Great's recognition of the value of this old channel as an eventual element in the realisation of his plans of Asiatic military or commercial enterprise—plans on which, we should observe, authentic information is as silent as it is on the hydraulic hints said to have been given to Peter by a certain Turcoman who visited Astrachan. Better informed than Peter, the Czar Alexander should know that the old bed of the Oxus, which General Stebnitzki examined for a length of four hundred and forty miles, belongs to geology, and not to history. The entire absence of all traces of anterior civilisation, such as remains of buildings or canals, along the line of the General's exploration shows that the abandoned channel dates from pre-historic Turkestan, whereas the present Oxus runs through comparatively modern alluvial formations of its own making. From time to time the river overflows its Khivan banks, pouring and filtering as far westward as Lake Sarykamish. Arrived at the 'Yellow Reeds' (ninety miles from the Khivan town Bend), the truant waters would have three hundred and forty miles to run before reaching Balkhan bay in the Caspian, and, says Professor Kiepert, the job of completely restoring their ancient bed, over such a length of desert isthmus, would overtask the financial resources of the richest State; so that "Slav credulity" must abandon this seductive dream in favour of the only practical method by which Russian commerce

4

can be conveniently brought to the heart of Central Asia—by the construction, that is, of a railway between the Caspian and the sea of Aral."

The question we have then to consider is, What is the most promising plan for effecting the diversion of the course of the Oxus? The following remarks represent more the opinions of a well-informed foreigner than those of the writer, who gives them here as the expression of one who is entitled to consideration upon Asian matters, and especially upon the question of the Oxus. It will be seen that at the least they qualify Herr Kiepert's strictures.

So far down its course as the Khivan town of Hazarasp the river Oxus flows in one unbroken stream. It is in its lower course from that place to the Aral— a distance of two hundred and fifty miles—that it is broken up into numerous channels, some on the right bank and others on the left. In the delta of the river which lies immediately below Nukus on the one side and Khodjeili on the other, the waste of its waters is extreme. It is computed that only half the volume of the river reaches the Aral, but there is no reason for disbelieving the assertion that the full volume extends as far down the river as Hazarasp. From that place the Doudon channel is traced in a north-westerly direction to Sarykamish, a distance of two hundred and fifty miles, and although we are not as well informed as we could wish of the present condition of this channel, which certainly has been dammed at several points, there is some evidence to show that to clear it out would be neither an arduous nor a lengthy proceeding. On that operation the whole undertaking would depend. The channel should be cleared out, levelled, and strengthened both in its embankments and its bottom, as the preliminary step. The Oxus should still be permitted to pursue its ordinary course towards the Aral while these works were in progress, and, if necessary, the first and principal dam might even be strengthened to prevent the river breaking through prematurely. The next step would be to execute the dredging operations that are no doubt necessary at Sarykamish; and it is probable that, to prevent waste and to secure the utmost economy in the volume of water, embankments on a large scale would also be required there. And then the Uzboi would have to be cleared out, levelled, and strengthened, just as the Doudon had been. The preliminary works would therefore consist in the preparation of two great channels—the one two hundred and fifty miles in length, the other rather more than four hundred miles—for the purpose of being the future bed of a great river, and in precautionary measures at the Sarykamish lakes lest some of the allvaluable stream should be wasted. In the scheme to which we have alluded these measures form the preliminary step.

When it becomes a matter of adapting means to ends, the great question of labour and expense has to be discussed, nor do the advocates of this particular proposal shirk the duty that of necessity devolves upon them. With regard to the question of labour, great stress is laid upon the fact that all the northern

4 *

Turcomans—the Yomults and the Chaudor in particular—would rejoice in a river being carried across Kara Kum, and would assist in securing this object so far as they could. The Khivans themselves would not be averse to the change, and whatever reputation they may enjoy for personal valour, they certainly have just claims to be considered admirable labourers and workmen. But perhaps the most favourable supply of labourers for these operations is to be found among the Karakalpaks* of the Delta of the Oxus, who have had experience in work of this kind, and are said to be desirous of following a settled life under any tolerable conditions. The labour question has never before prevented a Khivan khan carrying out either his works of construction or of destruction; and it would be strange indeed if Russia, with a wider field to obtain her workpeople from, and with greater influence and more money, should fail where the Usbeg rulers had succeeded. The labour difficulty is evidently not insuperable.

The question of expense is not so easy to be decided off-hand. The advocates of this scheme say that it would cost about fourteen million roubles,† and that the period required to carry it out would not be longer than two years. These views may be too sanguine; but they have been formed by men who have carefully worked the subject out. For that reason they may be considered to be approximate to the truth, even if not

* See "Shores of Lake Aral," page 157.
† About one million five hundred thousand pounds sterling at its present value.

strictly accurate. By comparison we shall best be able to test the question of expense. The alternative scheme which Herr Kiepert advocates is a railway across the desert from Krasnovodsk to Khiva, for which the cost even for a single line would certainly be four million pounds; and when we add the cost of wear and tear, the deficit in receipts as compared with expenditure, the capitalised amount necessary for the undertaking would probably amount to five or six millions sterling. For a third of this amount it is asserted that the Oxus could be diverted from its present course to one disemboguing in the Caspian. The time asked for the scheme would not be longer than that which would be required for the construction of a line of railway. Both as a matter of labour, expense, and time, the scheme with regard to the Oxus has the advantage over that for the construction of a railway. Of course that does not make the former feasible.

The preliminary steps have already been discussed. It is now necessary to consider how the crowning operation is to be carried out. The fundamental principle of this scheme is that no premature experiment should be made in effecting any modification in the existing course of the Oxus. The river should in no way be tampered with while the Doudon and Uzboi were being prepared for it. And regarding the question from this intelligent point of view, the rupture of the dam at Bend is a disaster and not a benefit. The absurd ejaculations on the part of the Russian press when news first came of the re-flooding of the petty Loudon canal —from the tone of which nothing less would be inferred than that the Oxus question had been solved—now appear revealed in all their absurdity beside the most intelligent scheme that has yet been devised by their countrymen. The Oxus cannot be brought into the Caspian save by very resolute action and considerable outlay. It will certainly not be accomplished in one stroke as if by a magician's wand.

The consummating act will only be undertaken when all the initial tasks, which have been specified, have been completed; but even then something more remains to be done than to break down the main dam at the entrance to the Doudon channel. The great recommendation of this channel over the others is that it branches off from the Oxus at a point where the river is in its full career; but is it to be only one arm of the river among others? Would the volume of the Oxus suffice to create a great river across the desert at the same time that a very considerable portion of its waters was diverted to the Aral and its other numerous outlets? There can be no hesitation in replying that it would not. It may even be questioned whether the volume of the Oxus would suffice to render a single channel across Kara Kum navigable. The destruction of the dam at the entrance of the Doudon channel would be only one portion of the consummating act. It should be followed, and that quickly, by the construction of another dam across the main channel of the river, and just below the point where the Doudon arm branched off. By this means the course of the river would be completely diverted into the Doudon channel, which would become the one bed of the River Oxus. By commencing operations at the Caspian end, and by completing the link from that sea to Sarykamish and thence to Khiva, the great problem of how to find a suitable channel for the river would be solved. It would only remain to decide how it was best to lead the river into that bed. By selecting the Doudon arm which branches off from the Oxus where that river is in full flow, not only is the greatest volume of water obtained, but there is only the necessity to construct one opposing dam. Of course that is in main stream, and would be no easy matter, although it would be simplified to a great extent by the destruction of the dam of the Doudon. On the other hand its advantages have already been stated, and must be apparent.

Lastly, there remains but one doubt, one unknown quantity. Assuming that the scheme has been carried out as suggested, that the main channel is arrested, that the embankments are strong, that the waste at Sarykamish is insignificant, and that the bottoms of the Uzboi and the Doudon are further excavated, if necessary, and made level,—assuming all these as accomplished, would the Oxus carry down sufficient water to flood the six hundred and fifty miles that intervene between Hazarasp and Balkhan bay to such an extent as to provide a stream navigable throughout its course? On that point there must be considerable doubt until the feat has been accomplished. And even if the answer be favourable it is one that assumes that there is not the slightest flaw in engineering judgment. But whatever the result, there can be no doubt that the Oxus can only be brought back to its Caspian outlet by damming the main channel to the Aral, and that can certainly be best accomplished at Hazarasp. The Russians themselves can only aspire to cope with this question in the spirit of those who have learnt the old Latin proverb that "Fortuna adjuvat fortes."

The question of the Amou Darya is a great question. The difficulty its solution presents is no slight one. Yet the Russians can have no claims to be held a great ruling power if they decline to attempt its solution because it is not easy. They cannot be compared to the Romans or the English, or even to several Asian nations, such as the Chinese and the Persians, if they treat with apathy and indifference this great problem on which the peaceful progress of their empire in Turkestan may be held to depend. It is improbable that they will much longer remain supine. They are urged into activity by the belief, well founded as it undoubtedly is, that to divert the Oxus into the Aral means increased prosperity for their Asiatic dominions; but they are still more impelled by a hope that in the solution of this question lies the best step towards an invasion of India. With a waterway from Derbend to Charjui, a distance of only nine hundred miles, Russia would have bridged that inhospitable gulf of steppe-land which intervenes between Orenburg and Tashkent. Without a war she would have connected the Caucasus and Western Turkestan, and by so doing enabled her generals to concentrate at Herat and Balkh those forces which, vast as they are, are now useless through their immobility and the distances which separate them from each other and from their common object, India. If the Afghan crisis passes away without an Anglo-Russian war, we may expect a very important development in the Oxus question; and the particular scheme referred to in these pages will in all probability be given precedence over every other.

It may be of general interest to insert here a brief narrative of the various attempts that have been made by the Russian Government in the past to solve the question connected with the course of the Amou Darya. It was during the reign of Peter the Great that information first reached Russia of the Amou Darya possessing more than one bed, and the news was brought to the Russian court by a Turcoman chief named Hodja Nefes. A Circassian prince, Alexander Bekovitch, who was high in favour with the Czar, introduced Hodja Nefes to Peter, and the question of the course of the Oxus was detailed for the first time to a Russian audience. It is not strange to find that the Turcoman placed a more seductive lure than geographical research before the Czar and his advisers. "In the country bordering the Amou gold sand was procured," and this raised a flutter of excitement in the bosoms of the Russian statesmen and courtiers, which operated far more potently upon their decision than any desire to lead the Oxus into the Caspian. But whatever the motives may have been, and however much Peter may have been induced by the representations of Hodja Nefes and his promises that the Turcomans would join heartily in any work to secure that end, we have only to judge of these things by the result.

Prince Bekovitch was authorised to undertake the enterprise.

In 1714 a reconnoitring expedition left the shores of the Caspian in the direction of Khiva. With this particular expedition everything went well, and maps were sent to Peter of the new region thus explored. The result was, of course, only partial, and much more remained to be done before even the old channel of the river could be determined. In the following year Prince Bekovitch was entrusted with a larger force, not less than six thousand men; but a large portion of this army remained at Krasnovodsk bay. He reached Karagash, on the Khivan frontier, with about three thousand troops. At first the Khan opposed his entry; but after a time, being won over by presents, and doubtless hoping to obtain more, he permitted him to remain. Prince Bekovitch did not hesitate to proclaim that he regarded Khiva merely as a half-way house in his progress through the States of Central Asia. But the Khan soon became discontented with his guests, and resolved to destroy them.

In a weak moment Bekovitch consented to the distribution of his force, and they were overcome and massacred in detail. The prince himself was reserved for a more cruel fate. He was flayed alive, and then murdered. Such was the termination of the Bekovitch enterprise, which at one time promised so auspiciously, and which was undertaken in so thorough and adequate a manner. Peter himself had no further opportunity of interfering beyond the Caspian, but he paved the way for fresh enterprises in this direction under his successors by the reduction of the harbour of Derbend.

From 1715 to 1837 nothing was done in this matter, and after more than one hundred and twenty years' interval the nominally scientific expedition of Peroffsky succeeded the more grandiose affair of Bekovitch. This expedition was a signal failure, since it was compelled to retreat before it had proceeded far into the desert, and was glad to find safety in the harbours on the shore of the Caspian, with the loss of nearly all its camels.

Since Peroffsky's year the attempts have been more frequent, and the bed of the Oxus has been more or less explored by Ivanof, Lomakine, and others. Lines of wells have been dug across in several directions from the Caspian to Khiva, and in one respect these would appear to have supplemented the absence of a railway or a waterway. But as a matter of fact it is not so. Communication between Krasnovodsk and Khiva is still attended by considerable danger both from man and nature; and there is no great caravan route here such as the Russians should in their own interests create. Military operations are hampered to a still greater extent, and the military sub-district of Trans-Caspiania is actually separated from that of Amou Darya by a greater distance than the latter is from Orenburg. These explorations will not be crowned with success until the Oxus or a railway forms a connecting link between the two seas of Caspian and Aral.

CHAPTER III.

THE RUSSIAN GOVERNMENT OF TURKESTAN.

IT is not easy to determine the modifications that have taken place since Mr. Schuyler penned his graphic description of the Russian administration in Central Asia,* and it is almost impossible to say whether there has been progress or retrogression. The Russian possessions in Turkestan at the present moment cover about four hundred and sixty thousand square miles, and the population of this vast region is at the highest computation under three millions. Yet within the confines of the Russian possessions are to be found the ruins of several powerful kingdoms, and the representatives of great conquering races and families, such as the Kipchak, the Usbeg, and the Kirghiz. The kingdom of Khokand has been completely absorbed, those of Bokhara and Khiva have been stripped of some of their possessions, and a province of the Chinese Empire has been retained at the cost

* "Turkistan," by Eugene Schuyler, vol. ii. chapter xiii.

of incurring the resentment of its Government and people. The total subjected population is between two millions and a half and three millions of human beings, scattered over a region which exceeds Western Europe in size. Among the subjected races there is no connecting link save that of religion, which has always in their case proved singularly valueless, and the Russian garrison is very nearly as large as that which is stationed in India. It will be more convenient to discuss the military situation in another chapter.

Up to the year 1867 affairs were conducted in Central Asia in what can only be called a hap-hazard fashion under the control of the Governor of Orenburg; but the triumphs of Generals Tchernaieff, Krjihanoffsky, and Romanoffsky, had resulted in the advance of Russian arms from Kazala at the mouth of the Syr Darya to Tashkent and Chinaz. It became necessary to constitute some definite authority in this new region. Whereas before that year the military and civil authority had been reposed in separate hands, they were henceforth to be wielded by the same functionary. A ukase (see Appendix), which appeared on the 11th (23rd) of July in that year, and which was published by the " Journal de St. Petersburg" a few days afterwards, announced the formation of the Central Asian possessions into a governor-generalship, with the seat of government at Tashkent. For the first four months General Romanoffsky filled this new and much-coveted post ; but it was in November found convenient to recall him in accordance with some State necessity, and on the 17th of that month General Kaufmann arrived in Tashkent as the representative of the Czar.

Before that time Kaufmann had been an officer attached to the staff of the Czar. He had never been in Central Asia, and he possessed no knowledge of the subject over which he was henceforth to exercise supreme control. But these were not his only faults, for, being naturally of an extremely vain disposition, it was not long before he became persuaded of his own special qualifications for the high office which he held, and strove in many ways to add a lustre to his administration by the prosecution of numerous campaigns, and by a series of conquests that have so far been unprofitable. The state which he maintains at Tashkent, his Cossack guard, the strict etiquette which fences him around, and the court balls that are given in close imitation of those held at St. Petersburg, all these are now well known, thanks to Mr. Schuyler, and have earned for the Czar's representative the nickname of Yarim Padishah, or half-king. But the actual result of all this sham State ceremony is that in practical affairs General Kaufmann is a cypher. He knows nothing of the subject which he is supposed to decide upon, and is consequently bound to guide his own impulse by the advice of such men as Abramoff and Kolpakoffsky. There are others in the civil administration who are equally influential, though less honourably distinguished, and in all directions in Turkestan an autocratic officialism works its own way and for its own ends, seeking only to flatter and to pander to the weaknesses of the Russian general, who is by a Czar's patronage supreme.

There have been many unfortunate results of this delusive condition of affairs, and disclosures have been made that the work of administration was not being conducted in a proper manner—only, however, to be hushed up again as quickly as possible. During the year 1877 there were circumstantial reports that serious discrepancies and errors had been discovered in the official returns from Tashkent; and officials high in the confidence of Kaufmann were said to be incriminated. The peculation referred to was of too systematic a kind to admit of the explanation that it was accidental, and a commission of inquiry was sent out to investigate the matter on the spot. From that day to this nothing has been heard of that commission, or of the result of its investigations.

It was understood at the time, on what was supposed to be good authority, that the peculations had been of the most systematic character, and had principally been carried on in fictitious transfers of land. But after all, this is only one instance of the discretion which is left, under General Kaufmann's regime, to subordinates; and there are many others. Ambitious officers have been permitted to undertake explorations —scientific and otherwise—which were far from being necessary or prudent, and there are even instances of wars having been sanctioned to propitiate inconvenient rivals. It is the system, however, that is rotten throughout. The service, military and civil, throughout the Russian possessions in Central Asia, aspires to make things pleasant for all of its members rather than, by any self-denying ordinance, to maintain the efficiency of the service at its highest point. There is undoubtedly an *esprit de corps*, but it exists at the expense of patriotism. Some travellers* have said that there is a laxity of morals among Russian officers and officials, which greatly detracts from their claims to be considered representatives of a civilised nation. Without pressing this charge home against them, there is abundant evidence on other points to prove that the Russian who seeks a career in Central Asia does so in a desperate mood, and never aspires to display any higher purpose than that of a somewhat reckless adventurer. He leaves the pleasures and luxuries of Moscow, or the capital, to find beyond the steppe that place of refuge which his folly or his crime in Europe has compelled him to seek. By such men as these is the vast dominion of Russia in Central Asia administered, and how can it be expected that such a governing body could be respectable, or respected by the sedate and dignified Mussulmans of Khokand and Samarcand? There is nothing in the ordinary Russian to attract sympathy or to command respect. Some affirm that under certain conditions he makes an amusing and gay companion; but if he be, as Professor Gregorieff asserts, the modern representative of the all-conquering Roman, it must be allowed that he has lost those personal attributes which were the mark of the coun-

* Even Major Wood, who cannot be called an anti-Russian writer, supports this accusation.

trymen of the Cæsars. To the more ordinary view a Russian does not present the same attractive or striking appearance that he evidently does to his panegyrist and compatriot; and some are found to maintain that he is only a Tartar of the same race as those whom, by the aid of Western science, he has subdued, and who may yet, in future times, drive back the Muscovite, by the same means that he himself has employed, to the walls of Moscow and the shores of the Euxine.

The formation of the governorship of Turkestan was not unopposed. It may even be said that it was carried out despite the opposition of many influential persons and the adverse opinion of at least one State inquiry. The Steppe Commission, which had been appointed to the task of exploring the steppe early in the year 1867, had done good service, and the principal and permanent result of its labours had been that a definite scheme was placed before the Russian Government for the prosecution of military enterprises in Central Asia on a settled plan. Once for all, the old hap-hazard way of attempting to achieve what had been foreshadowed in the mythical programme called Peter the Great's Will, was to give place to a logical and clearly defined method, which would enable a settled government to carry on systematic encroachments in Turkestan, beyond the Oxus, and at last in Cabul, and thus bring Russian bayonets in triumph to the Hindoo Koosh and Persia, and perhaps ultimately, in some weak hour of confidence on the part of a British Government, to the passes of the

Suleiman and the banks of the Indus. That was the object which loomed far ahead as the out-come of their task, and the Steppe Commission—of which M. de Giers, Head of the Asiatic Department of the Foreign Office, was a prominent member—more than any other person, or any other body of persons, laid the seeds from which in ten years has sprung the formidable aggressive power of Russia in Central Asia.

But there was a powerful opposition to its proposals, which were at one moment withdrawn. The Governor-General of Orenburg, under whose supervision all the previous military operations had been carried out along the Syr Darya and against the Kirghiz, was naturally loth that his old authority should be taken from him. General Krjihanoffsky was unable to turn the opinion of the Government against the changes advocated by the Steppe Commission, and—although his opinion, in so far as it protested against submitting the Kirghiz tribes to two different forms of government, has been proved accurate by later experience—those who take a larger view of the question must admit that the transfer of the central authority from Orenburg to Tashkent gave a vitality and *impetus* to Russia's progress towards India, that it is impossible as yet accurately to measure. With the installation of a Russian governor, and a settled administration at Tashkent, it became only a question of time when the neighbouring effete and tyrannical rulers should either sink into a state of subjection, or disappear altogether before the destroying influence of the Russian presence. The advance to Tashkent made a further progress also absolutely necessary. That city, strategically speaking, might be considered to be untenable so long as Samarcand was in hostile hands and Khokand occupied a flank position of great vantage. To render it as secure as a capital should be, and to dissipate the last vestige of resistance on the part of the Usbegs and the Kipchaks, those wars were undertaken which secured Samarcand as a possession for the Czar, and which ultimately laid Khokand at his feet. With Tashkent as the centre of a new power thrust into the heart of Turkestan, there was nothing strange or unexpected in those events; but had the report of the Steppe Commission been disregarded, and Tashkent remained only an advanced post of the Russian Empire, and not a new capital, it is very probable that the progress of Russian arms in a southerly direction would have been less precipitate, and less full of menace to India.

The Steppe Commission also was not content with the formation of a new government in Turkestan whose destiny would lie in the hands of a magnate only imperfectly under the control of the Imperial authorities. It was necessary to add to its dimensions before these had been rendered formidable by successful conquest; and with that object an immense tract of country was severed from the governorship of Semipalatinsk, and included in the new administration of Turkestan. This region was known as Semiretchinsk,* and may be roughly defined as all that country lying between Semipalatinsk and the Irtish on the one hand, and the

* Semiretchinsk means "the country of the seven rivers."

frontiers of Khokand on the other. It is divided into the following sub-districts:—Sergiopol, Kopal, Vernoe, Issik Kul, Tokmak, and Priilinsk (Kuldja). Therefore the Russian frontier from the neighbourhood of Chuguchak to the Aral Sea and the river Oxus is under the same head, the Governor-General at Tashkent. That authority is, it must be remembered, a military authority acting in conjunction with the War Office, and in obedience to, if to anyone at all, the Commander-in-Chief. In fact the official title of his jurisdiction is "The Turkestan Military District." There can be no doubt that whatever disadvantages there may be in regard to the management of internal affairs, and perhaps also as towards Russia's relations with China, in severing Semiretchinsk from Siberia, that change facilitated the adoption of a clearly defined and consistent policy towards those Mahomedan states which lay immediately beyond the actual Russian dominions. M. de Giers protested against this transfer in particular, but the military authorities over-ruled his opinion and advice. One effect of this change has certainly been that Russia in Central Asia has not pursued that successful policy of tact and gentle pressure towards China which she had always so skilfully followed in Siberia. At Tashkent there is evidently not such an intimate knowledge of Chinese character as there has been shown at Semipalatinsk and Kiachta.

The Governor-General of this extensive province, which since its creation has been increased by annexations in Bokhara, Khokand, Kuldja, and Khiva, is appointed by the Czar, and within the limits of his authority he exercises supreme power without control of any kind whatever. The military governors of Semiretchinsk, Syr Darya, Ferghana, and Amou Darya, are all equally subordinate to him, and although the appointment to these posts is vested in the hands of the War Minister, they possess no independent authority. The salary of the Governor-General is supposed to amount to only seven thousand pounds a year, but there appears to be an indiscriminate custom of setting down against the State revenue all expenditure. By this means General Kaufmann's salary becomes pocket-money.

The principal points to be considered in the Russian administration are the sources, and the amount, of the revenue; the expenditure; the dispensation of justice; the means of education that are placed at the disposal of the natives; and, lastly, what the effect of these various circumstances is upon the relations between the ruler and the subjected. Let us consider these in detail, and in the order given. When Russia advanced into Central Asia it was supposed that the khanates were naturally rich countries, and that they only required a very moderate amount of labour to become highly productive provinces, which would not only be self-supporting but would also contribute a handsome surplus either directly or indirectly to the State coffers. When it was found that the reality was of a completely different hue, and that the agricultural, commercial, and mineral resources of the country were all at their lowest ebb, the Russians, disappointed as they were, loudly proclaimed those military advantages which neither the improvidence of rulers, nor the feuds of races, could take from lands which were barren of everything else.

To bring prosperity back to these regions can only be accomplished by a very judicious, and also a very generous expenditure of money in the construction of roads and irrigation works; when with a settled peace, and the spread of tranquillity, they would become fairly prosperous in the course of several generations. But this prospect is one that the grandchildren only of those who rule now could hope to benefit by. It is too slow a method for the Russian rulers and soldiers of to-day. Works of such a kind as this are not approved of at Tashkent. In the eyes of Russian officers they can all wait their day. They will come in good time, after —I was going to say, the Russians had returned with the spoils of India—but then that is utterly visionary and impossible. At all events, undertakings of this description are not at present appreciated at Russian head-quarters. The tide of conquest has also carried Russia so rapidly along that there has been no time for looking behind or around. The goal lies before, and there is no sign as yet that its attractions have faded in any degree. In Russia's revenue account there figures therefore no return from public works. These are not, like ours in many instances in India, as yet unremunerative; they do not exist.

It is very strange to find that almost one-third of the revenue is contributed by Russians themselves in various ways, and that of the small sum collected in the gross only two-thirds actually proceed from the subject peoples. The most remunerative of all the sources of revenue is that from the land and house property. This, taking in the whole of the Central Asian region, now amounts to something more than eight hundred thousand roubles. Of course the tax paid by the Kirghiz nomads is included in this amount. There is also an impost on arable land and fruit; but of this we are unable to obtain any certain return.* It does not fall short of three hundred thousand roubles in any case. The road tax brings in some one hundred and sixty thousand roubles; that on licences twenty thousand roubles; customs two hundred and fifty thousand roubles; and several other minor sources of revenue, such as stamps, etc., about one hundred thousand roubles. These figures give a revenue derivable from the native subjects alone of about one million six hundred and thirty thousand roubles. A later but less authentic return gives a somewhat more favourable estimate of the revenue, placing that raised from native sources alone at two and a half million roubles, a large portion of which is derivable from the new districts of Amou Darya and Ferghana. But when we remember that this estimate is made on the basis of the rouble being worth only two shillings, and that the one before given takes it at its nominal equivalent of three shillings, it will be seen that the difference is not very material.

* Mr. Schuyler states that in 1872 it was two hundred and seventy-six thousand roubles. It is probably much more now, as Khokand and Amou Darya have been incorporated since then.

From the European branch of the community an additional sum of about eight hundred thousand roubles is raised, principally in excise dues, stamps, postage, etc. But more than a third of this amount is raised from excise alone, and this is paid almost exclusively by the Russians themselves. Of late years some considerable sum appears to have been derived from the sale of Government lands, but of this source of revenue no certain statement has been published. But including every impost of the most insignificant kind, the Tashkent exchequer does not receive annually in the shape of revenue three millions of roubles.* And the revenue shows no elements of elasticity. The figures given here are greater than those given by Mr. Schuyler in 1872, simply because Russia now draws from two additional provinces to those she ruled in that year. That surplus may be found to be an actual deficit when we come to consider the increased expenditure.

The excise tax, which falls as a burden on the not overpaid official Russian world, is the only tax that shows an increase each year. The benefits of Russian civilisation have not as yet resulted in any improvement in the material prosperity of Central Asiatics, principally because there has been no effort to produce that result. Glowing reports were circulated of the enormous impulse that had been given to the export of cotton from Turkestan. An official statement was published which

---

* It is doubtful also at what value the various official return compute the rouble.

announced that several millions of *poods* had been exported—during the year 1877 it was assumed, but as the report was careful not to state during what period of time, we are compelled to test its accuracy by reference to other sources of information. No proof of this assertion can be found, and it is evidently, from the state of the revenue, an exaggerated perversion of the facts. It is quite possible that the amount stated was from the commencement of the Russian government in Turkestan. Nor can there be discovered in any other article of commerce that rapid progress of which Russian journals have made so much talk. The Russian revenue in Central Asia appears to be as hopelessly stationary as it well can be, and the sources from which it is derived are limited. There is no elasticity to be perceived anywhere; while the expenditure which is necessary for the maintenance of Russian rule continues to increase, despite attempts at economy in some of the governments, and notwithstanding special commissions of inquiry to effect that object in them all.

The expenditure exceeds the enormous—relatively speaking—sum of nine millions of roubles, and of this sum about five millions, or more than one-half, are devoted to military expenditure of one kind or another. One million roubles are expended upon the civil service in the shape of salaries and expenses. Three-quarters of a million is absorbed by postal expenses; and half a million figures as extras, of which the greater portion is, we imagine, connected in some way with the army expenditure. Thirteen thousand roubles are set aside for the educational purposes of some three millions of people; and for those great undertakings which figure in our Indian Budget under the head of extraordinary expenditure we look entirely in vain. Judging the Russian rule in Central Asia exclusively by the light of its official budget, we find that its revenue is not only small, but that it is also stationary; and that its outlay is large and steadily increasing. Russian economists have a very serious question to ask themselves about this expenditure. Is it necessary? Is it unavoidable? Mr. Schuyler has pointed out several useless items in the bill which might be struck out at once. Of all the evils, that is certainly the greatest which is caused by the numerous staff appointments that are created apparently for the interest of their occupiers alone. But another and possibly an unavoidable difficulty is raised by the fact that provisions of all kinds are so enormously dear in Turkestan, that the cost of keeping European soldiers, more especially cavalry, there is very great. The taxes which are imposed upon flour, forage, and live stock seem only to be a fiction and a sham; for the native producer replies by adding the amount of the duty on to the regular price, thus incurring no loss whatever, and compelling Russia to pay in a great measure out of its own coffers the revenue of which it stands in need. Poor as Central Asia undoubtedly is, it would not require a financier of the first magnitude to restore something like an equilibrium to the finances, provided military expenditure were curtailed. If Russia's possessions are not as valuable as she supposed, they ought at least to be self-supporting; and where the khans were able to make both ends meet, it is not easy to see why Russia should so completely fail. We cannot accept as the cause of this deficit the explanation that Russia is so weak as to pay through the nose for what she purchases. As the matter stands, there is, according to the published accounts, an annual deficit of six million roubles which has to be made good by the Imperial exchequer. As the Turkestan army is technically a local army, Russia has not the satisfaction of possessing an actual addition to her military strength in it; and, as a matter of fact, for offensive purposes on a large scale the Turkestan army must be reinforced, and strengthened in artillery and munitions of war from Europe, before it could take the field. In the estimates of expenditure we have given, no allowance is made for any extraordinary expenses such as those connected with the military preparations in Turkestan during the summer of 1878, or for the expedition against Khokand; and these have to be added to make the absolute charge against the Russian exchequer understood. There are also the expenses of the Trans-Caspian district, which figure under the Caucasian returns. Considering the activity of General Lomakine, and the great cost of animals of transport, etc., the expenses connected with that general's governorship are not slight, and they certainly are a dead loss. It is probable that during last year the deficit has not been six millions but ten millions. Russia is not so rich that she can afford to waste that amount annually. The ruling powers cannot continue to demand that sacrifice, and the

Russian people will not consent to the continuance of that outlay unless some ultimate reward—showy or substantial—is placed very tangibly before them.

With regard to the dispensation of justice, we find that there is a law for the ruling and another for the ruled. So long as it is a matter of litigation between two persons, each equally a Russian subject, there is a civil court, presided over by a Russian official, which decides the dispute in accordance with the law of the empire. And if the ruled quarrel *inter se* they are allowed to decide the matter in dispute in their own courts and before their own judges. But in all criminal cases the Russian court exercises supreme jurisdiction; while for treason, murder, and other extreme offences there is the military court, which is above all. In this court cases are judged with military brevity and decision. In former times the kazis, or local magistrates, were appointed by the ruler; but now the Russians have lowered the old influence of these officials by deciding that they were to be elected by the people. The kazi, as an official created by their suffrage, lost all the claims to respect which he could claim as a ruler over them independent of their good will. Few Asiatics have yet learnt to regard representatives chosen by themselves as worthy of esteem and support. They appreciate force and superior energy alone.

The amount which figures in the estimate under the head of "Education" is, perhaps, the best proof that Russia has done literally nothing for her subjects in this matter. She has left them exactly as she found them, under the influence of their unlettered mollahs, and without any practical knowledge whatever. Were Turkestan a thickly-peopled country she would speedily reap the punishment for this neglect; as it is, she has no hold upon, nor, indeed, any certain mode of ascertaining what is, the opinion of the subject races. The few Russian schools there are are devoted exclusively to the education of the children of the Russian officials; but of these there is no necessity to say anything. The native schools are divided into *makhtabs*—the preparatory schools—and *madrassees*—colleges or more advanced schools—and all of these are religious in their character. The *makhtabs* are supported by voluntary contributions from the parents of the scholars, and these take the form of money, provisions, clothes, etc. There is no regular charge for any scholar, and the deficiencies of the poorer are made up out of the abundance of the wealthier.

The students of the *madrassees* are kept and educated free of charge. Each *madrassee* has a portion of land, or some other endowment, attached to it; and out of that revenue the Mahomedan youths are provided with the necessaries of life, and such literary knowledge as is extant among the *mollahs* who officiate as tutors and examiners in these colleges. Education commences at an early age, boys beginning to learn the Koran at six years old. But the range of subjects is limited, and although doubtless admirably calculated to improve the powers of recitation, the ability to recite passages from the Koran and from a few other Mahomedan authors scarcely tends to enlarge the ideas or to give a general knowledge of surrounding affairs. Without throwing any aspersion on the character of the teachers themselves, it may be said that the educational methods adopted in these *madrassees* are absurd, and an utter waste of time and money. For this the Russian Government is responsible. It cannot shirk its duties by proclaiming that it has desired to leave the natives to their own devices, and to interfere as little as possible with their customs, prejudices, and practices. The very reason which justifies Russia's presence in Turkestan is that it is a civilised country, which is bound to set a higher example to its subjects, and to see that they follow it in so far as it is possible or reasonable to expect them to adopt new and strange ways. The subject of education is the test question of whether a power is fit to govern inferior races or not. Russia has done nothing for Central Asiatics. She has left them in their own dark, narrow ways, and it is conceivable, from what we know of Russian character, that the day might arrive when there will be in Turkestan a race descended from Russian officials which will correspond, in its vices and its barbarism, with the Englishry of Ireland during the Middle Ages.

Thirteen thousand roubles are expended on the education of the children of Russian officials. Not a penny out of the State coffers goes for the instruction of the Mahomedan subject, who is permitted to remain in his own dark path. The day must come when Russia will repent her of this short-sighted policy, and then it is at least open to question whether the same gratitude will be evinced towards Russia's lenience in religious and educational matters as is too confidently expected. By taking over the estates and endowments of the *madrassees*, and by appointing European supervisors—Germans would be the best—Russia could secure a control over the people, that she has not at present, at the same time that she gave an impetus to education and learning in Asia. But it will be many years before such a scheme is undertaken. For once it came into operation the State would have to carry out in Russia itself some larger scheme of public instruction than at present exists, as otherwise the Russian would rapidly sink behind his Asiatic fellow-subject in point of education and knowledge. Improbable as it is, therefore, that Russia will for many years to come take any step in this direction, it may be confidently asserted that until it has been made Russia can lay no claims to having carried out that " civilising mission " which has so often been declared to be her peculiar duty in Central Asia.

The Russians have, however, performed one useful service for their subjects. They have given them tranquillity; and with tranquillity must come in the course of years an increase in material wealth and welfare. North of the Zarafshan range there is peace; and order prevails in all the cities, and among the Kirghiz on the steppe. The example has been infectious in Bokhara and Khiva, which are practically Russian provinces; and it is only among the Turcomans that something like the old condition of things exists. This is due to Russia, and to the credit of it she is fairly entitled. That benefit is in itself not sufficient to give the Russian Government claims to any general admiration, for the safety of her dominions in Asia depends, more than upon anything else, upon the preservation of order within them and in their immediate neighbourhood.

Something has also been done in the improvement of the roads, and there are several grand routes in different directions connecting the various dependencies of the State with each other, as well as with Europe. The telegraph has been laid down along all the principal roads, and Tashkent is in telegraphic communication with the most advanced out-post on the Naryn, as it is with that on the frontier of Bokhara.

It is by no means certain whether at this moment Russia is not in possession of a wire to the Oxus, for the Ameer of Bokhara not only consented to one being laid down, but even promised to supply the necessary poles. Kerkhi, or Khoja Salih, were named as the most likely places to which it would be laid down, but it is more than probable that the Russians would make an effort to induce the Ameer to permit it to pass through his capital to Charjui. Charjui is Russia's main object on the Oxus, and in considering the chief roads to India the importance of this position will be described. It would not be difficult to continue the wire along the banks of the Oxus to Kerkhi, and ultimately to Khoja Salih. The Ameer's offer, whether wholly voluntary or not, is of double importance, for it shows that he is entirely subservient to Russia, and also that he is not disposed to throw any serious opposition in the way of an army marching through his dominions. His interviews with the late M. Weinberg, one of the most skilled of all the Russian negotiators, apparently left him in a still more friendly mood, for it was after them that he made these suggestions concerning the construction of a telegraph wire to the Oxus.

The few irrigation works which have been commenced have been signal failures; but in the bridging of innumerable small rivers there has been greater success. The Syr Darya has been bridged in several places in Khokand, but below the town of Khodjent there has been no attempt to do so, although at Chinaz a bridge is much needed. At Khodjent, however, a wooden bridge has been erected by a M. Flavitsky within the last few years, and the tolls have been made over to him for a period of thirty years. That is consequently a private and not a public undertaking, for which the credit belongs to M. Flavitsky alone. Between Orenburg and Tashkent there are caravanserais and stations for post-horses at frequent intervals; and in Semiretchinsk there are equal facilities for State travelling. The old Chinese roads in Naryn and Kuldja have been repaired, and Mr. Schuyler speaks of these as being far superior to any others he had travelled by within the Russian dominions. In Europe it is well known that the roads are execrable. These improvements in means of locomotion are regarded simply as military necessaries, and are carried out as such. The distances are so great, and the time required to transport merchandise from one point to another so long, that there has been scarcely any increase in the trade carried on between Central Asia and Russia, although there has of course been a considerable development in the export of Russian goods into the khanates and Central Asia generally. When the railway which is at present in working order as far as Orenburg, and which is sanctioned as far as Orsk, has been continued up to Kazala, near the mouth of the Syr Darya, there will, in all probability, be a larger mutual trade between Russia and her Asiatic dependencies than there is at present. But as things are, Russia, despite the energy of her merchants—who are in many ways her most creditable representatives in Central Asia— does not possess an extensive trade in Turkestan. Such as it is, too, it is one-sided; for the Imperial Government derives no benefit from the latent resources of territory that should be most productive, and no assistance from races who are famed for their ingenuity and talent.

We have only to consider, in conclusion, what the effect of Russia's mode of government in Asia is upon the relations between herself and the subject races. Mr. Schuyler is evidently of opinion that the races will speedily assimilate, and that the rule of Russia, which is at present tolerated, will before long become popular. The great recommendation, in the eyes of a semi-civilised people such as those of Turkestan, that belongs to the Russian system of administration is that it leaves them mostly to their own devices. There is no fussiness; and the virtue of this want of public spirit—for such it actually is—is in no instance more clearly demonstrated than in the matter of religion.

The old state of things has not given place unto the new, but is rather becoming consolidated under the stolidity of the Russian Government. But Russia's success in dealing with the religious question is not very difficult of comprehension. She has only *one* religion to deal with. It is true that it is the fanatical creed of Mahomedanism, the religion which of all others has been most hostile to Russia; but in these apathetic times it seems to be possible to blunt the edge of that zeal when it is directed against the Czar. We have found the chief supporters of Islam in Central Asia, the Ameers of Bokhara and Afghanistan, become in turns the puppets of Russian schemers, and vent their spleen either in threats or in acts against England, who is the ostensible buttress of Turkey in Asia as well as on the Bosphorus.

At a first glance this appears very strange, if not incomprehensible. But it is not difficult to explain the religious apathy of the people of Russian Turkestan. Russia's treatment of the Mahomedan religion in Central Asia has been most judicious, but it has also been facilitated by the fact that Russia had only to observe one law towards all her Asiatic subjects. They were all Mahomedans. In India England can never achieve a similar result. The Mahomedans there are a minority, and an alien minority. They are dangerous, and they always will be dangerous. It may even be said that further precautions might be taken against the possibility of their combining, as they may combine so long as they are knit together by the ties of one faith, and so long as

Wahabeeism is only scotched and not killed. Russia's tolerance in religious matters has, therefore, had a practical result. It has enabled her to keep races, naturally turbulent, in a state of tranquillity; and it has given her some claim to general consideration in Central Asia. At the present moment, mainly through this wise indifference* in religion, the relations of Russia and her Central Asian subjects must be characterised as friendly and harmonious.

It would be wrong to leave out of sight that there are reasons why these should not always remain so. There are political factors as well as religious in the internal development of the Central Asian Question. There are deposed rulers, and exiled princes; powerful military castes which have lost their privileges and their supremacy; large nomadic confederacies which have been deprived of their freedom; and an administrative hierarchy which has been ousted from that career which lay open to it in the time of the old khans. All these discordant elements are present. No religious toleration will suffice to remove them, and until they are removed Russia's relations with her subjects in Central Asia cannot be held to be otherwise than insecure and uncertain. Russia's domination rests on the claim given it by the sword alone, and it will have to be maintained by that means, and no other.

* Mr. Schuyler mentions that General Kaufmann had sent back to Russia missionaries who had come to Tashkent with propagandist intentions.

CHAPTER IV.

RUSSIA'S MILITARY STRENGTH IN CENTRAL ASIA.

THERE is no point of greater interest to Englishmen, connected with the presence of Russia in Central Asia, than the military resources and power of that country. It is impossible for Englishmen to affect any philosophy in studying the conduct and movements of the great northern empire. Russians may be actuated by some honourable motive, or they may not; they may conquer and annex territory in the interests of humanity and civilisation, or the reverse; but whether they do or not is a very secondary matter for this country, whose interest in and concern at Russia's operations are solely occasioned by the menacing position Russia has assumed in Central Asia with regard to India. It will be said that this is indulging in a very idle fear, in a very unfair hostility. It will be called by one school un-English; by another, typical of England. It will be condemned as a selfish and as a *chauvinist* sentiment. But of the perfect accuracy of this statement there will be no doubt in the mind of any impartial observer of affairs. Our attitude towards Russia is one of watchful suspicion; and if events progress in the same direction as they have been progressing during the past ten years, that suspicion must so far become intensified that it will produce action of a decided character. Russia's attitude towards us is, if we are not wholly mistaken in reading the meaning of the policy she has pursued for so many years, one of covert hostility. The practical point to ascertain, then, is, what is the military strength which this covert hostility has at its disposal? For Englishmen the question which transcends all others in importance and interest is, how many men can Russia send across the Oxus? What troops can be conveyed by the Caspian to either Krasnovodsk or the Atrek? And what reserves can be pushed forward by the armies of the Caucasus and of Orenburg to reinforce the offensive army which should have taken up its position in the outskirts of Cabul?

The inquiry is not free from uncertainty and doubt. It is impossible to estimate exactly beforehand the degree of difficulty which the obstacles of nature—such as the badness of the roads, the want of water, and pasture for the horses and baggage animals, the delay in bridging rivers, the hindrances to be encountered in a mountainous region, and numerous other similar circumstances—would offer to the advance of a considerable army either towards the Hindoo Koosh or Herat. It is possible to minimise each and all of these; but it is also far easier to magnify them. Natural obstacles have a habit of vanishing before large armies and determined generals. In all directions, it should, however, be remembered that there are roads, although they have been for many years neglected, and have thus fallen into a state of disrepair. The rivers, which are neither very large nor very broad, are certainly in most cases unbridged; but none of them present any difficulties to pontooning. There are also fords on the Atrek, the Heri Rud, the Murghab, and the Oxus at many places and available during the greater part of the year; and where fords do not exist there are plenty of boats to be captured along the banks of the river. Readers of the campaign in Khiva will remember that it was by a lucky find of twelve of these river boats that Kaufmann was alone enabled to cross over from the right bank of the Oxus to the left.

It is pertinent to this subject to give here a list of the principal places where it is possible to cross the Oxus, which is the only great river in Central Asia. The Oxus is a very broad river, and also a very rapid one. At Charjui, the post on the main road from Bokhara to Merv, the river is six hundred and fifty yards wide; but it is very deep and rapid at this point. At Kerkhi, which is the next stage higher up the river, we have it on the authority of Professor Vambery, who used this crossing, that it is twice as wide as the Danube at Pesth (that is to say, about one thousand yards). It occupied half an hour in getting across. At Khoja Salih, which is the extreme north-western point of nominal Afghan soil, the river is very wide, being eight hundred yards across; but, on the other hand, it is shallower here, and the current is much slower. A Russian authority estimates it at three and a half miles an hour, and from the same source we are informed that the Cossack carriers, who have recently been travelling so frequently between Djam and Cabul, crossed the river in about thirty minutes. There is a ferry-boat at each of these places, which is generally a clumsy vessel pulled across by a couple of horses, the connecting ropes being attached to their manes. There is another ferry still higher up the river at Kilif; but this has not yet been used by Europeans. It is said to be eight hundred yards across, and is of great importance, as the one leading direct to Balkh; and should M. Maieff have reported favourably of the road leading to it from Karshi, it must become the main route for Russia in the future. There are also numerous fords in the upper reaches of the Oxus, more especially, perhaps, that at Sharwan, which was frequently used by Mourad Beg, the Kundus chief, in his raids into Kulab and Hissar. It is asserted, on the authority of Captain John Wood, that he even took cannon across at this point.

There are, therefore, several principal ferries across the Oxus which are in daily use, and also numerous fords and minor ferries in its upper course which present the means for crossing from one side of the Oxus to the other. The former are on the well known roads from Bokhara and Hissar to Merv, Maimenè, Balkh, and Khulm; the latter on those less known routes which lead towards Faizabad, Kila Panja, and Baroghil. But it must not be supposed that the appliances which a general would find ready to his hand for the conveyance of his army are exclusively the miserable ferry boats which have been described as "clumsy vessels." There is an Oxus fleet which is quite at the disposal of the strongest power in those waters. Since the time when Alexander had to cross on inflated skins, Genghis Khan and Tamerlane have crossed the Oxus in the boats of the fishermen and carriers of its banks; and those boats are still to be found there precisely the same in all essentials. It has been estimated that between Kilif and Hazarasp in Khiva there are three hundred of the large river boats, of which the following is a description. They are built with bows projecting very much at each end, in order to extend the more easily from the main bed of the river over the shallows to the shore. They are constructed of logs, squared, cut from the dwarf jungle tree, and these are fastened together by iron bands and clamps. As a rule they are fifty feet in length, eighteen feet in breadth, four feet deep, and have a displacement of only twelve inches of water. The tonnage of a vessel of this description is twenty tons, and at a very moderate allowance each should be able to carry one hundred and fifty foot soldiers. They would also be strong enough to admit of artillery, horses, and heavy baggage being conveyed across in them. Some have even said that they would be amply sufficient to form a strong and durable bridge across at Kerkhi; but on that point it is allowable to entertain a different opinion. The current of the Oxus is so strong, the exact direction of its course so uncertain, that it would be matter of serious difficulty, if not quite impossible, to construct a permanent bridge across the river at any of the principal passages.

But the means of crossing for an army of large dimensions are ready to hand. The Aral fleet of six steamers, and as many transports, supplies the nucleus of the force, and the native Oxus fleet the bulk. General Kaufmann's whole army once on the right bank of the river would experience no difficulty in crossing over to the left, and would leave behind it the ready means for the transport of reinforcements, or for the retreat of an army which had failed in its attack. The Russians would leave in their rear when advancing on the Hindoo Koosh no such formidable river as the Indus; and the difficulties that they have to encounter in crossing the Oxus would be almost entirely removed by the strongly-built vessels which are to be found in considerable numbers on that river. A little examination is therefore only required to show that one of the supposed obstacles of nature vanishes the moment it is boldly grappled with or considered. The Oxus is the only river of any importance which intervenes between the Russian frontier and the Indus, except the Helmund on the road to Candahar. During ten months of the year this is easily passable at Girishk. In the next chapter a description of the principal roads or routes leading from the Russian frontier to the British will be given.

The government of General Kaufmann is essentially a military government. Strictly speaking, as we have before pointed out, Central Asia is the military district of Turkestan; and military regulations predominate in the internal administration of affairs. We have seen how civil enterprises are permitted to languish, and how the material well-being of the province is neglected, because the grand desideratum in the eyes of the governing party is military efficiency; it becomes necessary then to inquire whether the Russian army in Central Asia can be held to be efficient? Is it in what may be termed fighting condition? Are its cadres full, its reserves actual or only imaginary, its supply departments in working order?

It is clear that if the reply to these questions were in the negative, the Russian Government would not have an excuse to offer for such gross neglect or for their indifference to other matters. It has disregarded things civil and peaceful, in order that matters military and warlike may receive every attention; and if the latter are not in the most perfect condition, it is obvious that the indictment against the administration is a very severe one indeed. It is not improbable that the indictment will be some day preferred. There is a growing dislike in Russia to the military penalties which accompany the privileges of Russian citizenship, and there are signs of the times that the day is approaching when the nation will raise a protesting voice against them. These penalties, which consist over and above the law of conscription—a very legitimate law and absolutely necessary to all nations with a land frontier—of the military repression of the rights of public speech and of the freedom of the press, are aggravated by the knowledge, which is becoming wide-spread throughout all circles of Russian society, that the military service is rotten in its higher branches, and that bureaucracy is only another name for dishonesty and corruption. The first symptom of an intention to proceed to extremities in this matter will be shown by an attack against the administration in Central Asia, which is rotten to the core. It is not thoroughly ascertained how far that corruption has impaired the value of the army in Turkestan, but it is known that that army costs a great deal more than it should.

In 1873 the Russian army under General Kaufmann's immediate orders numbered thirty-six thousand men. That was, however, before the war against Khiva, which resulted in the formation of a fresh district—the Amou Darya—along the banks of the Oxus. In this dependency of Kaufmann's there are several forts, notably those of Petro Alexandrovsk, Nukus, Chimbai, etc., and the garrison may be computed, at a moderate estimate, at three thousand men. This number is considered sufficient to overawe Khiva, which is prevented from keeping an armed force by the terms of its treaty with Russia. The larger and more important addition to the Central Asian army was caused by the despatch of large reinforcements to meet with the difficulties and dangers of the war in Khokand in the winter of 1875. When, as the result of that war, the remaining independent portion of Khokand became Russian territory under the name of Ferghana, a large addition of troops was made to the existing garrison. This addition was absolutely necessary, for the garrison duties of the army of Turkestan were almost doubled by the conquest of Ferghana.

The correctness of this assertion can easily be gauged by enumerating the fresh towns that had to receive a Russian garrison. These were Khokand, Namangan, Andijan, Margilan, Osh, and several other smaller and less known places. It also brought Russia into closer proximity with Kashgar, and one of the direct results of this conquest was that it opened up a road for Russian enterprise in Karategin and the neighbouring petty khanates, as well as on the Pamir. The natural consequence of Russia's annexation of Ferghana has been that her frontier, by some mysterious process, has embraced the northern half of the Pamir, including the Kara Kul lake, whence there are tracks followed by the Kirghiz, if not actual roads, which lead due east into Kashgar.

A trustworthy semi-official statement* gave the Russian forces in Turkestan and Semiretchinsk at fifty-five thousand men. It is not clear whether the Amou Darya garrison was included in this force. It may be assumed, however, that it was; as it is improbable that a greater addition than twenty thousand men in all has been made to Kaufmann's army since 1873. The garrison of Semiretchinsk, including Priilinsk (Kuldja), but excluding Naryn, is under ten thousand men, which leaves a force of forty thousand men under the immediate command of the Governor-General. Under anything like the present circumstances, when it is impossible to predict the moment at which a rupture may

---

* An article in the " Journal des Debats " in the summer of 1878 gave much higher numbers.

take place between Russia and China, or indeed at any time so long as China's hold on Chuguchak, Manas, and the cities of Eastern Turkestan remains firm, it would be out of the question to think of weakening the garrison of the vast district of Semiretchinsk by a single man. Under certain contingencies it might become even necessary to increase its garrison, either from Ferghana, or from Siberia, or from Europe. To some extent this has lately been done. Therefore as an offensive force it is unavailable. The frontier it has to defend is naturally a very strong one, being a mountain range of which it may be said to command the whole depth. The one weak point is on the due east, where it might be exposed to attack from several quarters if the enemy were of a sufficiently determined character and in strong force.

The Semiretchinsk army is held to be as efficient as any other branch of either the Russian or the Central Asian armies; and its commander-in-chief, General Kolpakoffsky, is one of the most distinguished officers in the army. Mr. Schuyler gives a graphic description of this officer and of his work. He appears to be the most practical of all the Russian governors, not excepting Abramoff. He is thoroughly acquainted with the people over whom he rules; and for almost thirty years he has been intimately connected with Central Asiatics. He possesses an excellent constitution, and his energy is so unwearied that he has obtained the name of "the Iron Seat" from the Kirghiz, themselves some of the hardest riders in the world. There have never been any insinuations against the moral character and integrity of Kolpakoffsky. With his practical experience, his zeal in the service, his energy enabling him to supervise details and to undertake all important matters himself, and his incorruptibility, General Kolpakoffsky appears to be the very man to restore the Russian finances in Turkestan, as well as to revive that sense of public duty which appears to have been banished from the bureau of General Kaufmann. In every respect the administration of Semiretchinsk presents a favourable contrast to that of Turkestan, and the credit of this contrast is due exclusively to the talent and moral qualities of Kolpakoffsky.

But in one respect the territorial army of Semiretchinsk is deficient, or rather its actual strength is diminished by the bad qualities of a force which would, if at all efficient, make it one of the most formidable armies in its way in Russian Asia. In various parts of Central Asia there are Cossack settlements. The origin of each of them has been at some past date the compulsory settlement of a body of Cossacks with their families in a district. The Government gives them land, tools, and arms; in some cases seed, grain, and a stock of implements are added. In return they owe military service to the Government, and are called out at certain periods, more especially when there is an intention to undertake some important expedition. The Cossacks who are settled along the Irtish river in Semipalatinsk are among the most efficient of their class. They are pure Cossacks, taken at various periods from the Ural, Orenburg, and Siberia armies. But the Cossacks of Semiretchinsk are not pure Cossacks—in fact they are not Cossacks at all. The supply of Cossacks did not suffice to people the immense tract of country lying between Semipalatinsk and Naryn, and consequently it became necessary to settle that line of country not with Cossacks but with Russian peasants, who, however, were styled Cossacks, and are generally known as the Cossacks of Semiretchinsk. They are, it is not very strange to learn considering their origin, held to be the worst of all the Cossacks in the Russian service. Despite their bad qualities they are the reserve, and the only recognised reserve, of the army of Semiretchinsk.

The army of Turkestan in the first place garrisons the numerous stations and towns along the Jaxartes, as well as Tashkent, Samarcand, and Ferghana. Of these places the garrisons of Tashkent, Samarcand, Khodjent, and Chinaz are among the most important. More than three-fourths of the number given is in garrison south of Tashkent, and it is from this force that the main body for any expedition towards the Oxus would be drawn. This army has also a small reserve in the Russian and Cossack colonists—principally the former—round Tashkent, and in the valley of the Zarafshan, where there are undoubtedly immense inducements to European settlers. It is, however, a very favourable estimate to say that this would raise General Kaufmann's own regular army by five thousand men; if it did, it would give him about forty thousand men to draw upon for the formation of an active army. This number is as it is stated to be on paper, but all accounts agree that the numbers taken here approximate very closely to the actual strength of the Russian army. The peace duties of this force are by no means trivial. It has to garrison an enormous tract of country, and to keep in order the Khokandians—one of the most turbulent races in Central Asia. In war time those duties would become more arduous. Let Russia take never so many precautions against sedition, the advance of a large army across the Oxus must be the signal for local disturbances that would require to be promptly repressed. They could not be repressed if the province were denuded of troops; and with each day of success or impunity their importance would increase, and from being only an annoyance they would become a danger.

It would, therefore, be impossible for the Russian authorities to withdraw the whole Turkestan army from the province, and, indeed, it must remain a matter of individual opinion how far it would be prudent to weaken that garrison so long as there existed such numerous causes of internal danger as there are at present, or so long as a semi-independent power like Bokhara retained an army which might, under possible contingencies, refuse to recognise the commands of a too-accommodating prince. It would certainly be extremely hazardous to take more than half that force away from its duties; and last summer barely a third was sent forward to Djam.

Under the most favourable circumstances, therefore, it would be impossible for Russia to weaken the Semiretchinsk garrison by a man, and from the garrisons of Tashkent, Samarcand, and Ferghana it would be difficult to bring a larger force than twenty thousand men into the field. From the Amou Darya district it would be possible to draw two thousand men, in addition to the Aral flotilla. The fighting army of Russia in Central Asia, which can be mobilised and directed by General Kaufmann, numbers scarcely more than twenty thousand men. This is Russia's offensive power at the present moment. It is at a first glance a very insignificant power; but weak as it is in total strength it is an effective power ready to be employed at the shortest notice.

In addition there is the Bokharan army, a portion of which as a matter of common prudence would be compelled to accompany a Russian army in its advance; and this with a little preparation might become a useful auxiliary. The Bokhariots are good horsemen, and fairly courageous. The people of Hissar and Kitab are still more to be relied upon. The "Turkestan Gazette" asserted that the begs of those places, as well as the Ameer of Bokhara himself, had promised to place twenty thousand men at the disposal of the Russian commander. This number may be taken to be too high, but there can be no doubt that Russia could obtain a very serviceable auxiliary corps, both for *etappen* duty and garrison work, from the Bokharan Government and chiefs. By a skilful manipulation of the desires that Government entertains to secure a fresh hold upon the khanates south of the Oxus, which are now known as Afghan Turkestan, it might even be possible to secure the hearty co-operation of Bokhara in the task of carrying on an extensive campaign south of the Hindoo Koosh.

The assistance that Khiva could give would be of a much vaguer character; but even from the khan of that dismembered state Russia would expect some service. At the least Khiva could provide guides for the desert of Kara Kum, and a considerable amount of labour for the construction of roads, and other necessary undertakings. The Kirghiz nomads would also be called upon to contribute their quota. These are the only allies Russia would find within her frontier, and on several of them it would be impossible for her to place implicit reliance. Yet her first line consists of them alone and the small nucleus of twenty thousand Russian troops. Assuredly, the advocate of " masterly inactivity" will exclaim, no danger to India from such a foe as this!

This is the effective total, available for offensive purposes, of the territorial army of Turkestan. Including all his immediate reserves and allies, General Kaufmann could not reach the northern bank of the Oxus with a greater force than forty thousand men, of whom only one half would be Russians. He would have left in his rear, too, a very inadequate garrison, and he could never feel certain that a rising in Khokand, or an *émeute* in Samarcand, would not paralyse his strength at some critical moment. The conclusion, therefore, at which we must arrive is that the Turkestan army, however efficient, is quite unequal to the task of crossing the Hindoo Koosh in face of an army of anything like equal numbers. It can dispose of a sufficiently large force to annex Bokhara, or to coerce an Ameer of Cabul; but on its own resources it could never dream of attacking India, or even of establishing itself in Cabul. It is too weak numerically, and therefore we have to consider how it can be strengthened.

It is strange, in our eyes, seeing what use we have made of the fighting-material that abounds in India, to discover that Russia has done nothing in a similar direction in Central Asia. She rules over warlike races to whom the noise of battle is by nature as the breath of their nostrils—Kirghiz and Kipchak, Usbeg and Turkman; but although there exist these numerous sources whence an army of native troops could be derived, Russia has not availed herself of their services. There is no native army in Central Asia. The Russian and the Cossack are the military races of Turkestan, and in the hands of the dominant power rests all the superiority of military strength. A few exceptions are to be found where natives have been permitted to join the Russian service, and, strictly speaking, there is no law which prevents a Khokandi, or a Samarcandi, becoming a Russian soldier. But if he does desire to become one, and some do, he must join a Russian regiment, and become a Russian individual. In the course of time, should Russia's rule remain strong and assured in Central Asia, it is conceivable that, without a native army proper having been established, the majority of the Russian soldiers in the Turkestan territorial army will be natives of Central Asia. In those days Central Asiatics will have been as firmly welded into the body of the empire as the Cossacks are now, and they will have as much affection for the Imperial Government as the bold riders of the Don and the Volga entertain at present. If nothing untoward takes place, no doubt can be held on this point, and the people of Turkestan almost imperceptibly will become merged in the mass of the other Russian subjects. Although we may be prepared to indulge in sneers at Russia's short-sightedness in not turning to immediate account the valuable fighting-material she possesses in Central Asia, let us not too hastily condemn her for what a little consideration must show to be a very prudent abnegation.

The safety which Russia feels against any intestine revolt far more than counterbalances the loss she temporarily incurs in not having a native standing army. There is no danger from the mutinous disposition of her soldiers; for all her soldiers are her own. There is no apprehension from the armies of semi-independent potentates within her frontier, because there are none. They have been all, with the exception of Bokhara, swept away. Let anyone compare these things with what obtains in India, and he must find that in many ways Russia's position is more assured in Central Asia than England's is in India. At the least her triumph is complete, whereas ours is founded on, and made secure alone by, the dissensions which keep races and religions divided into hostile camps. It hardly seems worth while to notice here the remark that a correspondent recently ventured to make in a daily paper, to the effect that Russia had much to fear from the bad feeling against the Government which was prevalent among a large portion of her army, recruited from Cossacks and Poles. The Russian Government has never had cause to complain of the fidelity of its army, heterogeneous though it is, and certainly its Central Asian army might be implicitly relied on for showing the utmost degree of fidelity and good service in undertaking a campaign which would be so popular as an invasion of India. All recent travellers, whether English, American, or French, concur in the view that the grand object of life in the bosoms of officers and soldiers alike in Turkestan is to invade Hindostan. From the highest rank down to the lowest the same feeling prevails; and how to reach India, and by what means to conquer it when reached, are the guiding motives in the policy of the Tashkent authorities. That being so, it is not probable that the declaration of a war with England would be followed by the outbreak of any disturbance within the ranks of the Russian army, whether among Polish exiles or political refugees.

The same correspondent also advanced the opinion that the prisoners who mainly constitute the population of Siberia would seize the opportunity to enfranchise themselves; but surely he must have forgotten the very efficient line of pickets which are maintained along the principal roads—and in Siberia, once the principal road is left, you are in the midst of a pathless waste, out of which it would be impossible for anyone to extricate himself. The settlements of the political or other exiles are separated from each other by immense distances, which for two-thirds of the year are wholly impassable. They have no organization, no common bond, and are perhaps in the main ignorant of each other's existence. Once they depart from the settlement to which the beneficent care of a paternal government has assigned them, they enter upon a wild and desolate region, in which they can find no friend. The terrors of a semi-Arctic climate become more terrible, and the dangers from man and beast grow greater and more difficult of being avoided, as the lonely settlement is left behind. Sometimes, despite all these difficulties and dangers, an unfortunate exile, gifted with more than usual boldness and strength, flees from the abode where he is safe from temporal want, to seek in or beyond the solitude that freedom of which he has been deprived. But of such an one all trace disappears. No one has ever broken out from that vast prison-house. The defences that nature has erected around it are impenetrable, and as completely shut out the interloper from beyond as they inclose the unfortunate occupant. If Russia's only internal danger is from either of these causes, she can banish all apprehension from her mind, for from them there is nought to fear.

The army of Orenburg has always been, and is still, considered the reserve of the army of Turkestan. This army is supposed to consist of eighty thousand men, but as this is the strength given on paper it is necessary to deduct a considerable number from it to arrive at its actual strength. It is also very weak in artillery, only two batteries—sixteen guns—being attached to it. Now it must not be supposed that the Orenburg army is an idle army—far from it, it is a very active one. Its duties are numerous and of various kinds. It has to garrison a vast tract of country; and it has to maintain order among the numerous and naturally very turbulent Kirghiz clans which hold the southern portion of this district. The Governor-General of Orenburg would raise strong objections to the weakening of his force. Even during the insignificant campaign against Khiva he insisted upon troops being despatched into the Ust Urt plateau to prevent the Kirghiz tribes making any inroad from that direction. In any more extended operation that necessity would still exist, and with double force. Events on the Hindoo Koosh would so far be reflected in the northern wastes of Ust Urt, that the Kirghiz of that quarter would seize the opportunity of any relaxing in Russia's vigilance to plunder and to ravage.

It is improbable that the effective strength of the Orenburg army is more than fifty thousand men, and of that number not more than one-fifth could be spared to reinforce the Turkestan army. In artillery, in which arm both the Turkestan ·army—sixty-four guns —and the Orenburg—sixteen guns—are extremely weak, no addition could be made from Orenburg. The Orenburg army, therefore, in so far as it is a reserve to the Turkestan, is a very insufficient one. It can scarcely do more than fulfil its own duties, and holding as it does the gateway to Northern and Central Asia, its garrison cannot be unduly weakened.

There is great jealousy also between the Governor-Generals of these provinces; and Kaufmann could not count on the hearty co-operation of Krjihanoffsky in an enterprise in which Kaufmann would be supreme. But even if ten thousand men were spared from Orenburg the Russian force would still be only thirty thousand strong, and it is doubtful whether more than four batteries—thirty-two guns—could be brought into the field. The first reserve may therefore be pronounced to be wholly inadequate to its purpose; and if General Kaufmann's force is to be brought up to an effective strength of fifty thousand men and one hundred and fifty guns, very nearly half the troops, and more than two-thirds of the guns, must be sent from Europe. It will require very little knowledge of the subject to perceive the truth of the assertion that to convey these troops and artillery, with the necessary amount of stores and ammunition, would be an Herculean undertaking. By exertions almost incredible Russia has built a railway as far as Orenburg, and its continuation to Orsk—one hundred and fifty miles further on—is sanctioned, if not actually commenced; but from Orsk to Tashkent the distance is more than one thousand miles.

The road—for there is a road—lies mainly through the steppe country, a waste expanse of treeless and grassless soil. Between Orsk and Kazala, at the mouth of the Syr Darya, there is no place where even a small army could be halted for a short period. It would be necessary therefore to push the detachments steadily forward, after depôts had been formed at all of the halting-places *en route*. To make those depôts would be a task of months of steady toil, and even then the advance of thirty thousand troops would be a matter which would require at least three months to accomplish. But the transport of artillery would be one of still greater difficulty. It is even open to question whether the road from Orsk to Kazala would bear of the conveyance of so much artillery over it; but even if it did, the time required for its transport would still be very long. At the present moment it takes the Russian reinforcements from Europe nearly three months to reach Tashkent, and it is very doubtful whether by using the greatest despatch a large army could accomplish the distance in a shorter space of time. The only means of expediting this journey would be by continuing the rail to Kazala across the steppe—an undertaking which must financially be ruinous—and by improving the navigation of the Syr Darya so that powerful river steamers of low draught may be able to ply between Kazala and Chinaz. To construct that railway, and to build a sufficient number of river steamers, must be the task of years and not months. Until these have been done it will be impossible for Russia to mobilise any large force north of the Oxus.

At the present moment Kaufmann can on his own resources assemble an army of twenty thousand men with thirty-two guns. With three months notice he can be reinforced from Orenburg by ten thousand men without any guns. By a supreme effort, involving the expenditure of several millions of pounds, he could receive twenty thousand more from Europe, and an adequate supply of artillery, within six months of the decision to adopt that extreme measure. But either of these proposals could only be consummated at a lavish outlay of money, and for that expenditure neither the Russian Government nor people is prepared. No minister would dare to recommend its being sanctioned, and therefore Russia will do nothing at present in Turkestan that would require to be backed up by a large display of force. The railway to Orsk and beyond will be prosecuted so far and so rapidly as is possible; but if foreign capital and sympathy hold aloof from the scheme, its execution must be both slow and uncertain. To General Kaufmann himself *carte blanche* may be given to do that which he can on his own resources, and by the aid of such small bodies of troops as can conveniently be spared from Orenburg.

With those means he possesses a sufficient force to take Merv, or Balkh, to advance on Faizabad in Badakshan, or to seize Wakhan and the approaches to Baroghil. And if each one of those acts were not sure to be the prelude to the great contest of all between England and Russia, he would carry one or all of them out to-morrow. There are great differences of opinion among military men as to what is the best strength for an army destined to effect, not so much the conquest of India, as the overthrow of our empire therein by a successful campaign in the Punjáb. Many hold that it should not exceed thirty thousand men, and if such were the case Russia has almost the necessary force.

Others say that double that number would be required for the main army, and that it should be supported by another column of twenty or thirty thousand men operating from another quarter. Between these it would be rash for a theoretical observer to decide; but it appears to be a safe assumption to say that whatever the strength of the army, it should be sufficiently numerous to deal with the Anglo-Indian army that would defend the Indian Empire from attack. In a later chapter we shall consider what the strength of that army would be; but here it may be said that it would be absurd to think of a smaller army than one hundred thousand Russian troops and auxiliaries beating it, under anything like present conditions.

Unless we remained as indifferent to a Russian advance south of the Oxus, to Herat as well as to Bamian, as we did to the progress of her arms from the Jaxartes to Samarcand and the Pamir, it would be impossible for Russia to take us off our guard; and unless we are taken off our guard, or sink into some state of political idiocy, we shall never permit Russia to acquire those strategical points which might supply her military deficiencies. But as things are at present—whether the Afghan crisis result only in a partial rectification of our frontier, or in a complete solution of the north-west danger by the annexation of Eastern Afghanistan, the only real remedy, and one which the present generation shall certainly yet witness—Russia cannot hope to secure any of those points save at the expense of a war, in which all the chances would be on our side, and none on hers.

Therefore, the army of Turkestan, even when reinforced from Orenburg, is utterly incapable of undertaking those extended operations which are necessary to carry Russian arms to the banks of the Indus. Its sphere is a more limited one, and must remain so as long as its communications with Europe are so imperfect as they are at present. If we stand aside, it could capture Merv, it could give a king to Afghan Turkestan. It could—had it chosen to strike in, as it was in honour bound, with Cabul—have made Afghan resistance more protracted. But for the invasion of India it as yet possesses neither the numbers nor the organization that are necessary. A bold policy in Afghanistan exposes at once the actual weakness of Russia's power in Central Asia, which is of too recent a growth to have become firm and consolidated.

So far we have only dealt with the forces that Russia can dispose of from Turkestan—that is to say, of those which recognise in General Kaufmann their superior officer. But this is only one phase of Russian activity in Asia—certainly the most prominent, but in many respects the least important for India and ourselves. We have now to consider that quarter of Asiatic events of which the Caspian is the base, and which was the original point from which Russia aspired to realise her designs against India, and which for a time forgotten has returned to a foremost place in public interest, mainly through the energy of General Lomakine. In November 1873 the Grand Duke Michael, Lieutenant of the Caucasus, acting, as it is believed, under the instigation of this general, induced the Czar to authorise the formation of a fresh district beyond the Caspian. This district was placed under the control of the Lieutenant of the Caucasus, and Trans-Caspiania, as it is called, was made an advanced post of the large army of the Caucasus. Now there can be no doubt that this step, which was one of the numerous results of the Khivan campaign, was of the highest importance. It gave Russia a hold on Turcomania which she had never obtained before; but at first that hold was purely nominal. As time went on it grew more assured, and Russia's frontier in Kara Kum became one of the most elastic of expressions. We defy anyone to define it, even at the present moment; and the Russian official map, which accompanies these volumes, admits its own inability to perform the task.

It would be quite a mistake to suppose that the ambition of invading India is confined to the headquarter staff of General Kaufmann. That general was not the inventor of the phrase that "the cost of absorbing the khanates is to be recouped in the spoil of Delhi and Lahore." The sentiment of which it is the expression exists wide-spread throughout the Russian army. Long before Russia had reached Khokand or the Oxus, she had broken ground in Persia, and with considerable effect. She had succeeded so far that on two occasions nominees of hers were supreme in Herat; and supremacy in Herat alone was worth more than all the conquests Russia has made in Turkestan since Peroffsky first advanced along the Jaxartes. But there can be no doubt that since the overthrow of Sultan Jan by Dost Mahomed in 1863 Russian activity had slumbered in Persia and on the shores of the Caspian.

The formation of a fresh Russian territory—with its future in its own hands—on the eastern shores of the Caspian in 1873 gave a fresh *impetus* to Russian schemes in that quarter where there is real danger to this country. General Lomakine is perhaps, of all the Russian generals in Asia, the man who is most to be feared, for he combines the dash of Scobelef to the practical knowledge of Kolpakoffsky and the calm prudence and scientific attainments of Abramoff. During five years Lomakine has guided affairs in Trans-Caspiania; and already Russian authority is recognised in a wide belt of territory beyond the Caspian. In the Atrek region, and along the Kuren and Kopet Daghs, the power of the Czar's lieutenant has become something more than the semblance of a name.

It is not our purpose to discuss here the relations between the Russian officers and the Turcomans, further than to say that the garrisons of Krasnovodsk and Chikishlar—the two principal posts of the Russians on the further side of the Caspian—can dispose of a combative army of five thousand men, which can easily be strengthened from Baku. At the present time it appears probable that Russia has an army of over ten thousand men in Trans-Caspiania; for not only has she established herself more firmly on the Atrek, but she has advanced far into the country of the Akhals. She has erected forts at Chat, near the junction of the

Atrek and the Sumbur, and at Kizil Arvat, and Kizil Tchesme in the Akhal region; and there is good reason for saying that the Cossacks have pushed beyond Ashkabad in the direction of Abiverd and the Tejend swamp. Later information says that Abiverd was occupied in force, but this has not been confirmed. These operations are carried on by an army of far different composition to, and acting under other conditions than, that which recognises General Kaufmann as supreme.

The army of Trans-Caspiania is but an advanced section of the army of the Caucasus, the same army which conquered Armenia and took Kars and Erzeroum. Its strength is computed at one hundred and fifty-five thousand regulars and forty thousand irregulars. It has an artillery of forty-three batteries—three hundred and forty-four guns—and is considered to be one of the most efficient forces at the Czar's disposal. It also has its garrison duties to perform. Tiflis, Ardahan, Batoum, Kars, Erivan, and Baku have to be garrisoned. The Circassians are not so cowed that they can be left unguarded. The frontier towards Turkey, strong as it now is, is not so impregnable that it does not need the presence of a strong garrison. Kars, Ardahan, and Batoum, the Armenian trilateral, require men to man their walls. Their possession, however, sets free a large portion of the army of the Caucasus. Fifty thousand men and one hundred and fifty guns could easily be spared for operations in Persia or in Turcomania; and with a slight effort that force could be doubled, its place being supplied by reinforcements from Europe.

To utilise this powerful military machine would require a much slighter effort than would be necessary to reinforce Kaufmann's army. There is only one point on which it is possible to entertain any difference of opinion, and that is with regard to the manner in which reinforcements are to be transported across the Caspian from Baku to Ashourada Bay or Krasnovodsk. The southern half of the Caspian is open at all times and seasons; but the northern half is closed during the winter months. The Caspian fleet is limited in numbers —consisting of only twenty steamers and as many sailing vessels—and quite inadequate to the conveyance of a large army. But there is no reason why the Volga boats should not be utilised for the purposes of transport on the Caspian; and they are amply sufficient for the purpose we are discussing. Without building a single fresh vessel, Russia possesses the means of carrying an army of fifty thousand men with its necessary artillery across the Caspian in the short space of one week, after the assemblage at Baku of the merchantmen and barges from Astrachan and Derbend. And the only difficulty that would beset an army in this direction would be this passage of the Caspian, for once across that sea it is plain sailing to the walls of Candahar, or, for the matter of that, up to the Indus itself.

It is a fact that is not realised in its full significance in this country that the northern provinces of Persia, and much of Western Afghanistan, are fertile districts, possessing water and herbage in abundance —the two great necessaries for an army—that the road from Astrabad to Meshed, and thence to Herat,

Candahar, and Shikarpore, is an actual road, and not a track, and that there are numerous places, such as Meshed and Herat in particular, where it would be possible to maintain an army of fifty thousand men permanently. From the shores of the Caspian to Meshed, from Meshed to Herat, and from Herat to Candahar, are all strides in a road which is practically at the mercy of Russia so far as Meshed, and which leads direct to the most vulnerable points in the frontier of India. At the base of that road in Trans-Caucasia stands the army of the Caucasus — two hundred thousand fighting-men. But although that road has not yet been traversed by Russian troops, and although Persian soil has not yet been violated, the forward movement which has been steadily going on north of the Attock,[*] under the auspices of General Lomakine, has carried Russia, by a parallel and a less advantageous road, far on towards the same goal, which is Herat.

With her hands fettered in this direction by the treaty which preserved the integrity of Persia, Russia had for long remained apparently apathetic in the region of the Atrek. The formation of the Trans-Caspian district provided the Tiflis authorities with that vent for which they had long been seeking, and afforded them the opportunity for entering into competition with the Tashkent Government, which had

---

[*] Attock means "the skirt," and is applied to the northern slope of the mountains of Khorasan; these are the Kuren and Kopet Daghs.

striven—and with some success—to monopolise the task of solving the Central Asian Question. By pushing their advanced posts from Krasnovodsk and Chikishlar forward to Kizil Arvat, and by fortifying that place, Lomakine secured the head of the road to Sarakhs, which, as far as Abiverd at the least, is outside the Persian border line. By carrying on this forward movement Russia may expect to find that she has secured possession of a large portion of the best road to India, and one which will also give her a hold upon Merv and the country of the Tekes. But the most important point is that it places an object before a Russian army which in numbers, efficiency, and position is immeasurably the superior of the Turkestan and Orenburg armies combined. We may now look forward to increased activity on the part of Russia through the emulation that will be caused between the authorities of Tiflis and Tashkent.

The conquest of India had come to be considered the perquisite of that army which had over-run Central Asia, and had carried the terror of the White Czar's name to the sources of the Oxus and the Jaxartes. The Persian phase of the question was, and is, distasteful to the generals at Tashkent; for in the Persian enterprise their share can only be secondary. It is because these facts were well appreciated that such energetic efforts have been made to find new roads to India across the Pamir, and to make the most of the passes which lead through the Hindoo Koosh to Cabul. In Tashkent, the favourite Indian conquerer of the

8 *

past is Baber ; in Tiflis, Nadir Shah and his numerous predecessors are quoted as the unanswerable authorities. In this rivalry the chances are mostly on the side of the Tiflis Government, and since the conquest of the Armenian fortresses those chances have still further increased.

It is difficult to persuade oneself that Kaufmann, that vain and meretricious ruler, will consent to forego the grand dream of his existence, and retire from a career which requires but a little further scope to bring upon him a war with England. It needs little judgment to perceive that Russia's national tendency is to absorb northern Persia, and to make the Caspian geographically the Russian lake which it practically is at present. We must judge of each of these movements by its practicability — Kaufmann absorbing Afghan Turkestan, and the Grand Duke Michael Azerbijan, Ghilan, or Mazanderan ; and, while remembering that upon neither could England look with anything but the utmost disfavour, it must be admitted that it would be a much easier task to drive Russia across the Oxus than to oust her from Persian provinces so remote from us as those specified.

In Kaufmann's path there, therefore, stands the grand obstacle of England's watchfulness. He can scarcely make a forward movement in any direction without encountering the opposition of this country. An advance on Merv from Charjui would assuredly be the prelude to a war that would rage within twelve months of the arrival of Russian troops at that place, and of English at Herat—the unavoidable and only reply to a Russian occupation of the Turcoman stronghold.

In Kara Kum, and even in Persia—despite the treaties—there is no such check on Russian impulse; and it would be difficult for anyone to define the point when encroachments on the Persian frontier would, in the eyes of the vast mass of the English people, constitute a just *casus belli*. And even if a war for the defence of Persia's integrity were decided upon, it is greatly to be feared that it would not be sanctioned because it was recognised that national interests of the highest importance were at stake. We have clearly to keep before us the fact that there is danger to India from Russia in two quarters; and that in many respects that from Persia is the more formidable. It is also in the present age the less recognised. Up to a certain point—in fact, up to the occupation of Meshed or Sarakhs, if Russia plays her cards with any of that astuteness with which she has been credited—it would be almost impossible to arrest the progress of Russia's army, and the very gravity of the danger in this quarter is its insidiousness.

Russia's military strength in Central Asia is limited and in an undeveloped stage. But there can be no doubt that it exists, and that for the accomplishment of any ordinary enterprise it would suffice. In the direction of the Caspian, where the army of the Caucasus—behind which stands the European army—can be called into play, it is formidable; and if ever India is to be wrested from England by external force, it will be from this direction that the attack will be made. But there is need to be on our guard against the movements of Kaufmann as well, although the Turkestan army is much too weak and unprepared to attempt the invasion of India. The vanity of that general—his ignorance is perhaps more dangerous than the knowledge of wiser men—will impel him to vie with Lomakine in expeditions against the Turcomans either from Charjui or Khiva. And for such operations he possesses the resources and the necessary strength. The efficiency of these armies may also increase every year, and the degree of offensive power they possess depends almost exclusively on the lines of communication that exist between Central Asia and Europe. At present these are almost as bad as they can be; but in a few years they will be better. Once they have been perfected, Russia's military strength will be most formidable. The certainty of that prospect carries a moral with it, which shall be considered later on, and with regard to which an unhesitating opinion must be expressed.

CHAPTER V.

THE PRINCIPAL ROUTES FROM THE RUSSIAN FRONTIER TO INDIA.

ON no point is it more necessary that clear views should obtain in this country than upon the nature of the region which lies between the English and Russian frontiers, more particularly of the territory which extends north of the Hindoo Koosh to the Aral, and the ranges of mountains known as Zarafshan and Alai Tau. Various books contain the necessary information with regard to different points, but even these have invariably placed the information in the Appendix; and Appendices, however useful, are not read or studied as carefully as they should be. Although the necessary *data* lie at the disposal of any inquirer who will take the trouble to seek for them in some score of books of travel,* and innumerable official reports, it is very few who will have either the inclination or the opportunity of making the necessary research.

---

* No book of travels is so valuable in this respect as Captain Burnaby's " Ride to Khiva."

For such reasons as these, it is in this place that we shall describe what some readers may think would have appeared more appropriately in the Appendix.

The Russian frontier in Asia is drawn in a line from the frontiers of Manchooria along the Chinese dominions to the Pamir; it then actually passes to the Oxus, which it follows to Hazarasp in Khiva. Beyond this river it strikes, by the old bed of the Oxus, across Kara Kum to Kizil Arvat, whence it is traced by the Sumbur and Atrek rivers to the fort at Chikishlar. That is its actual frontier, but its nominal one, after leaving the Pamir, is drawn along the Zarafshan range, and by a vague line in Kizil Kum to Petro-Alexandrovsk in the Amou Darya district. Bokhara and Khiva are, as a matter of fact, Russian vassal States; and just as we draw our Indian frontier beyond Cashmere, so Russia does hers at the Oxus. But although her frontier embraces Hissar, Bokhara, and Khiva, Russia as yet possesses only imperfect knowledge of those States, of the first more especially. For military purposes, then, the march of her armies would commence to be in a foreign and unknown country once the nominal frontier was crossed. In our review of all the known routes we will commence with that farthest to the east.

In this quarter China holds exclusively the country which leads up to whatever gateways there may be to India north or east of Cashmere. In any expedition, therefore, in this direction China must be either a willing agent or coerced. For many reasons it may be safely assumed that she will not be the former.

With matters arranged, however, with the Chinese, either by force or by some form of alliance, we find that there is an easy road from Osh in Russian territory by the Terek pass to Kashgar, Yarkand, and Sanju.

From Tashkent itself to Osh is a journey of some days—the distance being two hundred and fifty miles—and from Osh to the head of the Terek pass is sixty-five miles. The city of Kashgar is one hundred and twenty miles away from Sufi-Kurgan at the head of the Terek, so that that city is separated by a distance of four hundred and thirty-five miles from the centre of Russian power in Central Asia, and is at least three hundred miles away from the main garrison of the province of Ferghana.

It is not possible as yet to estimate accurately what change in this respect the exploration of a portion of the Pamir and the annexation of that plateau so far to the south as Lake Kara Kul have made. It seems probable, however, that a Russian column has been despatched from Margilan somewhere into this region, and that it is stationed close in on the Kashgarian frontier. The heights are by no means so extreme in this corner of the Pamir as might be supposed; and there would be no difficulty in following the course of the Kizil-su up to the immediate vicinity of the town of Kashgar. Farther to the south there is said to be a route to Tagharma and Sirikul, which is in common use by the Kirghiz from the Khargosh Pamir. If these routes do exist Russia could undoubtedly push her frontier not only to within fifty miles of Kashgar city, but to within less than that distance from Tashkurgan or Sirikul. Not only has the great Kara Kul been annexed, but the lesser Kara Kul and the Kan Kul could be absorbed to-morrow, provided such routes exist as those referred to. This is not the place to decide that point, nor should it be decided on slight evidence, or at the mere idle rumour that such ways exist. The heights of the surrounding region do not preclude their existence, and that is all that can be said.

So far then as our information goes, the Terek pass is the only road open to Russia into Kashgar. From Kashgar to Yarkand is one hundred and twenty miles by an excellent road. Beyond Yarkand several routes would lie at the choice of an invading army, but of these only two would practically be available. The straight road before it to Sanju, and thence over the Karakoram to Ladakh, is unavailable for any army. It is quite out of the question that even twenty thousand men should cross the Sanju Devan, or any other of those terrible passes which intervene between Kashgar and Cashmere. Unable to pursue the straight road, the invader would have to select either the road to the right or that to the left. For many reasons that to his right is the more important, and the one which he would most probably adopt. It may even be said that without the hearty co-operation of the Chinese that to the left would not be available for him.

The right road, following a south-westerly direction, leads to the town of Tashkurgan, in a valley the surrounding heights of which range from ten to fourteen thousand feet high. From Tashkurgan to Sarhadd, in Wakhan, there are two alternative routes, that by the Karachaukar pass, and that by Ongur and the course of the Oxus. The former is the one more generally used, and passes over a considerable portion of the Little Pamir. From Sarhadd—the neighbouring heights are eleven thousand feet—the Baroghil pass—twelve thousand feet—is under twenty miles distant. The distance from Yarkand to Sarhadd is three hundred and thirty miles. By the Terek pass Osh is therefore distant from Baroghil six hundred and fifty-five miles. Baroghil itself, by Mastuj and the Kunar valley, is two hundred and eighty miles away from Jellalabad; the alternative route viâ Yassin into Cashmere, where there are capital roads up to ten thousand feet, entails a journey of four hundred and fifty miles until British territory is reached immediately south of Jummoo. The occupation of the three passes, Baroghil, Karambar, and Darkot, would close this entrance to all invaders, and this has very wisely been carried out through the medium of the Maharajah of Cashmere.

The left-hand route to the south-east of Yarkand is an excellent road as far as Kiria. From that place, partly by the old Chinese road leading into Tibet, and partly by routes that are wholly unexplored, it would be hoped that Ruduk close in on the Indian frontier might be reached. It is not possible to give accurately the distances of this line of march, but Kiria is four hundred miles from Yarkand, and Ruduk is probably about three hundred and fifty more. There can be no doubt that from Ruduk itself into our territory there is an easy way, but this extreme dependency of China is in such an out-of-the-way corner that it may seem the height of fancy to select it as a quarter from which Russia might be expected to assail India. In this place we are simply obliged to point out that such a road is believed to exist, and that it must be seven hundred and fifty miles south-east of Yarkand. So long as Kashgar remains in independent hands, and free from the presence of a Russian garrison, so long is it extremely improbable that the road to India will be sought through Kashgaria. If it were selected for such a purpose Russia would have made one of the worst selections conceivable.

The next quarter whence it would be possible to advance against India would be from the Pamir, and its contiguous khanates, Karategin—virtually a Russian province—Darwaz, Roshan, and Shignan. In this direction the great river Panja, the upper course of the Oxus, which has not been wholly explored, would serve as the line along which troops might be able to advance. Here also the probable point of concentration would be Sarhadd. The Russian base would be Margilan, whence there are known passes into Karategin. At the most moderate computation Sarhadd is by this route four hundred miles from Margilan. In point of distance this route is preferable to the long, roundabout one through Kashgar. It is in fact one of the shortest.

The main point of doubt is what kind of country Darwaz is, of which neither Russia nor England knows anything definite. If it is possible to march an army from Karategin to Kilai Khumb on the Panja, then there can be no doubt that it is also possible to send an army along the banks of that river to Sarhadd. It is possible, however, to do more than this. By pursuing the same route as far as Ishkasm, in Badakshan, an army would be brought into the close neighbourhood of the Nuksan pass — about thirteen thousand feet high—through the Hindoo Koosh into the country of the Kashkars, which is on the flank of the Kunar valley route to India. Nor is the Nuksan pass the only one through the Hindoo Koosh in this quarter. There is known to be the Dora, and there is said to be a pass leading from Ishkasm itself. In no direction can Russia hope to reach the Indian border-lands by a shorter way than here, for by annexing the Pamir khanates up to the frontier of Badakshan and Wakhan she is within fifty miles of Nuksan, and Nuksan is only one hundred and eighty miles from Jellalabad. In a modified degree this road is also available to her for a flank advance through Hissar.

But if the Pamir route has to be abandoned as impracticable on account of the nature of the road, and the alternative roads still farther to the west through Hissar have to be adopted, then it will not be upon the Panja and Ishkasm that Russian troops will advance. They would strike straight at Faizabad, the chief town of Badakshan. Their base would be pushed forward to the town of Hissar, and advancing by Kurgan-tepe they would occupy Kulab, only twenty miles north of the Oxus, crossing at Sair Tchesme. Faizabad is two hundred miles from Hissar, and about eighty from the Nuksan pass. Faizabad is one of the most delightful places to reside in that can be imagined. During summer, in the close vicinity of fever-stricken haunts, such as Kundus and the banks of the Oxus, it preserves a temperature and equality of climate that would make it the San Remo of Central Asia when that continent becomes the abode of travellers. In winter it is sheltered alike from the bitter winds of the steppe or the mountain range. An army could pass the most severe of winters in comfort at Faizabad, and for this reason Badakshan must always be considered one of the out-works of India. It is not recognised as fully as it ought to be in this country that Badakshan must never be permitted to pass into the hands of a power of whose friendship we possess no security. Russian troops on the Kokcha would represent a most grave peril, and Faizabad must share with Balkh, Maimenè, and Herat the right to be called an out-work, or "key," of the Indian battlements. In any movement in this direction the rivers Surkhab and Panja must operate very much in the favour of an invading army. The former river turns out to be of much larger volume than had been supposed, and some Russians are sanguine enough to believe that there is a waterway for flat-bottomed boats from Kilai Darwaza to its entrance into the Oxus.

Of the roads we have up to this been considering, it may be said that it is uncertain whether they exist, except in the imagination of some enthusiastic Muscovites. If Russia should advance against India from that quarter, it would be the first occasion of which any historical record is preserved. It would be an experiment. By closing Baroghil, and by carefully watching any approach to Faizabad, all danger now, or at any future period, is removed from this direction. Of the various routes which might be followed in an advance on either Khulm or Balkh much more certain information is obtainable. The direct road to Khulm is that from Karatagh and Hissar, crossing the Oxus at Iwachik ferry. The communication between Karatagh and Hissar is defective, and in other ways Hissar is a base of much less value than Karshi, further to the west. The distances are from Samarcand to Hissar one hundred and fifty miles, Hissar to Oxus one hundred and twenty miles, and Khulm forty more. Khulm is the key to the main road to Bamian viâ Heibak—the most northern point to which British troops went in 1841—and is only two hundred and forty miles from Cabul. At Heibak a road also branches to the left, which at Khindjan turns off to the Salalang pass leading to Istalif, and beyond Inderaub to the Khawak pass, which debouches into the Panjkir valley. It was in this region that Dost Mahomed strove for many months to out-manœuvre our troops, and to some extent made up for the inferiority of his army by rapidity of motion and superior knowledge of the country. A road to Kundus from Hissar, crossing the Oxus at Hazrat-Imam, is still more direct for Inderaub and the Khawak. Kundus is, however, a very unhealthy place, and does not possess the same advantages in position that Khulm does.

To Balkh there is a greater number of roads. Roads from Kerkhi, Khoja Salih, Kilif, and Chuchka are all available, and present no inordinate difficulties. That from Kerkhi to Andkhoi is, perhaps, the most difficult, passing through the country of the Alieli Turcomans. The distance from Kerkhi to Andkhoi is one hundred and ten miles, and, so far as is ascertained, water is procurable only at the Zeyyid wells, about half way. The great value of Kerkhi is that it is the highest point to which the Aral flotilla has been able to ascend, but now that a Russian war-vessel is reported to have got as far as Khoja Salih it loses its special claims to be considered the best base for operations beyond. Khoja Salih can be reached from Karshi either by the Kerkhi road or the Kilif. Its ferry is one of the most used along the Oxus, and it is the extreme point of Afghan authority in a north-westerly direction. The Cossacks who have recently been travelling so repeatedly between Samarcand and Cabul have always used this ferry, and it was by it that the Stoletoff mission reached its destination. From Khoja Salih to Balkh there is a good road, with water procurable in abundance at at least five places, which is everything that could be desired, when we remember that the distance is only one hundred miles.

The road from Kilif is still shorter, being only fifty-five miles, and there is water in abundance on this road also. If the Russians have discovered a road from Shirabad to Kilif this is undoubtedly the way by which they will advance on Balkh, for the Gusar-Derbend-Shirabad road is superior in many respects to those leading south of Karshi. Its chief recommendation is that it completely avoids the desert, and that water, fuel, and herbage—the three vital necessaries for an army—are procurable in abundance along it. It is also as short as any other, the distance from Karshi to Balkh by it being only two hundred and eighty miles. These are the principal routes through Bokharan territory into Afghan Turkestan. We may look forward with comparative certainty to the imminent occupation by Russian troops of Karshi, if not of Hissar also. We may even witness the seizure of the Oxus fords.

It is necessary that this fact should be thoroughly grasped in this country. Its full significance time alone can show, but with Russian garrisons on the Oxus any Usbeg, or Afghan, or Turcoman authority in the country between it and the Hindoo Koosh could only be exercised on sufferance. An enemy with a strong force on the Oxus could select any line of advance that he chose, whether it were on Andkhoi and Maimenè, or Balkh, or Khulm, or Kundus, or Faizabad, or even Sarhadd; and with the actual absorption of Afghan Turkestan which would follow, the neutrality of England being assured, the passes of the Hindoo Koosh would be but an imperfect line of defence against an enemy possessing several approaches to each and all of them. To defend the half-dozen known passes would require one hundred thousand men, and even then the defence might fail against an enterprising enemy. It is important, therefore, to remember that when Russia has advanced to the Oxus, England will not have done enough by advancing to the Hindoo

9

Koosh alone. It would be absolutely necessary to hold a line of fortresses from Herat to Faizabad. Later on we may deal with this point in greater detail. Here it is only necessary to say that if, under these circumstances, we contented ourselves with the line of the Hindoo Koosh, we should have put ourselves in a less advantageous position, because of our greater distance from our base, than even our present hap-hazard frontier.

The Hindoo Koosh, with a line of fortresses from Herat to the capital of Badakshan, would be a perfect frontier, strong in every essential demanded by military strategy. The number of troops required would not be large—less than those needed to defend the Hindoo Koosh alone. Fifteen thousand men at Herat, five thousand at Faizabad, and two thousand at Maimenè, Shiborgan, Takhtapul — not Balkh — and Khulm, would be all that would be required, and only a third of these, ten thousand men, need be British. Against these garrisons the most desperate attempt that Russia will be able for the next century to make should recoil, and Anglo-Indians have certainly lost their skill if they could not raise thirty thousand of the best light cavalry—ready mounted and only lacking in arms—in the world from the Turcoman tribes. In the progress of events in Bokhara and Hissar the greatest interest should be taken during the next few years. We cannot watch Russia's relations with her vassal the Ameer of Bokhara too closely, for in them will be found the key to everything that must afterwards transpire in the country to the south of the Oxus.

The town of Charjui, opposite the Bokharan villages

of Batili and Ilik, is situated at one of the principal ferries over the Oxus. It is on the direct road from Bokhara to Merv, one of the chief trade-routes of Central Asia, and it is the only place from which Merv could be attacked on the north. There are various tracks from Khiva through Kara Kum, but on these the wells are so few, and separated by such great distances from each other, that, practically speaking, there is no way in this direction. From Bokhara itself to Charjui the road is neither so good nor the water so plentiful as a general would desire. Mr. Schuyler was unable to procure permission from the Bokharan authorities to proceed to this place, but from several other travellers we can obtain much information.

Charjui is exactly one hundred and forty-two miles from Merv, or six days' march according to military calculation by the wells; but as at this computation one day's march would be almost forty miles, it may be assumed that Charjui is a seven-days' march from Merv. Water is to be obtained at the following places: — Kaltaminar, twenty miles; Ishk Robat, twenty miles; Robitak, sixteen miles; Nizacher, forty miles; Khalka, twenty miles; and Merv, twenty-six miles. Balgoui has been given by Venyukoff in mistake for Robitak, the former place being on another route to the north of that generally used. Some maps give a place called Pindi, half way between Robitak and Nizacher, where there is said to be a supply of water. If this be so, then Charjui is only a seven-days' easy march from Merv. Charjui is two hundred and fifty miles distant from Samarcand, and consequently Merv is under four hundred miles from the second principal place in the Russian dominions.

It might be possible to advance on Merv by a triple line across the desert, but if the advance is only made in the small force that would be necessary, there is no reason for saying that an army of from five to ten thousand men would experience any delay in its onward march. The Turcomans might of course harass the expedition, but remembering the wretched way in which they are armed, and also that they, too, could not venture far from the vicinity of the Murghab without suffering from the same want of water as the invader, it must be concluded that a Russian occupation of Merv from Charjui would not require any more extended preparations, or a larger force, than did the expedition against Khiva. And once Merv is occupied, the road to Herat lies open by the banks of the Murghab, and the prosperous villages of Salor.

Herat is almost exactly two hundred miles south of Merv. Between those places there are no fewer than twenty villages *en route*, and these contain water, provisions, and shelter in abundance. By easy stages, or by long stages, in twenty days or in a week, a general and his army quartered in Merv could advance against and occupy Herat. From Herat to Candahar is only three hundred and fifty miles by the shortest road, and Candahar is the most vital point in the Indian frontier. It is the Metz of India. Before considering the roads from Herat to the Indian frontier —the point of all importance to be considered—it will be clearer to consider those other routes which lead from the Caspian and Persia to Herat. All these Persian and Turcomanian roads lead to Herat. It is the central point from which routes branch off in every direction. There are roads from Herat that, if followed up to their termination, will take one not only to Moscow or Calcutta, but to Pekin and the shores of the China Sea. It is one of the hearts of Asiatic life.

The first of these roads—and the one of which we have lately heard the most, owing to Russia's pledge not to violate the soil of Persia—is that from Krasnovodsk which leads to Kizil Arvat, and thence along the slopes of the Attock to Ashkabad, Abiverd, and Sarakhs. From Krasnovodsk to Kizil Arvat is two hundred and seventy-five miles, from Kizil Arvat to Sarakhs two hundred miles, and to Herat one hundred and thirty-three more. This road has been on several occasions used by General Lomakine in his advance into the Akhal country, and it certainly gives Russia a new route from the Caspian to the vicinity both of Merv and Herat. Without violating any treaty, and even without acting in direct contravention of the tacit understanding between the English and Russian Governments that Merv was not to be touched, Russia can push troops forward as far as Abiverd, thus bringing Merv and Sarakhs within her immediate control. The former place is one hundred and fifty miles from Abiverd, and the latter eighty. Although we do not possess as full information as necessary of this route, there appears to be no doubt but that it is available for the passage of ten thousand men, and that army, though quite inadequate for such a gigantic task as the invasion of India, would amply suffice for the occupation of Merv, or as a garrison for Herat. Moreover, this force is a reality; we are not now discussing suppositions. It is within three hundred miles of Herat, which it can easily reach by a violation of Persian territory. Even British troops at Girishk would be farther off from Herat than Lomakine's are now. By a new road, with European forces, with different aspirations to those that prevail in Tashkent, this general has more nearly jeoparded our controlling influence over the Heratees than it ever has been endangered since Eldred Pottinger baffled the Persians, or since Sultan Jan took Russian bribes.

By none of the roads which we have considered, not even the last, could more than thirty thousand troops be despatched. But the great superiority of those we have now to describe is that by them there is practically no limit to the number that might be sent by them. They all lie through Persian territory, and consequently the first move from the Caspian would be the signal for a declaration of war. Russia knows that, and will only seek to use these roads when she has resolved to cast aside the mask she has so long worn. Elsewhere she may strive to weaken our position by sap and mine; she may aim at detaching vassals from their allegiance, or at securing strategical points over against the Indus; and so long as there is ostensible peace between the two Powers, so long will she seek to secure her ends by fraud instead of by force. But when she has braced herself to the effort, and decides to fight no longer with concealed weapons, then she will throw aside all disguise. In that day the Persian road to India will be her road, and the contest will be one of giants. The victory will assuredly be to the one that is most strong and that has been most wise.

Nor can there be much doubt that that day must sooner or later arrive. It may even be precipitated by some premature move on Kaufmann's part which will meet with disaster, when Russia may turn her inert strength to the east to revindicate her name. Whenever she may do so, let us never blind ourselves to the fact that between the Caspian and Candahar nature has not raised a single obstacle. Every conqueror advancing from this quarter, whether he was Shah Abbas or Nadir, has only encountered one barrier—the ramparts of Herat. This road lies as available at the present moment for an army as it did two centuries ago, and does not require improvement to be rendered serviceable. The rivers, such as have to be crossed, are all fordable, and the climate is far from being severe. With very ordinary sanitary precautions there is nothing also to be feared from zymotic diseases such as fevers and cholera.

By this route Herat is five hundred and eighty miles distant from the Caspian, and between the two extreme points there are no fewer than thirty-seven recognised stages or halting-places. This particular road is the most northerly within the Persian frontier. It skirts in many places the southern slopes of the mountains of Khorasan. The principal places *en route* are Astrabad, Pisserook, Bujnoord, Kooshan, Meshed, Abbas-Abad, and Ghorian; but at all of the thirty-seven stages referred to every necessary for an army is procurable. But perhaps the vast superiority of this line of advance to every other is to be found in the fact that there are three roads between Astrabad Bay—the starting-point for each—and Meshed, their common goal. There is the Bujnoord route, which has just been mentioned, the Bostam-Sanghos road passing south of the Ala Dagh mountains and joining the road from Kooshan at the village of Saidan, and lastly there is the Shahrood, Sebzewar, Nishapore road to Meshed itself. The last of these is the most direct and the shortest; but, in actual condition, it is the worst. Meshed is three hundred and sixty miles from Astrabad, and between Shahrood and Meshed there are twenty-seven regular halting-places at short distances from each other.

Russia has therefore three roads to select from, or the option of using them all, in an advance so far as Meshed, and from that town to Herat there is also a capital road. By the Krasnovodsk route—six hundred and thirty-three miles from Herat—it is possible to reach the neighbourhood of the Tejend swamp—which is four hundred and seventy miles of the journey accomplished—without violating treaty stipulation or even exciting much suspicion, except from experts, in this country. An alliance with Persia, and an understanding with the Turcomans, would place Russia in possession of any or all of these highways to India, and would bring Russian bayonets to within two hundred miles of Herat before this country had awoke from the apathy and indifference into which it had sunk. As things are at present, there would be nothing to withstand a rapid advance against Herat. The sole obstacle that would then remain between the invader and his prey would be the three hundred and fifty miles of country that intervene between it and Candahar. It would be a mistake to suppose that that country is as fertile and productive as a hostile general would desire. Its character varies considerably, some portions being highly cultivated, and others barren and waste. There is a general balance of evidence, however, that naturally the region is rich, and its soil productive.

On this point no authority can be clearer, no document more explicit, than the remarkable letter which Sir John M'Niell wrote to Lord Palmerston from Meshed on the 25th of June 1838. It still retains all its freshness, and its principal assertions have been confirmed by more recent travellers. The following are the essential portions of the letter:—

" The key of all Afghanistan towards the north is Herat; and though I can have no right to press my personal opinions upon your Lordship after having already stated them, and although I must necessarily be ignorant of the many important considerations, not immediately connected with this question, which must influence the policy of Her Majesty's Government, still I cannot refrain from saying a few words more regarding the importance of preserving the independence of Herat.

" I have already informed your Lordship publicly that the country between the frontiers of Persia and India is far more productive than I had imagined it to be; and I can assure your Lordship that there is no impediment, either from the physical features of the country or from the deficiency of supplies, to the march of a large army from the frontiers of Georgia to Candahar, or, as I believe, to the Indus.

"Count Simonich, being lame from a wound, drove his carriage from Teheran to Herat, and could drive it to Candahar; and the Shah's army has now for nearly seven months subsisted almost exclusively on the supplies of the country immediately around Herat and Ghorian, leaving the still more productive districts of Sebzewar and Ferrah untouched.

"In short, I can state from personal observation that there is absolutely no impediment to the march of an army to Herat; and that from all the information I have received, the country between that city and Candahar not only presents no difficulty but affords remarkable facilities for the passage of armies.

"There is therefore, my Lord, no security for India in the nature of the country through which an army would have to pass to invade it from this side.

"On the contrary, the whole line is peculiarly favourable for such an enterprise; and I am the more anxious to state this opinion clearly, because it is at variance with my previous belief, and with statements which I may have previously hazarded, relying on more imperfect information.

"Under such circumstances, it appears to me that it would be a most hazardous policy to allow Persia to act as the pioneer of Russia, and, under protection of the article of the treaty, to break down the main defence of Afghanistan, and thereby make the country untenable to us, at a moment when the concert between Persia and Russia in these operations is avowed. . . . . .

"It is currently reported and believed here, though I cannot say on what grounds, that there is a secret arrangement between Persia and Russia to exchange Herat for some of the districts beyond the Arras which formerly belonged to Persia.

"This report was first mentioned to me at Teheran, in March last; but I then paid no attention to it, because I could not see how Russia was to get at Herat, and I still am inclined to regard it as probably unfounded, though Count Simonich certainly threatened Mahomed Ameen, a servant of Yar Mahomed Khan, (who was sent with a message from his master to the Persian camp,) that if Herat did not surrender to the Shah he would march a Russian army against it."

There is a choice in marching on Candahar of two main roads, that through Ferrah, and that through Daulatabad. There is still another farther to the north, passing through Kala-Yar-Mahomed. We need only consider the first two. They follow the same southerly road through Adreskan to a point a little way beyond Khwaja Uriah, and up to this place the road is most excellent. There is undoubtedly a scarcity of water, but even this appears to be procurable at certain places in any quantity. The caravanserais and wells have been equally neglected during the numerous periods of disturbance of which Herat, Sebzewar, and Ferrah have been the scene. The success, however, which attended our efforts in restoring these, and in keeping the road open during the maintenance of the Herat mission, should encourage us to believe that it would be possible to restore the wells and halting-places which are attributed to the public spirit of the Persians. At the present moment there can be no doubt that during the summer months it would be difficult for an army to march through this arid and thinly-populated portion of the country.

This portion of the road is, however, the worst, and the distance from Herat to Adreskan is only sixty miles, and to Khwaja Uriah fifteen miles more. The road by Ferrah continues still to the south through Sebzewar, while that through Daulatabad turns off to the left towards Asiabad. Sebzewar is a small fortress, half-way between Herat and Ferrah, and was at one time a place of considerable importance. Its position in a plain of some extent on the banks of the

Adreskan river is very favourable, and Sebzewar may yet recover that prosperity which Afghan feuds and Persian and Belooch hostility have taken from it. Between Sebzewar and Ferrah the scarcity of water still continues to be the great trouble; but this can be overcome to a great degree by following the course of the Haroot or Adreskan river; and by doing so, it is found that in this short journey —only eighty miles— there are at least seven distinct places where water can be procured in abundance. From Ferrah to Girishk, across the Khash-rud and through the Bukwa valley, the difficulties completely vanish. The Bukwa valley, watered by the Khash, is one of the most productive spots in the whole of Afghanistan, and could alone provide a host with supplies for an indefinite period. Between Ferrah and Girishk, a distance of one hundred and twenty miles, there are fifteen usual halting-places, and the country is well watered. The district of Khash to the south could also be drawn upon for supplies.

But although this road is the best, the alternative one is not wholly useless. There is also the cross road followed by Mons. Ferrier to Abkourmeh and Giraneh. Giraneh is certainly an important place, and, if garrisoned, would no doubt tend to the advantage of the authority that was recognised in Herat. Mons. Ferrier followed a route still to the south through Gurmab, and he suffered great inconvenience from the want of water. The road to the north, while passing through more mountainous country, is infinitely better in this respect. But of all, the Ferrah road is the best. That leads to Girishk on the Helmund, whence Candahar, by a well-known road, is seventy-five miles distant. The valley of the Helmund is the principal granary of southern Afghanistan, and although some portions of the roads into that valley from the west pass through an arid tract of country where water is scarce, and the heat during several months intense, it cannot be said that the difficulties even in this portion of the supposed move against the Indian frontier are such as would prevent an attempt at invasion. To give a comparison, they are not greater than those which beset an army in marching from Scinde upon Candahar, which has been thrice accomplished by English armies. Once in possession of Candahar, an enemy can strike at several points in the Indian frontier.

According to some authorities, and the maps are unanimous in supporting the assertion, there is another road leading from the Helmund almost in a straight line to the town of Khelat. There is no evidence that we can find of this route having been followed by a large army, or, indeed, by any army save small bodies of Belooch troops, either in raids into Seistan or when engaged on some petty mission of conquest. This route, commencing at Ferrah, passes by the Ferrah-rud and Lash into Seistan, thence by Nasirabad and the Helmund to a place on that river known as Pulatak, whence it takes a south-easterly course by Kuchan and Nushki to Khelat. Captain Christie used this route in his travels; and his account of it tends to show that it would be out of the question for a large army to follow it. Mons. Ferrier took a more hopeful view of this route, but in face of the contradictory evidence it is impossible to give any unhesitating opinion as to its value. There are certainly fifty miles of sandy desert to be traversed, and six separate passes of unknown difficulty. On the other hand, it also avoids much difficult country, and possesses the great recommendation of being short and direct. By it Herat is under six hundred miles from Khelat, whence, by the Mula pass, much easier than the Bolan, it is a matter of no difficulty to reach the Indian frontier. Of Nushki itself we possess some information, mainly from Pottinger. The productions to be found in this district are few, and, such as they are, of a very uncertain character, often failing altogether. No army could rely upon receiving a sufficient quantity of supplies from this district to enable it to pursue any great enterprise. As a matter of fact, the march from the Helmund to Khelat would have to be a forced march, made without any halts, and consequently in no great strength. Even then it would be a dangerous experiment. It is only mentioned here because such a route has been said to exist.

As little need be said of the Seistan or Persian Gulf routes, as these are only available to a strong power dominant in Isfahan and Shiraz. Russia is not, as yet, that power, nor is it likely that her immediate aspirations will so far have a practical result as to place her in the position of such a power. The Persian Gulf route is also only available for a country supreme upon the sea, and Russia is not in that enviable position, nor is it probable that she ever will be able to rival England or the United States in that respect. It may therefore be assumed that the road to India lies somewhere between the Kashgar and the Khorasan roads. For a large army—that is to say, for one of greater strength than thirty thousand men—the Persian and Turcoman roads are alone available; but for a smaller army, there can be no doubt that there are several which lead from the Russian frontier to Balkh and Afghan-Turkestan. There is danger in each direction; in the one part it will be more formidable, in the other it is more insidious. Each requires to be vigilantly observed, and estimated, and against both should precautions be taken, and in good time.

CHAPTER VI.

RUSSIA'S RELATIONS WITH KHIVA AND KHOKAND.

ALTHOUGH, practically speaking, Russia has overcome all the resistance that the two khanates of Khiva and Khokand are capable of offering her, and although they are now as much her vassals as any of the Indian feudatories is ours, yet it will not be out of place to give here a sketch of the past intercourse between them.* That retrospect will also afford the opportunity of qualifying the favourable opinion as to the security of Russia's position which would be formed from regarding the matter from the point of view of religion alone; and it may be found that, after all, religious fanaticism is the least potent sentiment that is at work adverse to the peace of Russia.

Russia's relations with Khiva are of old standing. It was the first Central Asian Court with which Russia had any intercourse, and it was also one of the last

* Works which may be consulted on this subject are Schuyler's "Turkistan," and Helwald's "Russians in Central Asia."

to feel the weight of Russia's hand. When it did feel it, however, it completely succumbed. So long ago as the year 1620 there are said to have been political relations between the two Courts. In those days there certainly was open hostility between the Cossacks of the Ural and the Khivans; and the former on several occasions carried their raids into the inhabited portion of Khivan territory. But out of this petty border warfare the Khan always emerged with success. The Cossack raiders were invariably cut off and often annihilated. In those days Khiva was strong, and the Turcomans were her allies.

We have already described the unfortunate expedition of Prince Beckovitch—the first official attempt on the part of the Russian Government to carry on intercourse with the States of Central Asia. The Beckovitch disaster gave the Khan a confidence in the security of his position, which had not deserted his successors even when General Kaufmann was sending ultimatums in 1873. A short time after the murder of Prince Beckovitch, of whose fate no certain tidings had then been received, the Czar Peter sent an ambassador to Khiva, but although he was well received he achieved nothing of importance. After Peter's death several fresh embassies were sent, but they all were practically abortive. The Khan would not surrender the Russian subjects whom he already possessed. He would not give up his privilege of capturing them whenever he could, and of enslaving them when captured. For more than two centuries Khiva bade defiance to Russia, and for a long time after the first triumphs on the Jaxartes the Khan continued to be hostile on the strength of his impunity in the past. As between Khiva and Russia there was, therefore, bitter ground for hostility, and Russia cannot be blamed for having at length indulged her pent-up indignation. The Khan had enslaved Russian subjects, when he had not murdered them. He had defied Russia as no civilised power can permit itself to be defied, and from the murder of Beckovitch down to the refusal to surrender the captives in 1869 there was a long score of misdeeds for which reparation should be given. The day of atonement was long coming, but it came at last.

Russian intrigues in Persia in 1837–38 had been one of the causes of an English invasion of Afghanistan in 1839; and Russia, foiled before the walls of Herat, mainly by the intrepidity and resolution of Eldred Pottinger, turned once more to the Khivan question, by the settlement of which it was hoped that not only would the old difficulties be removed, but that an equivalent might be secured round the Aral for the results of any British triumphs in Cabul. The two great empires made their first advance towards each other in the year 1839, and, strange to say, each was doomed to meet with disaster. In our case the disaster was relieved by the glory of two victorious campaigns; and in the Russian it was unqualified and complete. Both were capable of being permanently repaired, but while we remained apathetic after our military triumph, Russia turned in another direction to attain what she had failed in securing from the Caspian.

Yet the Russian expedition against Khiva in 1839 was one that, to judge from the care with which it had been prepared, should have succeeded. Its superiority over the Khivan army was not less unquestionable than the superiority of Lord Keane's army over that of Dost Mahomed. The officer who was entrusted with the command was General Peroffsky, certainly not an incompetent or an inexperienced soldier. His force consisted of five thousand fighting-men, twenty-two guns, and ten thousand camels, according to Mr. Schuyler; but Captain Abbott says that Peroffsky himself admitted that he had ten thousand men. There was also a large body of Kirghiz attached to the expedition. The march from Orenburg to Khiva lies through nine hundred and thirty miles of steppe beyond the Emba river, which is almost destitute of water during the summer, and well-nigh impassable in winter, on account of the depth of the snow and the extreme severity of the weather. For some reason or other—the Russians say through the treachery of a Polish officer*—it was considered that, although Russian soldiers could not do without water, there was no degree of cold to which they were not proof. It was in consequence resolved to begin the march in the autumn; but the fates were against the Russians in every way, for that year the winter set in unusually early, and with remarkable severity. Before Peroffsky had got more than half way to Khiva he

---

* I can find no trace of any officer having been tried for treachery after the close of the campaign.

was compelled to retreat, and those who witnessed that retreat say that its horrors could not have been surpassed. With scarcely one-third of his original force, and only one-tenth of his camels, Peroffsky was glad to find shelter and safety in Orenburg. Khiva was again triumphant, and Russia's Central Asian campaigns, which up to this had been a series of disasters, culminated in this the most disastrous of them all.

It was at once resolved to repair the catastrophe, and great preparations were set on foot for a fresh expedition. It was at this critical juncture that Captain Abbott's efforts at Khiva, and the arrival of Sir Richmond Shakespear on a special mission to that Court, were so far beneficial in the interests of peace that the Khan consented to restore the Russian subjects who had been enslaved in Khiva. These, to the number of four hundred and eighteen, according to one authority—four hundred and fifteen, according to another—were surrendered, and escorted in safety across the steppe to Novo-Alexandrovsk on the Caspian. The Russian Government in return was compelled to release the five hundred and fifty Khivan subjects who had been captured during the progress of the war.

The exact circumstances* of the case are the following:—When Sir Richmond Shakespear reached Khiva, and discovered that the threatened Russian invasion had failed, he lost no time in urging upon the

* This is mainly taken from Captain Abbott's "Herat to Khiva."

Khan the necessity for the immediate fulfilment of his promises to Captain Abbott—to whom greater credit is due than has as yet been accorded—to release the Russian captives, whom, in that spirit of chivalry which he possessed in so remarkable a degree, Sir Richmond volunteered to escort to the Russian frontier. For a time it seemed that the Khan was too much flushed by his recent success—for the retreat of the Russians was regarded as a triumph in the streets of Khiva, despite the small part that Usbeg or Turcoman valour played in bringing that result to pass—to listen to advice counselling him to concede willingly, and of his own accord, that which he had refused to force. But the English officer pursued the subject with such tact and resolution that he attained his object. The Russian captives were released. The Khan gave Sir Richmond Shakespear authority to search in all the houses wherein it was as much as reported that a Russian subject could be found. It is said that even the royal harem was not sacred from the investigation. This active assistance on the part of the Khan was turned to good account, and in a very short time more than four hundred Russian subjects were collected in readiness for departure. At this moment, when everything had been concluded, and the cortège was only awaiting the signal to set out on its journey, a rumour spread that there was another captive still immured in the city. The rumour was vague, but Sir Richmond was not the man to leave his work half-done. He hurried back to the Palace, obtained a fresh audience, and, to the amazement of the Court, urged the necessity for the most complete fulfilment of the engagement. The retention of a single captive would mar the completeness of the concession, and might destroy all its good effects. The captive was traced out, released, and joined his comrades in their journey to their native land, which they reached in safety under the personal charge of the gallant English officer. From about this period until the visit of Major Wood and Captain Burnaby, a short time ago, no Englishman visited Khiva, where, however, there still survived a remembrance of our old embassies.

Although the idea of a second Russian expedition against Khiva was abandoned, two embassies—the first under Nikiforof, and the second under Danilefsky —were sent to that country in 1841 and 1842, with the object of securing trade concessions, and the Khan's consent to the ratification of a formal treaty with the Czar. The former was a complete failure; but M. Danilefsky succeeded in inducing the Khan to sign a treaty of friendship. The terms of this treaty remained a dead letter, but its signature was a triumph for Russian diplomacy. This concession is clearly traceable to the effect produced on the Khan's mind by the Cabul disasters in 1841. But, confident in the strength of his position, the Khan showed little respect for the stipulations which he had ratified. The Khivans in a short time forgot that there had ever been such a treaty as that with Danilefsky, and even denied that it had existed. In fact, from 1842 down to 1870, Khiva was as covertly hostile to Russia as it was possible for her to be. She ravaged the borders, she stirred up the Kirghiz, she gave sanctuary to several of the most proclaimed of Russia's foes, and whenever the chance offered she carried off Russian subjects into captivity, there to subject them to the most harsh of punishments—the loss of freedom. Long impunity had made the Khan and his people reckless. The day of reckoning had been so long coming that the Usbeg, in his vanity, thought it would never come.

General Tchernaieff thinks that the part assigned to Khiva, by authority, as the author of the Kirghiz troubles, was exaggerated; and he supported this view in the columns of the "Russki Mir." He is probably correct, in so far as the Kirghiz raids are concerned, but of the generally hostile tone of Khiva towards Russia there can be no question. During the years 1871 and 1872 great preparations were being made for the Khivan campaign. Not only were stores collected, and fresh troops despatched from Europe and Orenburg, but the country surrounding Khiva was explored on all sides, and the greatest precautions were taken to ensure speedy and unqualified success.

The Khan was very naturally alarmed at these preparations, and strove to avert, by diplomatic means, the storm which he saw was gathering over his head. He made overtures both to the authorities at Tiflis and at Orenburg, thinking to secure better terms from them than if he treated with Tashkent direct. In this he was mistaken, for with the demands made upon him he found it impossible to comply. For the campaign against Khiva in 1873 it is impossible to blame Russia, in so far as it was designed as a punishment for Khiva's hostility in the past; but at the root of the decision to attack Khiva there were less creditable motives. Attention had, so long ago as 1872, been called to the maladministration of the Tashkent authorities, and by no one with greater force and eloquence than General Tchernaieff. It was necessary to drown hostile criticism in some triumph that should attract popular sympathy to the cause of General Kaufmann, and no task lay easier to hand than an invasion of Khiva.

Russia could, however, bring a serious bill of indictment against this State, as has been observed; and so long as Khiva remained the slave-mart for the Kirghiz in the north and the Turcomans in the south, so long was it impossible for any civilised power to look upon its ruler with a friendly eye. Against Khiva's receiving the chastisement she had deserved it is impossible to say anything, and it would be unfair to condemn Russia for inflicting punishment so well merited as that meted out to the Khan of Khiva. Let it be conceded that Russia's right to punish an aggressor is as clear as our own—and that the Khan of Khiva was an aggressor there can be no question— that concession does not in the slightest affect the argument that Russia committed a breach of faith, for which there is no justification, towards this country in annexing the whole of the khanate of Khiva which lay on the right bank of the Oxus, and in imposing such terms upon the remaining portion that it has become completely at the mercy of the small

Russian garrison of the Amou Darya district. The conduct of Khiva justified an invasion, and the imposition of a suitable fine. Russia's engagements to this country forbade the annexation of territory; yet territory was annexed. Both to the spirit and the letter of her bond Russia was proved to be utterly false.

The failure of Colonel Markozof's expedition from the Caspian, in September 1872, when that officer was compelled to retreat with the loss of most of his camels, rendered an expedition against Khiva more necessary than ever before. After some months' delay General Kaufmann received the necessary permission to attack Khiva, and thereupon at once set about the final preparations for the forthcoming campaign. The following is a summary of the principal events of this war, of which the fullest and most graphic description is to be found in the pages of the late Mr. Macgahan's book, "Campaigning on the Oxus." In all there were five columns directed against Khiva from as many different points, viz., from Orenburg, Chikishlar, Fort Alexandrofsky, on the Caspian, and from Kazala and Jizakh. The total strength of the Turkestan army was said to be under six thousand men; but when we add to that the other corps we find the number of troops comprising the five columns to have been considerably higher than the figure given of twelve thousand men. The Aral flotilla of four steam-vessels, and a considerable number of barges filled with provisions, also assisted in the enterprise. The column from Chikishlar, under the command of Colonel Markozof, was obliged to retreat for the second time after reaching a point a little way beyond the Igdy wells. It returned to Krasnovodsk after having suffered serious loss, and utterly demoralised. The column starting from Alexandrofsky reached Kungrad in tolerably good condition, mainly through the care of its commander, Colonel Lomakine, where it joined the Orenburg force under General Verefkin, who had also reached his destination in safety.

The principal column starting from Jizakh across the Kizil Kum desert was originally to have advanced upon its destination by a road that had been explored and was well-known through the Bukan mountains, reaching the Amou at Shurakhana. This road was, as we have just said, well-known, and had it been followed there is little doubt but that General Kaufmann's own division would have reached Khiva without undergoing any extraordinary deprivations. By the rules of the Order, the chief of the staff of an army can only receive the Cross of St. George when the route followed has been prepared by him. In this case this had not been done under the personal supervision of Colonel Trotzky, Kaufmann's *adlatus*, and in order to qualify that officer for the decoration, it was resolved to depart from the proposed route, and to follow what on the map appeared to be a shorter way to the Amou. At this point the Kazala column effected a junction with the Jizakh, and the united force prepared for that short march to the Oxus, which was intended to secure a decoration for a popular officer. So far as Khalata the difficulties, though far from slight, proved not insurmountable;* but beyond that point the true arduousness of the enterprise revealed itself.

Between Khalata and the Oxus there intervened one hundred and twenty miles of deep and shifting sand, without any wells upon which an army could rely with any degree of confidence for a sufficient supply of water. In fact the only known well on the march was that at Adam Krylgan, and the character of that well may be perceived from its name, which signifies "man's destruction." A day's journey beyond this well the Russian army was on the point of despair,— the men were exhausted, the heat was intense, and the transport had broken down. There can be little doubt that, had the remaining transport been sufficiently serviceable, General Kaufmann would have ordered a retreat to Khalata; but even to retreat was denied to the distressed army. General Kaufmann gave himself up as lost, and ordered that, in the event of anything happening to him, the chief command should devolve upon Colonel Trotzky instead of upon General Golovatchef, the next senior officer. At this critical moment a preserver appeared for the whole army in the person of a "ragged Kirghiz," who had joined the Kazala column at Irkibai. He declared that wells at a place called Alty Kuduk were only a few miles away, and his declaration turned out to be correct.

A Russian general and army were thus saved, on the very point of destruction, by the fidelity and good

* This description is taken, with trivial alterations, from the pages of Mr. Schuyler.

memory of a Kirghiz peasant. The folly of the commander-in-chief had brought six thousand soldiers to the verge of ruin; and the necessity of obtaining a petty distinction for an unknown officer had almost wrecked the whole enterprise. Had General Kaufmann's force met with a disaster at this point, it is doubtful if any of his followers would have escaped. It would also have been extremely probable that the other columns, which had reached Kungrad in safety, would have been compelled to beat a hasty retreat. On the 28th of May the force arrived on the banks of the Amou, and on the 30th the passage of the river commenced. On the 3rd of June the whole army was across the river, ready to advance against the capital, and on the 4th the town of Hazarasp was occupied. In the meanwhile the Orenburg column was advancing against the capital, and before Kaufmann had quitted Hazarasp General Verefkin was encamped only three miles from Khiva.

After waiting for some days in this position, General Verefkin resolved to assault Khiva by himself, considering that it would be unsafe to put off the attack any longer, as it was rumoured that Kaufmann's army was retreating. During the 9th a smart cannonade took place between the Khivan artillery and the Russian. The Khan's artillery was well served, and during this day's fighting the Russians lost forty killed and wounded, including among the latter General Verefkin himself. The firing recommenced the following morning, and Colonel Scobelef was compelled to storm one of the gates. This was successfully accomplished with a loss of fifteen killed and wounded; and Khiva was then in the hands of the Russian army. Great credit is undoubtedly due to both General Verefkin and Colonel Lomakine for the remarkably able manner in which they conducted their operations and brought them to a successful termination; but it is impossible to give praise to the rashness which characterised General Kaufmann's measures, and to the haphazard way in which he and his staff carried out their plans.

The first and principal result of the Khivan campaign was the liberation of the Persian slaves who were immured in the country. These were computed to number thirty thousand persons. Such little interest was taken, however, by the Russian authorities in the fate of these unfortunate persons that they had no idea how many out of this multitude actually availed themselves of the permission to recover their liberty. It is supposed that not more than five thousand were freed before the departure of the Russian troops. If such was the case, we may be sure that very few were released afterwards. The freed slaves were sent in detachments across the steppe to Krasnovodsk, whence they were to be conveyed by steamer to Persia. Mr. Schuyler was only able to discover traces of two of these detachments, but of the nature of their fate it is impossible to entertain any doubt. The first of these was attacked by the Turcomans, who either killed the fugitives or carried them off to be re-enslaved. The second appears to have met with the same fate. It is estimated that of these five thousand persons nearly one half perished or became captive to the Turcomans. To judge from some evidence that was produced in the Russian journals the massacre of Persians increased rather than declined after the departure of the Russian troops. Couriers across the steppe reported that they had met hundreds of corpses of Persians by the road-side, and similar tales were told of the road both to Krasnovodsk and to Mangishlak.

The one benefit which Russia might have conferred upon a suffering body of human beings was turned into a curse by her mismanagement and downright carelessness and disregard for human life. Russia is so far a civilised power that she can imitate England's example, and enfranchise slaves both within and without her frontier; but her native barbarousness is at once made apparent in the improvidence and callousness which she shows in working out what, in some freak of sentiment, she may have ordained. What Russia gives lavishly with the one hand, she takes away, either through obtuseness or deceit, with the other. Her favours are to be shunned rather than solicited. Of the expeditions against the Turcomans subsequent to the fall of Khiva nothing need here be said. Mr. Schuyler's graphic description still lives in the memory and lies at the service of the English reader.

At the present moment Russia's relations with Khiva may be summed up in the one word, dependency. The Khan has no army. His subjects are not even allowed to carry arms, and but for the presence of Russian troops across the river he would be at the complete mercy of the Kirghiz and Turcoman tribes which haunt the neighbourhood of Khiva. On several occasions Russian troops have crossed over to the left bank to punish the marauders and to assist the Khan in the collection of his revenue. The nominal authority of the Khan still continues, but his actual authority has disappeared. He is as much a vassal of the Czar as the Ameer of Bokhara, and he is so far a more completely subjected prince in that he no longer possesses an army.

Of Russia's breach of faith to this country in retaining possession of a large portion of Khivan territory, when she had formally bound herself down not to annex a yard of it, it is impossible to speak in terms too strong. Nor was the acquisition so valueless as some would have had us suppose. The territory itself, which became the Amou-Darya sub-district, was not remarkable for its fertility; but such as it was it sustained a population of a quarter of a million. It had two fairly-populated towns, Chimbai and Surakhana. But above all, it commanded the navigation of the Oxus. The possession of the right bank of the Oxus gave Russia a new road to Central Asia, and placed at her disposal a waterway from Kazala to Charjui, and it is now said even to Kerkhi and Khoja Salih. Those advantages are due to the campaign against Khiva. They were obtained, it is true, at the cost of a perjured word, but that did not greatly affect the Muscovite conscience. The offence having been condoned by England it is now too late to take action upon it; but the lesson of Russia's falseness then learnt should hold good for all time.

When, in 1841, General Peroffsky's scheme of revenge for the failure of the Khivan expedition had to give way before the amicable measures of the Khan, acting under the influence of British officers, the Russians for the first time began to consider the proposal of making a bold advance across the Orenburg steppe into the country held by the Middle Horde of Kirghiz and the Khan of Khokand. The first stage in these later campaigns was the chastisement and coercion of the Kirghiz, which was effected in the first place by a series of expeditions being despatched against them, and in the second by the construction of a line of forts in advantageous positions across the steppe. These measures were carried out with energy by General Peroffsky and the Governor-General Obrutchef. Several of the leading Kirghiz chieftains were either killed in fight or captured, and peace gradually settled down over the vast region held by the Kirghiz tribes. Thus was the path cleared for the main enterprise, an advance upon the Jaxartes. In 1848 Russia had reached that river, she had planted her foot upon its banks, and since then her forward march has been steady and persistent. A fort was constructed almost at the mouth of the river, and it became known as either Fort Raim or Fort Aralsk. The Aral flotilla was simultaneously commenced. The position of this fort was, however, unhealthy, and liable to be flooded, so that after a brief stay there the Russians moved their first fort higher up the river to Kazala in 1855. During these years a continual war was waged along the border, and while General Peroffsky was maturing his plans for future campaigns, alarm and fear were spreading among the Khokandians and the Khivans at Russia's appearance north of Turkestan. "We are lost," exclaimed these Asiatics, "if the Russians drink of the waters of the Syr Darya." The Russians were, however, doing more than drink of the waters of that river. They were making them an ally in their warfare with the peoples of Turkestan.

In 1852 an attack was made in small force upon the very important Khokandian outpost of Ak Musjid, situate three hundred miles from the mouth of the Syr Darya. It failed in its main object, and during the winter the Khokandian garrison made strenuous efforts to strengthen its defences in anticipation of a renewal of the attack. General Peroffsky on his side was not less diligent, and a considerable force was assembled at Aralsk for the forthcoming campaign. The siege of Ak Musjid, which was defended with such gallantry by the late Yakoob Beg, of Kashgar, closed with the triumph of the Russians, who successfully maintained themselves in the position they had won against the utmost efforts of the Khan to retake it. On the ruins of Ak Musjid rose Fort Peroffsky, after the name of its captor; but for many years after this event Russia remained inactive upon the Syr Darya through the prostration resulting from the Crimean war.

But although Fort Peroffsky was for many years Russia's advanced post in Central Asia, her officers and troops were not wholly unemployed. There was work still to be done within the advanced line they had so rapidly secured. The Kirghiz were beginning to perceive that Russian fetters were not more silken than Khokandian; and that they had by affording assistance to Russia only made their loss of independence more hopeless of recovery. While these sentiments were rising in the bosoms of the Kirghiz there appeared amongst them a man capable of exciting their passions to the utmost, and of leading them against even an organized foe. The name of this leader was Izzet Kutebar. His eloquence roused his kinsmen to the highest pitch of frenzy; and his war proclamation against the Russians went the round of the Kirghiz kibitkas. "Steeds and arms they have; have we not the like? Are we not as numerous as the sands of the ocean? Wheresoever ye turn—whether towards the east or the west, or towards the north or the south—ye surely find Kirghiz. Wherefore, then, should we submit to a handful of strangers?"

With such bold words as these did Kutebar inspire courage into the bosoms of the Kirghiz. His example shamed many of the chiefs into imitation, and for a time the disunited Kirghiz found union in a common hostility to Russia. During five years Kutebar waged an irregular kind of border warfare with Russia, and on more than one occasion his skill and rapidity of movement turned the scale against the better arms and superior discipline of the Russian troops. At length, for reasons not clearly ascertained, but probably because he found dissensions breaking out in the ranks of his followers, he accepted the honourable terms which the Russian authorities offered him, and with his surrender to the Czar the life of the Kirghiz cause died out. This event took place in the year 1858, when Russia was again in a position to assume her activity, temporarily laid aside, in Central Asia, and to follow up those early triumphs on the Jaxartes which had been suspended after the departure of General Peroffsky.

It is unnecessary to describe the past history of Khokand in any greater detail than to say that this khanate had, in the year we have arrived at, as its ruler a prince named Khudayar Khan. In the year 1842 Mahomed Ali Khan of Khokand was executed by his bitter foe Nasrullah of Bokhara. In the confusion which then broke out, his cousin, Shere Ali Khan, was proclaimed ruler; and he in turn was succeeded by his younger son Khudayar. The real arbiter of the State was, however, the minister Mussulman Kuli, a Kipchak chief. For a long time it was thought that Khudayar was the son of Mahomed Ali, but Mr. Schuyler discovered the mistake, and there is little doubt of the accuracy of his information. During ten years Khudayar ruled tranquilly in the country mainly through the ability of Mussulman Kuli; but in 1853, the same year that witnessed the appearance of Kutebar, the Khan chafing—as jealous despots often chafe at the restraints imposed upon their caprice by their wisest advisers—at his Wazir's expostulations, intrigued against him. He even availed himself of the deadly feud between Kipchak and Kirghiz to crush more completely the man to whom he owed his throne.

From that year things in Khokand went from bad to worse. There were fresh intrigues, under the guidance of another chief, Alim Kuli, who on several occasions drove Khudayar into exile. The only person who survived these constant changes in the ruler of the State, these palace brawls, and this civil strife, was Khudayar himself, whose eventful career, even now not concluded, seems to embrace the old and the new in Central Asian life, the time when Russia was not a Central Asian power at all, and also the period when her supremacy was uncontested. As a matter of fact, however, the death of Mussulman Kuli, and the strife for which that event was the signal, marked the crisis in the fate of Khokand. Those occurrences paved the way for an easy Russian triumph, and for the incorporation of the khanate in the Russian empire.

Immediately after the surrender of Kutebar, the Russians began their second advance along the banks of the Syr Darya. They attacked in the year 1859 the Khokandian fortress of Chulak Kurgan, eighty miles south-east of Fort Peroffsky, and two years later on they had also seized Yany Kurgan, fifty miles nearer Khokand. After another interval of the same period an advance was made on a larger scale against the town of Turkestan, near the Syr Darya, and also against Auliata in the Kirghiz country north of the Kara Tau range. Both of these operations had to be postponed until the following year through the outbreak of the rising in Poland. In 1864 they were carried out on a large scale and with complete success. Both towns fell into the possession of the Russians, and the intermediate country with its line of forts shared the same fate. This was the first important success of the

Russians in Central Asia. They had remained inactive during ten years; they were now to reap the full benefit of the preparations they had been so diligently preparing. The credit of these successes belongs to General Tchernaieff, who completed the task which Peroffsky had commenced. The eventful campaign of 1864 did not, however, close with these triumphs.

The Khokandians, unable to oppose Russia in the open field, devoted all their energies to the strengthening of their towns, hoping that by this means they might offer a more protracted resistance to the advance of Russia. The town of Tchimkent, which forms the apex of a triangle of which a line drawn from the city of Turkestan to Auliata would be the base, was the next defence of Khokand on the north; and no effort was spared in making it as strong as circumstances would permit. A garrison of ten thousand men was left in it, and it was also fairly provided with artillery. Tchernaieff, recognising the importance of this place, and the danger which might arise from the presence of so large a hostile force in his neighbourhood, resolved to attack it, and to seize it by a *coup de main*. He delivered his attack with remarkable skill and boldness, and despite the resolution of the garrison, who fought with great determination, and were skilfully handled during the earlier part of the day, the town and fortress were carried at what may be called a rush. The Russian army numbered between four and five thousand men, and was exceptionally strong in artillery. There can be no question that the capture of Tchimkent was a most brilliant affair, ably conceived and boldly carried out. That achievement alone would justify General Tchernaieff being placed in the first rank of Russian generals.

This successful campaign, resulting in the annexation of a vast tract of country, including three fortified towns of great importance, naturally caused uneasiness in England. Official representations were made at St. Petersburg, and in reply Prince Gortchakoff despatched one of those circulars in which he has attained an eminence unequalled by any other statesman, assuring England that there was no cause for apprehension, that the extension of Russia's frontier was demanded by local necessities, and could not be avoided, but that in the future no further extension was contemplated. This may be taken to be Russia's programme in Central Asia (see Appendix). This interesting document deserves the most careful consideration. Once mastered, the key-note of Russian policy is revealed by it. When the philosophical historian comes to analyse the past, and he peruses this remarkable document, which has done such good service on so many occasions during fifteen years—perhaps its virtues have not yet wholly departed—with what veneration must he regard it! Having expended, however, his powers of admiration upon it, his next thought may be to consider what manner of people those English must have been who permitted its specious phrases to dupe them so far as to make them blind to practical interests and national necessities. Assuredly from such a historian we shall not receive words of praise.

The Khokandians did not succumb under the intelligence that Tchimkent had fallen. Their national existence was at stake. They resolved to defend it manfully. The fortifications of Tashkent were repaired. A large army was hurriedly collected and pushed forward to that town, and the regent Alim Kuli and his lieutenants took every precaution in their power to avert an overthrow. Once more Tchernaieff thought there was prudence in audacity, and that by dealing an equally prompt blow against Tashkent he might fare as successfully as he had at Tchimkent. According to one version, and that adopted by Mr. Schuyler, he delivered an assault upon the city, which was repulsed with serious loss to the Russians—sixteen men killed and sixty-two wounded. The Khokandian troops, under the late Yakoob Beg of Kashgar, attempted to follow up their success, but were checked at the small town of Ikan by the valour of a small detachment of Cossacks. Here, again, the Russians lost severely, and the Cossacks narrowly escaped annihilation. Another version merely says that there was a battle in the open field between the Khokandians and Russians, in which the latter were victorious, but with such heavy loss that they were compelled to retreat. This version is derived from native Khokandian sources, and is given by Dr. Bellew in his historical portion of the Report on Mission to Kashgar. In either case the Russian design against Tashkent failed, and Tchimkent for some months longer remained the most advanced post of Russia in the south.

At this crisis of their fate the internal feuds in the

State, and the encroachments of Bokhara, still further detracted from the vigour of the Khokandian resistance. While Bokhara was wresting the town of Khodjent from the Khokandians in the south, Tchernaieff was tightening his hold upon Tashkent. In April 1865 he had cut off its principal water-supply from the Cherchik river, and had entered into intrigues with a party of the citizens, who felt no sympathy for the government which Alim Kuli had forced upon them. Early in the month of May Alim Kuli arrived in person with reinforcements, and shortly afterwards a battle was fought outside the walls, in which Tchernaieff was of course victorious. There is a discrepancy of authorities on this point also, but it seems probable that Alim Kuli attacked the Russian camp on the 21st of May, and, although at one moment things looked black for the Muscovites, the attack was repulsed on all points. The victory itself assumed most of its importance from the death of Alim Kuli, for with him passed away the last possible defender of the country. In the meanwhile the Ameer of Bokhara was assuming a threatening attitude, and his army was rumoured to be marching to the relief of Tashkent. General Tchernaieff in consequence detached a force to occupy the ferry over the Syr Darya opposite Chinaz, while he prosecuted the siege of Tashkent with greater vigour than before. On the 27th of June a successful assault was delivered against two of the gates, in which Captain, now General, Abramoff first distinguished himself, and on the 28th the whole city was occupied. For this exploit, perhaps the most remarkable of all the exploits of Russia in Central Asia, General Tchernaieff received great praise, which he fully deserved. Amongst not the least honourable of his rewards was the nickname which he received from the natives of Shir-Naib, "the Lion Viceroy," a tribute at once to his courage and magnanimity.

In the following year Tchernaieff was succeeded by Romanoffsky, in consequence of an abortive expedition into Bokhara. When considering Russia's relations with Bokhara in our next chapter, it will be more appropriate to describe the course of this campaign. The further conquests which Russia made on Khokandian soil were snatched rather from Bokhara than Khokand. With the capture of Khodjent in 1866 there followed a peace of nine years' duration between Khokand and the Russian generals. The rebellion which broke out in that khanate in the winter of 1875, under the auspices of Abderrahman Aftobatcha, son of Mussulman Kuli, against the authority of Khudayar, afforded General Kaufmann that excuse for the absorption of the remaining portion of the khanate for which he had long been seeking. The independence of Khokand completely disappeared in April 1876, when it became the Russian province of Ferghana.

Khudayar Khan himself became a Russian pensioner, and for some time resided at Orenburg. At last, pining for liberty, he fled in December 1877 to the steppe, and was reported to have reached Cabul. It is impossible yet to say that this extraordinary career has seen its last vicissitude. He was an independent ruler before the Russians had reached the Jaxartes and the task of Central Asian conquest had begun. He alone has survived four or five civil wars, which aimed chiefly at his destruction, and the feuds of Kirghiz and Kipchak. He has escaped assassination and death at the hands of open enemies when every other member of his house has been less fortunate. And although he can scarcely hope to witness the decadence and fall of Russia's power, he may live long enough to see its curtailment.

In twelve years after the capture of Tchimkent Russia had absorbed the whole of Khokand, and, despite the valour of the Khokandians, her domination seems to be nowhere so secure as it is there. Tashkent has become the metropolis of a mighty empire, and its admirable position fully justifies the selection. But in the mountains of Ferghana, and along the banks of the Naryn, travellers say that there exists the remembrance of independence that is now lost. A powerful caste, and an ambitious and capable race, have been overthrown. The Kipchak is apparently as subdued as the Kirghiz, and from neither is it possible to expect any formidable resistance. But they have lost their career, Russia has deprived them of their supremacy, and it is not in human nature to suppose that they love their masters any better than the Mahratta loves us. They, too, are in a worse position than the Mahratta, for they cannot play at those martial exercises which still, perhaps, in India afford relief to the warlike sentiments of a bold people. Russia's rule in Khokand is secure to almost all intents and purposes; but should ever the opportunity offer for striking a blow for freedom, not a Khokandian would be backward in manifesting his actual hostility to Russia. The people of Khokand must live upon their aspirations. The day of emancipation now appears far distant, impossible of arrival. Yet it may come, and a bold and prudent people can prepare in quiet for the dangers and the duties of that time.

CHAPTER VII.

RUSSIA'S RELATIONS WITH BOKHARA.

BOKHARA had for many years been in close intercourse with Russia by means of the caravan trade that was carried on between the two States. In fact, until the Russians laid siege to Tashkent there had been marked cordiality between the two countries. The Ameer of Bokhara had always been on good terms with Russia, and the extent of that alliance is proved by nothing more strongly than by the position M. de Boutinieff occupied at the Court of the tyrant Nasrullah when compared with that of the unfortunate Stoddart. That *entente cordiale* stood every test until the Ameer Mozaffur Eddin perceived that Khokand, which he regarded as his legitimate prey, was slipping from his hands into those of the great northern Power. The siege of Tashkent, which could be very conveniently attacked from the Bokharan town of Chinaz, brought home to the mind of the Ameer the fact that Russia was about to secure that to which he considered himself to be entitled. Hence arose that dubious attitude in 1865, which was to become more pronounced as events progressed.

General Tchernaieff's prompt advance upon the Syr Darya, and capture of the ferry at Chinaz, averted the danger that was then imminent from a Bokharan intervention. But after Tashkent had surrendered, this Russian success did not prevent the Ameer revealing his hostility. An embassy, composed of Messrs. Struve, son of the distinguished astronomer, Tatarinof, and Glukhoffsky, and other officers, was sent by Russia to Bokhara, with the intention of discovering what was the feeling which the Ameer entertained towards Russia. The Ameer's reply was to throw several of them into prison. Before Khokand, therefore, was more than half conquered, Russia's relations with Bokhara had changed from friendship to hostility.

In January 1866 Tchernaieff crossed the Syr Darya, and advanced from Chinaz upon Jizakh. But his force was very weak, and he found that Jizakh was stronger than he had expected, and that the Ameer had assembled a considerable army for the defence of his dominions. Mozaffur at the same time pretended to be disposed to yield to the Russian demands, which Tchernaieff was weak enough to credit. He was consequently compelled or induced to retreat, and the Russian envoys still remained imprisoned.

When Mozaffur Eddin interfered, in 1864, in the affairs of Khokand, and placed Khudayar again on the throne, he retained possession of the important town of Khodjent in the southern portion of the State, on the banks of the Syr Darya. The Russians coveted this highly important position, and were by no means disposed to admit the justice of Bokhara's claim over a town which should so clearly belong to Khokand as Khodjent. General Tchernaieff had been replaced by General Romanoffsky, in consequence of the retreat from Jizakh, and it became his successor's immediate task to repair that disaster, and effectually to curb the hostility of Bokhara. In April 1866 Romanoffsky was already moving down upon Khodjent, and was collecting at Chinaz a large supply of provisions, etc., which had been sent up the river by water from Kazala. In that month he routed a considerable body of Bokharan cavalry, and in May had advanced across the Syr Darya to encounter the main army of the Ameer.

The Russian army with which this important campaign was commenced certainly did not number more than four thousand men, with an artillery of twenty guns. It was, however, well supplied with rockets in addition. The two armies came face to face on the plain of Irjar on the 20th of May, and a battle was immediately commenced. The Bokharan army is computed to have numbered forty thousand men, with twenty-one guns; but it is only fair to state that of these barely five thousand were regular Bokharan troops. Such confidence was there at this time in the valour and efficiency of the Bokharan army, that the Ameer had already announced his intention of retaking Tashkent. Von Helwald has stated that this army was armed with excellent English weapons, but this is one of those sweeping statements in which this writer sometimes permits himself to indulge when he thinks that it may be prejudicial to this country.

The battle commenced with a skirmish with the swarms of irregular cavalry that covered the front of the Bokharan entrenchments, but these were slowly and completely driven in upon the main body. Even after this success the battle raged furiously, and several of the entrenchments had to be carried at the point of the bayonet. The arrival of a fresh Russian detachment on the opposite bank of the river with artillery was the decisive turning point in the day; and after that event the Bokharan army broke and fled in all directions. The Ameer, who was present, retired with a small detachment to Jizakh, leaving in the hands of the Russians his artillery, his treasure, and untold stores of warlike munitions and provisions. No official statement was published of the loss on either side; but it has been computed that the Bokharans lost over one thousand—a total which seems moderate considering the bitterness of the fight—and that the Russians only lost twenty or thirty wounded. But although the price paid for this victory is not exactly known, its results were so great and so important that it would not have been dearly purchased at great slaughter. The prestige of Bokhara was annihilated on that field of battle, and Russia, secure in her own strength, became doubly secure through the panic that unnerved all Asiatics after the great overthrow at Irjar. The practical results of the battle were immediate, and the greatest of these was the capture of the fortress of Nau, which stands half-way between

Khodjent and Ura-tepe. The first step in the siege of the former of these towns was to garrison and provision Nau, which was accomplished in the short space of two days. An advance was thereupon at once made upon Khodjent. On the 29th of May the city was surrounded and attacked from two sides. The inhabitants had made some imperfect preparations for defence, but, as Mr. Schuyler observes, the resistance here was not so great as might have been expected from a town of such importance and one so strongly situated. The garrison, too, comprised some of the regular Bokharan army, under the command of a relative of the Ameer. After a heavy bombardment of five days it surrendered at discretion, the Russians admitting a loss of eleven killed and one hundred and twenty-two wounded.

After his defeat at Irjar, Mozaffur sent back the Russian envoys to Tashkent laden with presents. But the Ameer had not yet given up the game as lost. He had been beaten in the field, several of his fortresses had been wrested from him, but there still remained to the reputed head of Islam in Central Asia other armies and other fortresses wherewith to carry on a war. After the fall of Khodjent there was a truce of some months' duration, but in the early winter of the same year the attitude of Bokhara was held to be so unsatisfactory that a further advance was considered to be necessary. Ura-tepe and Jizakh were the two principal outposts remaining to the Ameer now that Chinaz and Khodjent had been taken from him. They each guarded a road to Samarcand, the former one from the east and the latter one from the north-east. The Russians closely besieged Ura-tepe on the 6th of October, and on the 14th it was in their hands. The greater part of the garrison appears to have escaped, and the Russians admitted a loss of two hundred killed and wounded.

Almost on the same day Jizakh shared the same fate, being carried by assault, despite its natural strength and the number of its garrison, after a short bombardment. The garrison fought bravely—particularly its leaders, who were nearly all killed on the walls—but apparently with little skill. The official numbers given of the loss on either side appear strange when we remember that the large garrison fought under cover and stood manfully to its post. The Russian official statement gave the Russian loss at six killed and ninety-two wounded, and that of the Bokharans at six thousand men *hors de combat*, and two thousand prisoners! If these figures are to be relied upon this is certainly the battle in which the superiority of European discipline and arms over brute courage has been most clearly demonstrated. The result of these triumphs—so complete, and obtained with such little loss—was that Bokhara was perforce compelled to sue for peace. Mozaffur Eddin himself recognised the impossibility of continuing the struggle alone.

He made overtures for an alliance to the Ameer of Afghanistan, and as affairs happened at that time to be in a very troubled state in Cabul, he entered into particularly close relations with Faiz Mahomed Khan,

12

Governor of Balkh and one of the sons of Dost Mahomed. Some clue is to be found as to the nature of these negotiations in the Blue Book on Afghan affairs published in November 1878 (see pages 15 and 18). He even made propositions to our Government, which politely snubbed him; but although he could find no allies in his extremity, the turbulence and fanaticism of his people were urging him more and more to again draw the sword which had been for the moment sheathed.

After the fall of Jizakh the Russian generals, who had been continually reprimanded for their activity, took so sanguine a view of the condition of things in Turkestan that the following official announcement was sent home. "Perfect tranquillity reigns throughout the country of Turkestan. The war with Bokhara, as far as regards Russia, is at an end. The Governor-General (Orenburg) hopes for a long continuance of tranquillity, provided the Ameer of Bokhara abstains from a renewal of hostilities. Amicable relations with Khokand are confirmed, and commerce is everywhere re-established. Many caravans come from Bokhara, and go thither. Even the West Siberian corps, ordered to the territory of Turkestan, returns home again." But although there was a lull in the strife, it was uncertain how long it would continue. Six months after the capture of Jizakh the "Invalide Russe" declared that Russia had entertained no negotiations or diplomatic relations with the Ameer Mozaffur.

In September, 1867, Kaufmann became Governor-General of the newly-constituted province of Turkestan, and he at once pursued the negotiation of a treaty which had been drawn up by his predecessor, General Krjihanoffsky. The draft of this treaty was sent to the Ameer for approval, but instead of replying to the proposal made him he began to discuss other matters and to correspond with Kaufmann upon other topics. Mozaffur's procrastination assumed a more dubious aspect when he refused to surrender a Russian officer and three soldiers who had been carried off by robbers on the Jizakh road. The officer—Slushenko by name —was tortured and compelled to adopt the Mahomedan religion. The immediate consequence of that act was that Kaufmann began to mass troops for an advance on Samarcand, and the Ameer to raise levies from amongst his subjects.

Unfortunately for him, he no longer ruled an united State. His internal foes were not less dreadful to him than his external. If his own inclinations had been alone consulted, it is probable that he would not have gone to war with Russia under any pretext whatever. He had already tasted enough of the pleasures of such warfare. But he was no longer a free agent. The *ulemas* of Bokhara and Samarcand were urging him on to resume the "holy" war. His eldest son, Katti Torah, was intriguing against his authority, while his nephew, Seyyid Khan, was in open defiance at Shahr-i-sebz. The latter was soon in the position of an independent prince, for Shahr-i-sebz cast off the Bokharan yoke, and became independent under the leadership of a chief known as Jura Beg. It was at such a moment as this, when Bokhara was as a house divided against itself, that its final war with the Russians began.

Colonel Abramoff, as commandant of Jizakh, took the first step towards punishing the assailants of Lieutenant Slushenko by making an attack upon the village of the robbers. In the meanwhile Mozaffur had been deserted by the Afghan prince, Iskander Khan, with some 2,000 followers, who had gone over to the Russians; yet unable to resist the demands of his people, he declared a holy war against Russia. General Kaufmann, who was said to be on the eve of setting out for St. Petersburg, but who had previously, there is good reason to believe, sent a letter to the Kazi Kalian of Samarcand, demanding the surrender of that city, thereupon ordered an advance to be made into Bokharan territory. This decision was come to early in the month of May, 1868, and on the 13th the first brush with the Bokharan army took place at the hill of Tchupan-ata on the banks of the Zarafshan river. The result was an easy triumph for the Russians, who crossed the river in the face of a heavy fire and drove the enemy out of their entrenchments. The result of this success was the surrender of Samarcand itself, for the inhabitants of their own accord shut their gates upon the Bokharan army, and voluntarily welcomed the Russian army. After the surrender of Samarcand desultory fighting took place between the Russian army and irregulars from Shahr-i-sebz and other cities. In all of these the Russians were uniformly victorious, but these attacks necessitated a scattering of the Russian forces which gave confidence to the Ameer.

He was collecting a fresh army near Katti Kurgan, a town forty miles west of Samarcand, which had been garrisoned with a small force by General Golovatcheff, and his cavalry had already cut the Russian general's communications with Jizakh and Tashkent. The neighbourhood of Samarcand was also swarming with armed men, who, if not very formidable in the line of battle, were certainly much to be feared in more irregular warfare. A large body of cavalry—said to number fifteen thousand men—was at Chelik threatening Yany Kurgan and even Jizakh, and wherever General Kaufmann turned there was a foe to be encountered whom it was most difficult to get at. In this emergency General Kaufmann thought his best plan was to advance to the relief of Katti Kurgan, but the moment he left Samarcand the Shahr-i-sebz army attacked it; and although Major Stempel and the small garrison defended the citadel with the greatest heroism, it was very nearly captured. In fact, it was only saved from surrender by the withdrawal of the troops from Shahr-i-sebz under their leader Jura Beg, who was misled by a report that Kaufmann was returning.

In the meanwhile Kaufmann had relieved the garrison of Katti Kurgan and defeated the army of the Ameer in a pitched battle at Zera-bulak. It was only several days after the attack upon Samarcand that Kaufmann heard of what was taking place in his rear, and he hurried back with all despatch to rescue the much-reduced garrison. Mozaffur Eddin then made an unconditional surrender, and had the Russian

Government given Kaufmann the necessary permission he could have annexed the khanate in its entirety. The annexation of Samarcand was in itself a triumph with which any governor-general might have rested content, and the practical results of this 1868 campaign were so great as to be scarcely realisable at the time. Mozaffur Eddin was, however, permitted to retain his personal authority, and received assistance in putting down the seditious movement which his son, Katti Torah, and several other chiefs raised up against him. These were all repressed, and in 1869 Katti Torah was a fugitive, and his father's authority more firmly established than it had been during the three previous years. He had conceived a stronger friendship for the Russians since they had occupied in his name the town of Karshi, and then handed it over to him. On the strength of such friendly acts as these a younger son of the Ameer, Jan Torah, was sent on an embassy to St. Petersburg, where he stayed for some time. One of his principal objects was to obtain the restoration of Samarcand, but in this, it is scarcely necessary to say, he completely failed.

With the annexation of Samarcand Russia's warlike policy in Bokhara came to a close. Since that year, if we except the brief misunderstanding which manifested itself during the progress of the Khivan campaign, the relations of Russia and Bokhara have assumed their old cordiality. The same Ameer who threatened Russia so nearly when Tchernaieff was besieging Tashkent is now her very good ally. His old dreams of ambition have vanished. He is content with his temporal advantages. The army which he is permitted to retain numbers some twenty thousand men; but it is of the most nondescript character, and wholly unadapted for modern warfare. He bears precisely the same relation to Russia that the Khan of Khelat did to us after the signature of the Treaty of 1854. The principal strategical points within his frontier, such as Charjui, may be garrisoned whenever Russia deems fit; and a right of way has been obtained to the Oxus. Ten years and more have elapsed since these events, yet there is no more instructive paper on the subject than the statesman-like memorandum of Sir Henry Rawlinson (dated July 20th, 1868). Samarcand had not then fallen, but a fortified post had been erected at "Jizakh almost within hail of Samarcand, bearding the Ameer, as it were, in the high place of his power, encouraging the malcontents throughout the province, and holding out a standing menace of invasion." The consequences of that act were clear. Bokhara and Khokand would cease either in substance or in form to be independent governments. That was the prediction, and it has been verified. We may expect it to be realised to the letter the moment the present Ameer dies. He has no successor who would be absolutely pleasing to the Russians, and he has several relations who lay claims to the succession who would be positively displeasing to them. That event may be expected to produce the actual dismemberment of the Bokharan State and its incorporation with the government of Turkestan. At the present moment, and under the conditions that exist, the Bokharan

Government has no discretionary power over its acts, and in whatever Russia decides upon it must acquiesce. The people themselves are said to be extremely hostile to Russia, but from what Mr. Schuyler has told us it is clear that this sentiment is neither so bitterly inimical, nor so deeply rooted as has been asserted. Mozaffur Eddin does not possess the power to disobey the orders sent from Tashkent, and it is very doubtful whether he possesses the inclination.

It must also be remembered that the Ameer has nowhere to look to for assistance. He appealed to this country in 1867, and he received neither sympathy nor encouragement. He had previously made overtures to the Cabul Ameer for a defensive alliance against both Russia and England, and he has subsequently to his reconciliation with Russia inveighed against this country in his correspondence with Shere Ali. It is impossible to say what part he played in the negotiations which led up to the despatch of the Stoletof mission, but as all the native emissaries from Tashkent came through his court, we may be sure that it was not a neutral part. The long-standing relations between Cabul and Bokhara, the claims that Bokhara has over Balkh and the neighbouring districts, forbid the supposition that Mozaffur Eddin would be an unconcerned spectator of the dismemberment of Cabul. He will remember the part his father played in the days of Dost Mahomed, and he will aspire either to be the protector of the cause of the Barucksyes, or, if that cause be utterly wrecked, will strive to extend his dominion up to the slopes of the Hindoo Koosh. In either case he will be eager to be the puppet of the Russians and to play the game they may sketch out for him. His ambition and his vanity will urge him to prosecute whatever aggressive design General Kaufmann may entrust to him, and his hostility to England has been but thinly veiled.

There is a reason, too, though it is now seldom mentioned, why England can never hold out the hand of friendship and alliance to Bokhara, why the Ameer of that State can never receive assistance from our countrymen against any foe, even though it should be Russia herself. The story has been told so seldom, and is now so utterly forgotten, save by the few contemporaries who still survive of the unfortunate sufferers, that it will bear repetition, even though little fresh can be said to that already so forcibly pronounced by Mons. Ferrier. In the year 1839 not only had Afghanistan been conquered by a British army, but the bold scheme had been conceived by a few men, remarkable for their foresight, of raising a powerful barrier in Central Asia from amongst the Tartar States of Turkestan to any encroachment on the part of Russia. With that object in view Colonel Charles Stoddart, one of M'Niell's most trusted officers, went to Bokhara, and for the same purpose Captain Arthur Conolly arrived at Khiva, and travelled thence to Khokand. For the moment "the great game in Central Asia" found favour in the eyes of the authorities, but the fit passed rapidly off. There can be no doubt that Charles Stoddart, splendid fellow as he was, was not the man most suited to work out an intricate negotiation in so base a Court as that of the Ameer of Bokhara. In those days that ruler considered himself to be a great prince; and he had already had some experience in dealing with European nations in his long-standing diplomatic relations with Russia. Our representative treated him in a manner that was at once imperious and dictatorial. The personal character of Nasrullah, the Ameer at the time, made this mistake still more unfortunate, for of all Central Asian despots Nasrullah was certainly the most tyrannical and unreasonable. His antipathy once roused was most difficult to be appeased, and he readily believed all the tales that were brought to him of those who had fallen under his displeasure.

There can be no question that Colonel Stoddart, in setting all the customs and etiquette of the strict Bokharan Court at defiance, behaved very foolishly, and rushed upon his fate. He might well have taken a leaf out of the book of Sir Alexander Burnes, that most accomplished of all Asiatic travellers, and by humouring the Ameer have advanced the cause he had so dearly at heart more than he possibly could by any rashly-bold demeanour. But those were the *Civis Romanus sum* days, and no one had a higher opinion of the superiority of England over every other country under the sun than Charles Stoddart. From one mistake he passed to the commission of another. He refused to abide by the Court forms, he assaulted the palace officials, he treated the Ameer with defiance, he insulted the vizier, and to all these acts he added the crime of coming without presents, and the weakness of bringing no credentials. He came to treat with the proudest ruler in Central Asia as the bearer of a letter from the East India Company's agent in Persia, and he had only *vivâ voce* instructions for the conclusion of a treaty of the highest importance. No mission was ever more unfortunate, no envoy worse selected or less prepared.

Within three days of his arrival at Bokhara Colonel Stoddart found himself a prisoner. At first he was confined in a house, but after a short time spent there he was transferred to the Siah-tchah, or Black well. " This horrible abode,* which is in the centre of the town, is twenty-one feet in depth; and here the greatest malefactors are generally confined. The descent into it is made by means of a rope; and when Stoddart was let down he found there two thieves and a murderer, the latter having been incarcerated here for several years. With these criminals for his companions, the Colonel remained *two months in this loathsome and filthy hole, covered with vermin and surrounded by reptiles, in killing which they were constantly occupied.* Their food, such as it was, was lowered to them by the rope with which they had themselves descended, and much of their time was passed in smoking. When the furious caprice of Nasrullah had been satisfied, and he thought he had humbled the pride of the Englishman and impressed him with the terror of his power, he gave an order to the chief of the police to remove him from the Siah-

---

* Ferrier's " History of the Afghans," page 447.

tchah in which he had been immured, and keep him a prisoner in his own house; but two days after this the public executioner came to Stoddart with an order to put him to death unless he consented to become a Mussulman. To this alternative, borne down by the dreadful sufferings he had endured, and the exhaustion of his mental and bodily powers, he gave a reluctant consent, repeating the Mahomedan confession of faith, after which he was taken to the public square, and circumcised in the presence of an immense crowd who had been attracted there by the novelty of the event. Austere and sensitive in his religious feelings, Colonel Stoddart never forgave himself this act of weakness, of which he bitterly repented during the remainder of his wretched existence."

The Russian minister then interested himself in his fate, and the continued triumphs of the English armies in Afghanistan occurred at the same moment of time to induce Nasrullah to alter his treatment of the unfortunate English officer. But when the fortune of war changed in Cabul, and tidings came of the disasters of 1841, Nasrullah reverted to his former cruel treatment. War had in the meanwhile broken out between Khokand and Bokhara, and there were those in Bokhara who asserted that English counsel was at the root of this quarrel. The Ameer readily believed these stories, and was only biding his time to obtain a complete revenge.

In order to obtain that, it was necessary to get the other British officer in Central Asia, Captain Conolly, who was residing at the Court of Khokand, into his power. He accordingly invited him to his Court, and Colonel Stoddart in a weak moment aided in the plot by innocently advising Conolly to come. Despite the warnings of the Khan of Khokand, and notwithstanding the advice repeatedly given by his old friend the Khan of Khiva never to trust himself into the hands of Nasrullah, Conolly went to Bokhara. The bait had been taken, and the birds were caged. For a brief season the tact and diplomatic ability of Conolly staved off the danger. But it was not for long. Before the month of November, 1841, closed, both officers were imprisoned. For more than six months they were kept in close confinement, and at last, having undergone torments indescribable, the most brutal treatment, and the most writhing contumely, the end came on the 24th of June, 1842. "Stoddart was put to death like a sheep, in some ruins at the back of his prison, and in the presence of a few passers-by, who had been attracted to the spot by his cries and his invectives." Conolly was offered his life on the condition of his turning Mussulman; but, with that moral fortitude which is the highest courage, he refused. " Stoddart and Yusuf (Conolly's Greek servant) turned Mahomedans, and you put them to death," he said. "Your proposal is a snare, for you will not spare me any more than you did them. I have no confidence in your promises; I will be no renegade. I die firm in my faith. Finish your work!" So died Arthur Conolly, as every Englishman should die, true to his country and himself, vindicating the real superiority of his race to the last by the calm resolution with which he could face death. Long years afterwards a mysterious stranger left at the door of a house in London a prayer-book which had belonged to Arthur Conolly, in which he had entered a touching record of his sufferings and aspirations in the well at Bokhara, and then vanished. The house belonged to Conolly's sister, but of the stranger no trace could be found.*

It is thirty-seven years ago since this tragedy was enacted in Bokhara. For more than a generation English vengeance has slumbered. But it cannot be because the bloodthirsty act of Nasrullah has been forgotten or condoned. Time works many changes, and smooths down the bitterest of wrongs. But the inhuman treatment of those English officers, who went to Bokhara not through any weak desire to gain notoriety, but through a sense of duty, in fulfilment of a great national design, can never be forgotten. It is the one instance in history of the representatives of England having failed to find a vindicator in their country, the solitary occasion when the remembrance of a crime has been sought to be mollified. Yet the story lives in history, and will ever live. The stoicism of Conolly, the intrepidity of Stoddart, are not the least striking proofs our countrymen have afforded before the world of Asia of the possession of great imperial characteristics. It is upon such conduct as theirs that the fabric of British superiority rests in

* See Colonel Malleson's "Recreations of an Indian Official," page 293.

India, and wherever else we are called upon to face superior numbers and the brute force of semi-civilised peoples. Conolly's brave words are still ringing in our ears, and they, more than any feeble language I can use, should teach his countrymen never to forget his fate. The day must come when Bokhara shall dearly repay the wrong she did our countrymen, and when the inevitable punishment which England exacts for wrongs inflicted upon her subjects shall be meted out to the city of the bloodthirsty Nasrullah.

Until that deed of retribution has been wrought, England's prestige can never be great in Central Asia, but we may confidently expect that, when the citadel of Bokhara goes up in the air with a loud explosion to the *manes* of Charles Stoddart and Arthur Conolly, all the peoples of Turkestan will remember that, though they are separated from this country by a great distance, by mountain ranges, and steppes, and mighty rivers, yet they are not safe from the just wrath of England. The day may be nearer at hand than we at present suppose when we shall be sufficiently near to Bokhara to deal out that retribution which, no matter how long put off, must most assuredly be exacted eventually; and if we then abstain from exacting it, we shall have failed in the duty England owes to herself and every one of her subjects.

CHAPTER VIII.

RUSSIA AND PERSIA.

FOR practical purposes Russia and Persia may be said to have first come into contact with each other in the reign of Peter the Great. In the year 1722, when an Afghan prince was seated upon the throne of Isfahan, a Russian embassy arrived in that capital. It came to demand the redress of various wrongs, and the settlement of several grievances. But there can be little doubt that its ostensible object was not the real cause of the rupture between the States which shortly afterwards took place. Mir Mahmoud, Afghan ruler, replied that he could not be responsible for the acts of the previous Persian sovereign, and that, moreover, his authority did not extend over the Usbegs or the Lesghians. The principal cause of offence was the injury Russian subjects had incurred at the hands of the Lesghians at Shamakee; but there is much better reason for supposing that the Czar, piqued by the failure of his Central Asian projects elsewhere, had turned to the task of securing complete possession of the Caspian Sea as the means towards attaining the end he had always in view of forming a mighty empire in the vast border lands of the two continents of Europe and Asia.

Therefore he brought imaginary charges against Persia—it is even said that he held her responsible for the acts of the Khan of Khiva,—and when no redress could be given to him he took the matter into his own hands. Mr. P. H. Bruce, an English gentleman who accompanied Peter in this war, says, in his interesting "Travels," that "the motives which occasioned the Emperor of Russia to undertake this enterprise were the desire of avenging the insults and wrongs which his subjects settled on the shores of the Caspian had suffered, particularly in the plunder of Shamakee, and a desire to succour the King of Persia against the Afghans, who offered important cessions in return for the aid of the Russian monarch." Peter's first object of attack was the important town and harbour of Derbend, situated on the shores of the Caspian. A large portion of the army destined for what was called the war with Persia was conveyed in boats down the rivers Occa and Volga to the Caspian, and thence to Astrakhan. This portion of the army was composed exclusively of infantry, of which there were thirty-three thousand men on board the fleet. Russia has, therefore, had some experience in the conveyance of large bodies of troops upon the Caspian, and that in days when there was no Caspian fleet, and when the merchant vessels plying upon it were much fewer than they are at present. In addition to the infantry a large force of cavalry proceeded by land to the vicinity of Derbend, where the whole army concentrated without accident. Derbend surrendered after a short siege; and with Derbend in her possession Russia held the most important position on the western shores of the Caspian. She did not, however, acquire permanent possession of it until fifty years after the death of Nadir. The Russian Government then entered upon a course of intrigues with the Porte and the Prince of Georgia, which had as their object the dismemberment of the Persian Empire. It was with no half-hearted design, nor with any vague object before it, that the Russian Government concluded treaties of the very highest importance with the rival and the tributary of the Shah. The triumph of the Afghan adventurers, the apparently complete disruption of the power of the Suffavean rulers, the general disorders prevailing in the State, the insubordination of Turcoman and Arab vassals, and all those other disturbing elements which seemed to have permanently destroyed the vitality of the Persian power, inspired its ambitious neighbours with a belief in the possibility of dividing the spoil amongst themselves. The prize which Peter, and at a later period the Empress Catherine, aimed at securing was no slight one. It was not so much a mere question of obtaining a strong frontier in the Caucasian range, or even of placing Russian administrators in Georgia and Daghestan, as it was of constructing round the southern shores of the Caspian a belt of provinces immediately dependent upon the Czar. The partition treaty between Russia and Turkey during the reign of

Peter was, it is said, brought about by the French Ambassador at Constantinople, the Marquis Bannac; but its sweeping character may be best appreciated when it is said that Ghilan and Mazanderan, Azerbijan and Astrabad, were to pass away from Persia to the Russian State. Fortunately for England the genius of Nadir Shah averted that catastrophe. But the speculative observer may for a moment ponder over the changes that that treaty, if its terms had been carried out, would have wrought in the later history of Europe and Asia.

One hundred and fifty years ago Russia was almost in possession of those fertile provinces on the shores of the Caspian which are the practical base of an army advancing on Herat and the Indus. Astrabad and its invaluable bay were on the point of falling into her hands. These, too, at a moment when India was defenceless, lying exposed to the audacious demands of every military adventurer. The vigour of the Afghans had also been sapped by the greatness of the effort they had made in Persia. Once the garrisoning army of the Afghan ruler was overthrown, there remained nothing capable of checking a Russian army of fifty thousand men between Astrabad and Delhi. The question of the possession of India was nearly being solved in a manner wholly favourable to Russia a generation before Robert Clive contested with Dupleix for supremacy in Southern India.

The genius of Nadir Shah fortunately prevented these audacious schemes having any practical result. He, after expelling the Afghans, defeated the Turks, and pushed Russian pretensions back from the Persian frontier. During his reign and for about forty years after his death Russian ambition remained quiescent upon the shores of the Caspian; but in the year 1783 the Empress Catherine conceived that affairs in Persia had so far taken a favourable turn for the prosecution of fresh enterprises, that she resolved to resume those intrigues which the death of Peter and the appearance of Nadir had upset. At this time the Prince of Georgia was Heraclius, an aged man, who saw in the intestine troubles of Persia a danger to the tranquillity of his own State and to the permanence of his personal power. He looked about him, consequently, for an ally to support him against the pretensions of the new Persian ruler, Aga Mahomed Khan, and there was none at once able and willing to protect him save the Czarina of Russia. He accordingly transferred his allegiance to St. Petersburg, and a treaty (given in the Appendix) was signed at the fortress of Georges' in July, 1783. The transfer of allegiance was so far unfortunate for Heraclius that the Persian ruler twelve years after the signature of the treaty invaded Georgia and portions of Armenia with a large army. He routed the small Georgian army near Tiflis, and occupied that city, which he handed over to his soldiery to plunder. The Persian wished to make an example of this city as Heraclius's capital, and he certainly did so, for, as the Persian historian puts it, "on this glorious occasion the valiant warriors of Persia gave to the unbelievers of Georgia a specimen of what they were to expect on the Day of Judgment." In this campaign the power of Georgia as an independent State was shattered, and Aga Mahomed Khan continued to follow up the brilliant success which he had already obtained by the capture of Tiflis. His attention was for some time diverted from the west to the east, that is, from Georgia to Khorasan; but the advance of a Russian army recalled him to the Araxes.

In 1796 the Russian armies laid siege to Derbend, Baku, and other fortresses, all of which offered but slight resistance. Before the close of that winter the Russians had pushed forward two armies to the frontier of Azerbijan, and were threatening not only Enzeli and Resht, but even Teheran itself. Aga Mahomed made during the winter months the most energetic preparations for the approaching campaign. He summoned from all parts of the kingdom the great chiefs and the frontier garrisons; and he appealed to the support of the whole nation " in order to punish the insolent unbelievers of Europe who had dared to invade the territories of the faithful." There was, however, no collision between the two armies, for, as they were preparing for the decisive war, Catherine died, and her successor, the Emperor Paul, at once recalled his army. In some respects it is much to be regretted that this campaign was never fought out. Aga Mahomed had made such careful preparations, and had drawn up so clear and sensible a plan of campaign, that it would have been an interesting problem to have watched the result of his skilful tactics when brought into opposition with the superior discipline and arms of a Russian army. The future course of Persian history might have been very different had this very capable ruler achieved a striking success over the Russian army. As it was, he slowly followed up the retreating Russians, and had the satisfaction of obtaining possession of the strong Georgian fortress of Sheshah, which had for long resisted his greatest efforts. But his triumph was brief, for a few days afterwards he was murdered by some servants whom he had condemned to death. With the death of Aga Mahomed Khan the vigorous period of Persia's rule came to a close. Since then there has been a steady and never varying decadence, and Persia owes much that she still retains to the active interference of England.

With the death of Aga Mahomed Russian encroachments recommenced more actively than ever before, and before the Treaty of Gulistan in 1813 (see Appendix) Persia had lost all the provinces north of the Kur. His successor, Futteh Ali, was unable to stem the tide of invasion, although at peace within his State, and he owed the preservation of some of his more immediate provinces exclusively to the intervention of the British Government. But the Treaty of Gulistan left many points unsettled and vague; and neither the Russian nor the Persian Government seemed disposed to acquiesce in the various suggestions that were made by friendly advisers. In 1826 the question was again referred for settlement to the sword, in consequence of Russia having forcibly occupied the district of Gokcha, which she refused to surrender. Thereupon Abbas Mirza, the prince royal of Persia, advanced into the Russian territory. At the same time Persia appealed to us for aid on the strength of a treaty we had concluded with her in 1814. That aid was refused. Persia had been the assailant, and her just cause of grievance in the forcible occupation of Gokcha was overlooked, or treated as of little consequence. Of the war which then broke out, it need only be said that it was an unvaried Russian triumph—thanks to the ability of Paskevitch—and that when a peace was patched up again under the auspices of this country Persia came out of the struggle *minus* the provinces of Erivan and Nakhitchevan.

This treaty, the text of which will be found in the Appendix to the next volume, was called that of Turkomanchai, and it indubitably marks a turning point in the modern history of Persia. Up to that point the Shah had not failed to assert his claims to equality with the Czar of Russia, and certainly the fortune of war had not been so crushingly against his side as to render it probable that he would willingly cede his position as a great independent prince. The missions of Sir John Malcolm and other English officers to his Court had inspired Futteh Ali with a belief that England would be willing to support him against any undue pretensions on the part of Russia. His expectations were not, however, realised, and after the signature of the Treaty of Turkomanchai we find that Russia and Persia became more intimate, while the friendly feeling between England and Persia waned more and more. A most significant piece of evidence of the manner in which Persia was becoming regarded by English statesmen at this time is to be found in the fact that we paid a considerable sum of money to be absolved from our obligations under some of the clauses of the treaty of 1814. It is true that it is asserted on good authority that the abrogation of these clauses was a benefit to each country, but this may be doubted, for the very value of the two clauses abrogated consisted in the fact that they were tantamount to a guarantee of the integrity of Persia—the point which of all others is perhaps the most important towards the attainment of a definitive solution of the Central Asian Question. The Treaty of Turkomanchai was a great triumph for Russia and a severe blow to this country, and after its ratification Russia commenced those intrigues at Teheran which, carried on during the next ten years, made the Shah a tool of the Czar, and produced a rupture between England and Persia; and, among other incidents, occasioned the siege of Herat and the occupation of the island of Kharrack.

The disorders which prevailed during this period in Afghanistan, and the independent government which was established by Shah Kamran, Sudosye, at Herat, gave those facilities for intrigue to Persia, of which the Shah Mahomed, acting on the instigation of Count Simonitch, the Russian Minister at his Court, was not slow to avail himself. Russia did not owe her predominance in the council chamber of the Shah to the superior abilities of her representative over our own, for no one could have taken a clearer or a broader view of the question than Mr. Ellis during the earlier stages of the negotiations, or than Sir John M'Niell during the later. The fault was rather on the part of the Home authorities, who realised neither the importance of Persian affairs in general nor of the Herat question in particular. We concealed our hand up to the last moment, and our representative, left without instructions, was out-bid by the Russian envoy, whose promises and threats were uttered officially and in full accordance with his instructions from Count Nesselrode. When at last Sir John M'Niell received during the progress of the siege of Herat authority to present to the Shah what may most accurately be described as an ultimatum, it was too late. Although Herat still held out, the Shah refused to accede to the demands made upon him by the English Minister, and several acts of discourtesy were added to render the refusal more offensive. Our Minister was withdrawn, and an expeditionary force established itself in the Persian Gulf upon the island of Kharrack. But the real settlement of the rivalry in Persia between England and Russia was on this occasion effected before the walls of Herat, when the resolution and courage of Eldred Pottinger foiled the machinations that had been for so many years in course of preparation to the detriment of his country.

But the intrigues of Simonitch in Persia were only one part of the scheme that had been formed by Russian statesmen and adventurers against England. In those days England had identified herself with the Sudosye cause in Afghanistan in more than one respect. She had given sanctuary to Shuja-ul-Mulk, and she had assisted him in undertaking at least one expedition into Afghanistan for the recovery of his rights, and was in this year (1838) preparing for a more declared and a more important step. Shah Kamran, Shuja's nephew, had also been supported in his possession of Herat; and the Barucksye chiefs of Cabul and Candahar, Dost Mahomed and Kohundil Khans, were neglected, and regarded in the light of usurpers. The key-note to our policy was to be found in the belief that it was the highest wisdom to assist in the aggrandisement of Runjeet Sing and the Sikhs; but even at Lahore, where the rule of its astute prince was drawing to a close, there was a strong party hostile to the interests of England. The Russians saw their chance in the internal divisions of Afghanistan and in the growing distrust between Lahore and Calcutta; and they were not slow to avail themselves of it. A Russian officer, Captain Vickovitch, was sent to Candahar in the first place, where his efforts to conclude a treaty with Kohundil were crowned with complete success. That treaty undoubtedly precipitated the war in Afghanistan, for any movement on the part of Kohundil must have decided the fate of Herat. Captain Vickovitch went on to Cabul, where the good sense of Dost Mahomed for a time prevented his attaining any great success; but unfortunately we had chosen our course, and that able ruler was compelled to fall in with the proposed Perso-Russian alliance. He was never as hearty in it, however, as his brother Kohundil; but, although his sympathies were not with the cause, Vickovitch had virtually secured his alliance while the siege of Herat was still in progress. The foothold Russia had by these means secured in Persia and Afghanistan was made more firm by a somewhat lavish expenditure of money, but this system perhaps defeated its own ends. It raised up expectations which the Russian agents were incapable of meeting, and thus bred disappointments among the prominent supporters of the Russian alliance which completely destroyed the fruits of the skilful diplomacy of Simonitch and his subordinate.

The grand question was, however, to obtain possession of Herat, and when that siege failed Russian intrigues lost their sting, if they could not be cleared from the charge of malice. Count Nesselrode disowned Simonitch with as little compunction as generals have more recently been disowned in Central Asia, and Captain Vickovitch, smarting under a sense of the wrongs which he received from his Government, put an end to his existence. The grand scheme, which had been constructed with such care and some skill, went to pieces before the sturdy defence of Herat, and when the English army advanced on Candahar the Afghan princes were left to bear alone the brunt of our indignation. Yet the plot had nearly succeeded. Had Herat fallen, as it well might, during the first few weeks of the siege, the later events would have been widely different. The Persians, established in Herat with a considerable army, backed up by Russian gold and auxiliaries, would not easily have been driven out again. The very fact of Herat being in the hands of their ally would have given an impulse to Russia's designs against India that might have been pregnant with results of the highest importance. The army which Mahomed Shah had assembled round Herat was composed of at least thirty thousand men, many of whom were trained soldiers and quite trustworthy. There can be little doubt that, despite the treachery and divisions which existed within the army, Herat must have surrendered had even the plans of the French officer, Semineau, been adopted. On several occasions the bravery of certain portions of the Persian army was worthy of all praise, and almost made up for the deficiencies of their leaders. It may be said that ever since this year Russia's schemes in Persia have not been marked by their old vigour, and that, although she has never ceased to maintain her position in the Persian Court, it is even now not so supreme as it was in the old days of Nesselrode and Simonitch.

But that Russia had not completely abandoned her Persian schemes, as Count Nesselrode so emphatically declared in his despatch of the 20th of October, 1838, may be seen from the fact that Count Simonitch was succeeded at the Persian Court by General Duhamel, the same officer who fifteen years later proposed the despatch of an expedition against India during the Crimean war. The future course of these relations depends more upon the development of the Afghan question by our war with Dost Mahomed than upon Persia, and this can be considered more conveniently in a later chapter. It is not clear what part Russia played in the later phases of the Herat question, or in the rupture that took place between England and Persia in 1856; but it is probable that during the earlier portion of the reign of the present Shah Nasireddin the Russians were not so active as they had been during the life-time of his father.

The border dispute between Persia and Turkey, which is not yet settled, has also brought England and Russia into contact upon this question, as well as upon those to the East. The root of this dispute is to be found in the acts of nomad tribes upon the borders of the pashalik of Bagdad, and in the grievance Persia conceived she had received by several political exiles being afforded sanctuary within the Turkish frontier, and at Bagdad in particular. There was also the dispute with regard to the sacred shrines at Kerbella and Nedjef, and numerous other trivial circumstances arising from the fluctuating character of the Turco-Persian frontier that were fruitful causes of disagreement between the two Governments. In the year 1823 Persia and Turkey were on the point of war, when the active intervention of the British Government averted the catastrophe. With the cooperation of Russia a peace was concluded at Erzeroum between the rival powers, the principal clauses of which granted a free road for Persian pilgrims to the holy places, the extradition of political offenders, and the acceptance by the Porte of a certain responsibility for the acts of the border tribes of Hyderanloo and Sibbikee. These provisions soon became a dead letter, and once more the two great Powers had actively to intervene. A second treaty was signed in

Erzeroum in May 1847, and two years afterwards a Commission, with one representative from each of the four Powers interested, was appointed to define a frontier for the two States. The task was a very complicated one, and the Crimean war threw considerable obstacles in the way of accomplishing a satisfactory result, but at last the Commission gave some proof of its work by issuing maps of the border districts. With that act its labours ceased for the time, as the representatives of England and Russia decided that their functions were exhausted with the definition of the country through which the frontier line should pass. In 1869 the Turkish and Persian Commissioners agreed that the *status quo* should be maintained until a definite solution had been arrived at; but in 1871 the old troubles revived, and a Commission from the four Powers met at Constantinople to decide what could be done in the matter. Difficulties were, however, raised in the path of a settlement by the representative of Persia, and the sittings of the Commission were suspended. In 1875 a convention was agreed upon between Persia and Turkey defining the position of their subjects when in the neighbouring State, but nothing more was said about the frontier question. The international Commission still exists, however, and Lord Derby said, in 1877, that it was only awaiting a favourable opportunity for the resumption of its task. After a discussion extending over more than half a century, it may be doubted whether this frontier dispute admits of satisfactory solution under anything like present circumstances. It is undoubtedly a misfortune both for Turkey and for Persia, neither of whom can afford to exhaust its strength in quarrelling with the other.

During the progress of these negotiations Russia had done much to identify herself with the cause of Persia, and the litigants and their supporters, instead of being impartial hearers, appeared to be divided into sides whose demands and views it was found to be impossible to reconcile. Russia's sympathy with the Persian cause was made clearer by the insertion in the Treaty of Berlin of a clause securing for the Shah the small border district of Khotour. This little-known place, with a small town of the same name, lies eighty miles south-east of Bayazid, in the neighbourhood of Khoi, and in the same latitude as Van. It always formed part of the province of Khoi until wrested from Persia by the Turks in the last century. Its actual importance is more nominal than real; but the significance of its restoration to Persia is to be found in the fact that it is a proof of Russia's desire to champion the Persian cause. It has been put in the light of a reward to Persia for her neutrality during the late war, and it certainly admits of being considered as such, although its practical value is doubtful. Moreover, at this date (January 20th) it has not been surrendered by Turkey. The frontier question is quite apart from this, and still remains as unsettled as ever before.

There can be no doubt on this point, that Russia has not abandoned her old designs in Persia. The annexation of the Armenian fortresses and of the harbour of Batoum has placed at the disposal of Russia a fresh line of advance upon the Persian capital and Herat. The Caspian is still an open highway during the greater portion of the year, and the railroad now continues, with the exception of the break over the Caucasus, to Tiflis; but in addition to both of those routes, there is the shortest and best of all from Odessa or the Crimea to Batoum. It only needs the construction of a light railway from Batoum to Erivan to bring the Russian army of the south within a week's journey of the Persian frontier; and already bolder schemes than the construction of so short a line as that have been discussed and have found favour with the Russian authorities. The collapse of the Turkish power in Armenia enables the Russian Government to devote closer attention to the Persian question, and although some of the Shah's ministers have lately manifested symptoms of alarm at the intentions of Russia, as expressed by the demands of her representative at Teheran, there can be no doubt that they have neither the power nor the disposition to refuse obedience to what is required of them. It has often been said—and it has been considered one of the safe-guards of English interests —that we can always cow the Persian Court by despatching a fleet to the gulf; but in the next stage of the Central Asian Question this hope would be quite delusive. The amount of pressure we can bring to bear upon the Shah is as nothing compared to that which Russia can employ. Teheran lies at the complete mercy of the Russians, and so it must until Persia has been regenerated, or until a great change has taken place in the condition of things upon her eastern frontier. It is because these facts are so palpable that it is necessary to remember the lesson they teach, which above all is, that when Russia finds the time ripe for revealing her hand in Persia, it will not be by underhand intrigues such as those of Simonitch or Duhamel that she will utilise what she has so long been preparing; but by declared acts and open hostility will she demonstrate that Persia is her principal base in operations against India, and that Persia, *nolens volens*, is at her complete disposal. On several occasions, as we have seen, Russia has been on the point of absorbing northern Persia; but although she has not for long made any ostensible advance, her power was never more assured in those provinces than it is at the present moment, when she has not violated the letter of any of those engagements which were intended to secure the integrity of Persia. This fact being ascertained, it follows that the danger to India from her predominance in Persia could never have been greater than at the present time; yet there is an apathy and a confidence in the security of our interests in Persia that are extraordinary, and that cannot but be hollow and utterly to be distrusted.

CHAPTER IX.

THE TURCOMANS.

FAR and wide, although no longer so far or so wide as formerly, over the waste expanse of Kara Kum there roam tribes who are independent of all earthly authority, whose hand is against every˙ man, and who are known as Turkmen or Turcomans. The great desert of Kara Kum, extending from the Caspian to the Oxus, and from Khiva to Persia, has been their home for centuries; and they are still to be found there in the same wild state of independence as their fathers were seven centuries ago. Their irregular confederacy has stood the test of time far better than some more regular modes of government, and so far as matters have yet progressed they appear to be better able to defend their rights than the other States and nationalities of Central Asia. The practical importance of the Turcomans in the present phase of the Central Asian Question cannot be over-estimated. They are evidently the next opponent with which Russia will come into contact, and to some degree the contest may be said to have already begun. Before entering upon the consideration of any of the numerous topics suggested by the aspect of political affairs, it will be instructive to consider the past history and present condition of these tribes.

When the Persian province of Khorasan extended to Merv the Turcomans were Persian subjects, when the Khan of Khwaresm was strong they were Khivan; but at all other times they have been independent. They themselves trace their origin back to the Mongols, and D'Herbelot states, on the authority of Mirkhond, that they look upon Oghuz Khan, grandson of Moghul Khan, as their great ancestor. A more recent authority says that the Turcomans are the Ghuz of Oriental history, who crossed the Oxus with the Seljukians about the year 1030. These continued to be for two centuries the dominant Turk tribe of Western Asia. Colonies of these Turcoman Ghuz, as they are called by contemporary historians, are still to be found in Persia, Anatolia, and Syria, the descendants probably of the original settlers. The main body has always held the country between the Oxus and the Caspian, that is to say, Turcomania. From the earliest times it had been their custom to break into Persia or the countries of the Oxus at any moment of internal anarchy, and the havoc they thus wrought has been untold. Timour inflicted severe punishment upon them, and for a time they were more disposed to follow a peaceful career. Although claiming a Mongol origin their resemblance to the Turks earned them the name of Turcoman, which means " resembling (*mánind*) the

14 *

Turk," and the Turcomans both of Kara Kum and of Asia Minor derive their name from the same cause. In both cases it is morally certain that they are the descendants of military settlers, who, separated from their main stem, have not possessed the necessary numbers or organization to become great conquerors, although they have never lost their warlike proclivities and ambition.

It is probable that most of the Turcomans of Kara Kum participated in the wars of Timour, although their kinsmen in Asia Minor suffered severely at his hands; but it was not until the time of Nadir Shah that we find them possessing any real sympathy with a great ruler.

Shah Abbas the Great endeavoured to curb effectually and for ever the turbulence of the Turcomans by settling a belt of Kurd colonists along the frontier, principally at Bujnoord, Kooshan, and Dereges. During his reign and that of several of his successors the plan worked well. The Kurds effectually checked the Turcomans; and the Khorasan frontier was for that space of time settled. The Persians benefited by the scheme, but soon the Kurds combined with the Turcomans, and then it is difficult to say whether there was greater danger from Turcoman hostility or from Kurd treachery. So recently as the year 1832 the Persian Government had to wage a regular war with the Kurds in order to compel them to revert to their allegiance. This the prince royal Abbas Mirza accomplished, but since that time the old state of things has revived, and quite recently there was much uncertainty with regard to the sentiment of the Kurds. In modern times the efforts of Nadir Shah to settle this question have been the most successful. Nadir Shah, as one of themselves—a Turcoman of the tribe of Affshar—had claims upon their sympathy such as no other ruler ever possessed, and consequently we find that during his life-time they were not only remarkably tranquil, but also ardent in the support they afforded him in his numerous enterprises. But considering that Nadir Shah himself was in his earlier days the leader of a band of robbers, it is safe to assume that the condition of the Khorasan frontier was not then greatly different to what it is at present. From a robber chief Nadir soon became the leader of a small but organised band of Turcomans; and this was the beginning of that army with which, composed of many nationalities, Turcoman, Persian, and Afghan, he afterwards achieved such remarkable triumphs.

During his life-time the Turcomans were well content to share in his success, and the alteration of his capital from Isfahan to Meshed, and the construction of the strong fortress of Khelat-i-Nadiri in the Turcoman country, made his power most vigorous and firmly established in that region which had before been most disturbed. But upon his death they relapsed into their old habits, and again became a thorn in the side of their more peaceful neighbours, whether Persian or Khivan, but more especially the former. From the death of Nadir to the close of the eighteenth century the Turcomans carried on their raiding expeditions into Khorasan, sometimes penetrating still farther into the country to

Irak and Seistan. It is said that they even dared, in parties of twenty or thirty, to molest the dwellers in the suburbs of Isfahan.

But in the last years of the century they incurred the enmity of the Persian ruler, Aga Mahomed Khan, not, indeed, through their marauding propensities so much as by an act of personal hostility. Although the Turcomans had been on sympathetic terms with Aga Mahomed and his father, they murdered the former's brother when he fled to them for refuge from the pursuit of Zuckee Khan, brother of the Shah Kurrum Khan. For that act Aga Mahomed resolved to exact the most ample reparation, and he accordingly collected a large army at Astrabad, in the neighbourhood of which place the offending Turcomans dwelt. His operations were completely successful, and the Turcomans—who were probably either Goklans or Yomults—paid bitterly for their treachery. So severe were the retaliatory measures adopted by Aga Mahomed, and so resolutely did he carry out his plan of revenge, that the Turcomans were thoroughly cowed, and for a long time afterwards the frontier near Astrabad was more settled than it had ever been before since the days of Nadir. Aga Mahomed carried a large number of prisoners into captivity, and in addition obtained hostages for the future behaviour of the tribe. But the lesson which was then read the Turcomans was only an exceptional occurrence, and has never been repeated. For a time it tranquillised the border, but in order to have been permanently effectual it should have been followed up.

About the same year that Aga Mahomed was dealing out well-merited punishment to the Turcomans of Astrabad, their kinsmen of Merv were being hard pressed by the ruler of Bokhara, Mourad Shah, or Beggee Jan, as Sir John Malcolm calls him, who had over-run a considerable portion of Central Asia, and had warned the Persians of Khorasan that unless they turned Sunnis he would return and proceed to convert them after a summary fashion. In this campaign he had indeed laid siege to the town of Meshed, but finding that town stronger than he had anticipated, and being unwilling to admit his inability to capture it, he informed his soldiers that the holy Imaum Reza, who was buried in Meshed, had appeared to him in a dream and forbidden him to prosecute the siege any further. The story goes that the daily supplications to the Imaum by the distressed inhabitants deprived that sacred personage of sleep, and that when Mourad learnt this, he said, " I know that the Imaum liveth, and he shall not have to reproach me with disturbing his rest."

The career of this Bokharan ruler was so remarkable that some sketch of it here may prove interesting. Shah Mourad, or Beggee Jan, was the eldest son of the Ameer Daniel, who had established himself upon the throne of Bokhara at the expense of its legitimate ruler, Abdul Ghazi Khan. When he died he left Mourad his heir. But Mourad had many brothers and other relations, all of whom aspired to the chief place; and there was no doubt that if he put forward his own claims he would have to compete with several formidable rivals. From a deep policy, and not through any excess of zeal, Shah Mourad became a fakeer, and on the death of his father shut himself up in a mosque, forbidding entrance to all. He also handed over the private property left him by his father to the public charities; and then he visited all the quarters of the city of Bokhara in a penitential garb, imploring the prayers of all persons for his deceased father, and the forgiveness of those whom he might have wronged.

For several months the Government of Bokhara remained in an unsettled state, and during that period Shah Mourad lived in close confinement within a mosque, wrapt up in religious devotions, and employed in composing some of those works, such as the " Eye of Science," which have earned for him a high literary reputation in the East. The necessities of the State, which was threatened both by internal and by external enemies, at last called him from his solitude; and at first as regent, and later on as ruler, Mourad restored the failing fortunes of Bokhara. He was not more widely famed for his conquests than he was for his justice and skilful administration. His code of justice was admired throughout Central Asia. No one was too high to escape receiving his deserts, and no one too low to be unable to obtain the justice which was fairly meted out to all. A slave could cite his master, and wherever that is possible in a slave-holding country, we may be sure that the guiding spirit must be actuated by the greatest desire for impartiality. Against drunkards and gambling Shah Mourad was particularly severe; indeed, one of his first acts was to destroy all the drinking and gambling houses in Bokhara.

He was also very stern in his measures for the promotion of religious fervour, as indeed behoved a true fakeer. Five times a day were loiterers in the streets driven into prayers, and a sense of devotion was quickened by the liberal employment of the whip. His police also carried a small memorandum book with a catechism to test the orthodoxy of the citizen who appeared to be neglecting his religious exercises; and in the event of his failing to give a correct answer, a punishment was inflicted upon so lax a Mussulman. But this ruler did something more for the advancement of his religion than by a mere enforcement of its rites. He held out numerous inducements, such as free education and subsistence, to all such as desired to become *mollahs*, and it is said that his patronage of the *madrassees*—colleges—produced such great fervour among the people, that at one period the students in them exceeded thirty thousand in number. Much more might be said of the justice and the vigour of Mourad's government, but enough has been related to show that, in his way, this seldom-mentioned prince of Bokhara possessed many striking qualities of greatness.

The capture of Merv caused a rupture between the Courts of Bokhara and Cabul, and Timour Shah, the son of Ahmed Khan, advanced with a large army upon the Oxus. It is computed that the Afghan army consisted of one hundred thousand men, but whether this number is correct or not we may be sure that it was a very formidable army, being commanded by Timour in person. The Afghan army advanced to Akche, on the borders of the Merv desert, and there halted. The Bokharan army boldly crossed the Oxus at Kilif, and several skirmishes occurred between small detachments of either army. In these fortune favoured Shah Mourad, whose principal strength lay in his cavalry; but he had the good sense to perceive that his interests would be better served by a peace than by a continuation of the war. Timour, who was by this time wearied of the contest, readily made peace, and Shah Mourad was permitted to retain Merv —his sole object. A few years later on he died, and was succeeded by his son Hyder Torah.

With the death of Shah Mourad, Merv speedily obtained its independence, becoming the chief possession of the Salor Turcomans. From that time to this it has been independent. Khiva has at several times sent armies against it, and even levied tribute from it; but the claims of Persia, Khiva, and Bokhara, and the aspirations of Cabul, have slumbered with regard to this ancient city of Khorasan during the present century. For seventy years and more the Turcoman confederacy—only, unfortunately for themselves, the confederacy has existed only in name—has been supreme in Kara Kum; and the various clans have maintained in their districts that freedom which has become their boast. The circumstances under which these clans exist are by no means identical with what they used to be, nor are they even similar with each other. Some are peaceful agriculturists, others are irreclaimable (?) robbers; this tribe is actually subjected to Russia, that is as free as the wind of its own steppe. Let us consider one and all of these clans.

Firstly, let us take those who are most to the north. The Chaudors dwell in the country between the Caspian and northern Khiva—that is to say, on the southern slopes of the Ust Urt. They are computed to number twelve thousand tents, with certainly not fewer than five and possibly six or seven persons to each tent. As they have of late years been undisturbed, and have settled down into a regular mode of earning their existence, it is possible that their numbers have increased since Vambery computed them to be of the number mentioned. Far to the south of the Chaudors, but still in the vicinity of the Caspian, come the Goklans. These are, for the most part, subjects of Persia, dwelling along the banks of the Gurgan river, but some of them are to be found across the Atrek in the Sumbur region. Vambery computed them at twelve thousand tents, or at sixty thousand persons at the least. Mr. Schuyler gives them only a fourth of that number, but as very little is yet known of this portion of the Persian frontier it is impossible to affix accurately what the number of the Goklans may be. They are a settled people, carrying on agricultural pursuits, and the breeding of the silkworm; and they give the Persian authorities little trouble.

Their neighbours, the Yomuds, or Yomults, are certainly among the very foremost of these tribes. Those of the Atrek, who hold the country between the Persian frontier and the Caspian, as well as several islands in that sea as well, are computed to number forty thousand tents; but, although this large number may be exaggerated, Mr. Schuyler testifies to the fact that one single encampment of the Tcharva branch of the tribe numbered four thousand tents, while another of the Ak Atabai consisted of half that number. It is amongst the Yomults that the Russians have been most markedly busy, and the efforts of Lomakine, Markozof, and others, have not been in vain in this quarter. Through the intervention of the Russian authorities old feuds have been settled, and bitter opponents reconciled to each other. The Yomults are divided into the two grand divisions, the settled—Tchomura—and the nomad—Tcharva; but there are clannish distinctions of which we do not as yet possess full information. In the khanate of Khiva itself there is a large colony of Yomults, who, it will be remembered, were chiefly settled on the lake Aibughir, and played a certain part in the Khivan campaign.

It was against these that those never-to-be-forgotten operations, commanded by General Kaufmann, and carried out by General Golovatcheff, were prosecuted with such vigour and relentless cruelty after the fall of Khiva, when they underwent such sufferings that it is doubtful if they can ever recover from their effect. Both Mr. MacGahan and Mr. Schuyler have exhausted this topic, and it is only introduced here to show that the Khivan Yomults must have greatly fallen off in numbers. It is probable that the Yomults of the Atrek, and their kinsmen of Khiva together amount to the total given by M. Vambery. Their relations with Russia have within the last few years been cordial, but it is permissible to believe that the past is too clearly impressed upon the minds of the Yomults ever to be forgotten. Quite recently, too, they had cause for complaint at the severe treatment of the Russian authorities, who hired a large number of camels from them, and when many of these were lost upon the steppe refused to give any compensation for them. This is an old trick that has often been played the natives by Russia. It has done service often enough, but its virtue does not yet appear to be extinct. From the reports which reach us through Teheran from Bujnoord, and even from narratives that have appeared in the " Tiflis Gazette," it is patent that there is great dissatisfaction among the Yomults at this harsh treatment. The Yomults do not possess any large number of camels, and consequently the loss is to them doubly severe. Such acts as these cannot but generate in the bosom of the Yomults—not the best-disposed of human creatures—feelings of hatred against Russia that must sooner or later manifest themselves; and as the event has only occurred recently, there has not been a sufficient interval for its results to be rendered perceptible.

The great tribe of the Erszari, who hold the left banks of the Oxus from Charjui to Khoja Salih and perhaps also to some distance within Afghan territory, are the least known of all these tribes, and except at the passages of the Oxus Europeans have not been brought into much contact with them. It appears to be probable, from what we have learnt from those sources, that the Erszari are a peace-loving and good-tempered set of people, of whom it would be interesting to procure further information. Their number has been computed at as many as fifty thousand tents, or a quarter of a million of people. This is, however, derived from very vague authority, and all we know for certain is that there are about five thousand in and near Charjui, and about the same number at Kerkhi. There are also settlements of this tribe at Kilif and Balkh itself.

South of the Erszari are the Alieli, a much smaller clan, who are confined to the small khanate of Andchui. Their number is probably under twelve thousand people; and if Ferrier's inquiries may be trusted, these are not a distinct tribe, but only a branch of the Tekes who were removed to Andchui in the reign of Shah Abbas the Great. He calls them descendants of the Affshars—that tribe of which Nadir Shah was a member. We then come to the Kara tribe, which occupies the desert between Andchui and Merv, but of them we know less than of either the Alieli or Erszari. Professor Vambery computes their numbers at one thousand five hundred tents, or seven thousand five hundred persons. Their political importance is practically *nil*, and so far as it is possible to express an unhesitating opinion, these clans on the frontiers of Afghan Turkestan are of considerably less importance than their kinsmen further west. In the triangle formed by lines drawn between the three points,

Charjui, Khoja Salih, and Shiborgan, there live these tribes, the Erszari, the Alieli, and the Kara, with a total approximate strength of seventy thousand persons. These are scattered over so large a surface, and the soil they till is so barren, that they possess neither the cohesion nor the resources to play any great part. The chances are that if the opportunity were offered them they would eagerly take up their residence within Afghan Turkestan, and speedily become merged in the Usbeg population.

The Turcomans of Merv and the region of Sarakhs and Dereges are for every reason the most important of all the Turcomans, and these are divided into three clans, the Teke, the Salor, and the Sarik. The Salor clan, which in happier days possessed Merv, has been ousted from its post of vantage on the Murghab, and compelled to seek in the country to the south that sanctuary which the superiority of the Tekes obliged it to discover. Its head-quarters are now round Martshag or Merutshag; but it is highly improbable that this clan still possesses anything like the forty thousand persons which Professor Vambery estimated it to number. It is possible that the Salor have recognised the necessity of war and have become subservient to the domineering Tekes. But on the other hand they may be biding their time in the hope of turning the tables upon their rivals. The Sarik clan, which is rather more peacefully inclined than the tribes to the north, holds the country close in on the Afghan frontier towards Herat. Many of the two tribes are Afghan subjects, and the numbers of the Sarik are certainly not over-stated at fifty thousand persons. Their head-quarters are generally considered to be Pendjdeh on the Murghab. For the present Russia, not having come into contact with these two tribes, knows little or nothing of them, but it is with them that she would be called upon to deal after the fall of Merv. It is just possible, particularly if a friend held Herat, that by skilful negotiation these clans might be secured by her as allies in a war with the Tekes, who are certainly no favourites with the smaller tribes.

But of all the clans the Tekes, whom we have now to consider, are by far the most important. They are the most numerous, warlike, and united. They hold the best strategical positions, and their principal stronghold is as inaccessible as it well can be. Their horses are also the best specimens of the kind, and their arms, inferior as they are when compared with those of Russia, are superior to any possessed by any other Turcoman tribe. The Teke country commences in the north-west at the post of Kizil Arvat, and continues down the valley which lies between the Kuren and Kopet Daghs on the one side, and a range of sand-hills on the other, as far as Abiverd. Beyond the Tejend they hold Merv, and its vicinity as well. This valley is extremely fertile, owing to the numerous rivers that flow down to it from the crests of the mountains of Khorasan. The Akhal branch of the Tekes hold the country between Kizil Arvat and Anef, and their region is marked throughout by a line of forts—forty-three in number. The Akhals alone are reckoned to have nearly ten thousand tents, and the other Tekes are said to have fifty thousand more. It has been computed that the whole tribe could put thirty thousand men into the field, more than half of whom would be admirably mounted. Although the Tekes are the most formidable of the robbers on the Persian frontier, they yet follow in their villages a busy life as agriculturists and silk weavers. Those villages are also much larger and more permanently occupied than is wont with these nomads; and as one consequence of these regular communities there is a more definite mode of government existing among them than anywhere else among the Turcomans. The Aksakal's authority is respected, but the most important check over the turbulent spirits of these strange people is that given by " custom."

The *deb*, as it is called, rules everything; and all disputes are decided, not by reference to the Koran, but to precedent. All travellers agree that the order and tranquillity in a Turcoman camp is wonderful, considering the character of its occupants, and also bearing in mind the very ineffectual punishments it lies at the disposal of the community to inflict. This may be traceable to two causes; in the first place to the numerous ties which bind each member of a clan to the other. So strong is the clannish feeling among the Turcomans that it has been said that a child of a very early age can distinguish the sub-division of the clan to which it belongs. And in the second place it may be due to the fact that, though the Turcoman can engage in a foray and execute it in an unequalled manner, he cannot commit a petty larceny—more especially against one of his own kin. The very hostility between the clans makes the connection between all the members of each clan the more binding; and thus it is that a village of marauding Tekes is as tranquil as and less disturbed by domestic strife than many a hamlet in this broad England.

In this fact, and in the high opinion English officers have formed of the personal characteristics of the Turcoman, an opinion not more favourably expressed by Conolly and Burnes more than forty years ago than by Butler and Napier the other day, lies a reply to those who would assert that the man-hunting Teke is an irreclaimable savage. His faults are exposed to the light of day, and they are those which incur the most strongly adverse sentiment of a civilised and free people; but it should be remembered as a point in his favour that once the evil has been cured by giving him a settled career in place of that to which he has been brought up, there remains no exhaustive process to be carried out of eradicating innumerable evil propensities. When it is said that the Turcoman is a man-hunter and a robber, everything that can be said against him has been said. It may without hesitation be asserted that that is a fault which admits of easy remedy.

On the other hand, the Turcoman possesses great merits. He is honourable and sincere in his dealings; and up to a certain point he possesses courage. It would be a mistake to suppose, however, that at the present moment the Turcoman is a very formidable antagonist. He will never attack even a caravan except in overwhelming numbers, and on several occasions the best men of the Tekes have been worsted by a small band of regular Persian troops or armed villagers. Against the Russians they have, with one exception, been uniformly unsuccessful. In 1872, 1873, 1875, 1876, and 1877, the Akhals have been assailed by Russian troops advancing into their territory, and on each occasion they appear to have had much the worst of it, except in the last-mentioned year, when General Lomakine, after occupying Kizil Arvat, was forced to beat a retreat, either through want of supplies or some other cause. But that was a solitary instance, and this has been more than redeemed by the successful operations of the same general in 1878.

With regard to the Akhal Tekes, it may be here useful to state that they are divided into two sections, the Tokhtamish and the Utamish, which are bitterly hostile to each other. The former are the more numerous, and generally have been supreme; but the Utamish have not rendered a very willing obedience. After a vain attempt in 1875 to reconcile these rival sections by the election of a common head, the Akhal clan broke up into several fragments; and when Lomakine advanced upon their line of forts, it was with a disunited clan that he had to deal. It is more than probable that the Russian general succeeded in establishing some kind of relationship with the Utamish branch of the Tekes, and that the resistance of the Akhals—of which the Russian press makes no mention—collapsed early in the last campaign. The main body of the Tekes must be discouraged by the disasters incurred

15 *

by the Akhals, and it is far from improbable that they may, failing the discovery of any ally, strive to come to an understanding with the Russians whereby Merv may be saved and their independence for a short time prolonged.

Upon the action of the main body of the Tekes undoubtedly depends the future of all the Turcomans who are still independent. These, perhaps, can bring thirty thousand fighting-men into the field, half of whom would be mounted. The line of the Murghab, and the position of Merv itself, is strong, and can be made stronger by inundating the country. On the other hand, the Turcomans possess no artillery, and are proverbially bad fighters behind walls. Their valour in the field has been questioned, but this may have been by unfriendly critics. It will be admitted, however, by their greatest admirer, that they are most formidable in the open. At the present moment it is our object to consider rather whether they would offer any opposition to the advance of a Russian army than to discuss the probable result of that resistance, which can be better considered in the next chapter.

There will be no question that the instinct of the Turcoman would impel him to resist the advance of a Russian army into his camping-places, but at the same time he is gifted with some prudence, and knows that on his own resources, and as his fighting strength is at present constituted, he has no chance in a fray with Russia unless he is backed up by foreign aid. The Turcomans of Merv have never been able to resist the advance of a disciplined army. Persia has often occupied that place from Meshed and Sarakhs; Khiva has also on several occasions advanced through the worst portion of Kara Kum upon the Murghab; and even Bokhara, under Shah Mourad, overthrew the Turcomans, and for a time annexed Merv. Against a small disciplined army, which is accompanied by a sufficient baggage train, the Tekes have always been impotent; and in this century the chances are still more against them than they have ever been at any previous time. There can be no doubt that the Turcomans are aware of their own weakness as compared with the power of Russia, and there is no reason to suppose that the Tekes will be more resolved in their determination to resist to the bitter death than the Yomults were.

It may be conceded that, despite the very gallant journeys of Captain Butler amongst them, and notwithstanding the information which that officer and Captain Napier collected concerning them, we do not possess as intimate an acquaintance with the Tekes as is desirable. Of course to English officers their talk is of nothing but of the unflinching manner with which they will resist Lomakine; yet their want of confidence in their own ability to do so is proved by nothing more clearly than by their repeated inquiries as to what England will do in their behalf. Their heroism is unfortunately belied by their own history, for they have never resisted the Persian or the Usbeg in the desperate fashion which they assert they intend to adopt when their opponent is the Muscovite.

But for one circumstance there would have been no recent evidence to show what the more probable attitude of the Turcomans in the coming crisis of their fate will be; and that circumstance is the mysterious reconciliation that took place in the early part of 1878 between the Tekes and the Government of the Shah. It was in March 1878 that tidings of this transaction first reached India, whence the news was transmitted to this country. It came suddenly, and without any previous intimation. That it signified something was evident, but what its actual signification was, was far from being clear. Even after this lapse of time nothing has occurred to elucidate its meaning, and much has since been written and said of the Turcomans as if such a transaction had never taken place. A revolution had occurred in the condition of affairs upon the Persian frontier, but when it was found impossible to measure the extent of that change it was assumed that its importance was slight and that it might be disregarded.

The terms of this arrangement, so far as they have been revealed, were the following :—The Teke Turcomans of Merv acknowledged the supremacy of Persia, and admitted that their city is held in obedience to the Governor of Khorasan, of which province the Persian Government has always considered that it formed part. They promised to commit no more raids upon Persian territory. In token of their complete submission to the Shah they gave one hundred hostages, who are to reside at Meshed, and permitted an agent from the Shah to reside at Merv; and as some contribution towards the military strength of Persia, they were to send a detachment of one thousand mounted

Turcomans to serve in the army. These very substantial concessions were made on the part of the Tekes by sixteen of their principal chiefs. They have given the Shah the form of vassalage which he has always claimed, they have conceded the substance of good conduct which, among purely Persian rulers, Shah Abbas the Great was the only one who could exact. So far as our information goes, the raids along the Khorasan frontier have ceased, and this fact proves that the hostages stipulated for have been surrendered. There is indirect evidence that a portion of the armed contingent has actually entered the Persian service as arranged. In addition to these very substantial concessions the town of Sarakhs, which had long been a debateable possession between the Persians, the Tekes, and the Salors, has been admitted to be a Persian possession, and with that admission a garrison from Meshed has been installed there. Without having received any defeat from Persian troops, and apparently of their own voluntary act, the Tekes have declared themselves vassals of the Shah, and, still more important and singular, have given tangible guarantees that for the future they intend to keep the peace towards Persia.

What urgent cause induced the Teke Turcomans to concede that which Persia has for so many years been unable to wring from them? The reply can only be surmised. Before considering the probabilities of the case it is as well to state what Persia on her part granted to the Tekes in return for their newly-found loyalty. In the first place the Shah condoned their past misconduct, and he gave a firman to the Tekes declaring *that they were and always had been his subjects*. He went beyond this declaration by remarking in this document that in consideration of their promise of future good conduct he would bestow on them his protection and favour. With regard to the surrender of their claims on Sarakhs, permission was given to one thousand Tekes—more probably one thousand families —to reside there and along the course of the Tejend. The favours granted by the Shah appear on the face of them to be wholly inadequate to the concessions made by the Tekes. The latter are substantial, and solid guarantees have been given for their due fulfilment. The former are at the least vague, and rest upon the word or promise of a Persian ruler alone. They also represent very little, unless that elastic phrase of "favour and protection" and the reference to the Tekes being Persian subjects mean more than such expressions generally do in Persian documents.

The objects of the Persian Government in making this arrangement are clear. They have secured by it everything that a difficult and costly campaign could have obtained for them. They have pacified their frontier, enforced their nominal rights, and obtained a valuable auxiliary force, without any effort and with apparently little outlay. From their point of view nothing could have been more opportune than the twinge of conscience which suddenly troubled the peace of mind of the marauding Tekes. But it is difficult to discover the potent argument which induced the Tekes to concede such substantial points as those referred to in this arrangement. As has been observed, they have often and often promised, when it happened to suit them, obedience to the behests of the Shah; but these have been mere promises to be broken at the first opportunity, and not to be compared for an instant to the very succinct engagements contracted between them in January, 1878.

There are two ways of looking at this matter, the first being that which assumes that the stipulations made by the Turcomans are worthless and that the whole proceeding is a sham. This view is based on the fact that it is difficult to explain the action of the Tekes, and that consequently the easiest theory is to assume that it is a farce and that bribery is at the root of the whole transaction. In the mere fact of Persian governors distributing bribes and in Teke chiefs pocketing them there is nothing to excite surprise. It has often been done before, and there is no reason why the plan, although it has always failed in attaining definite results, should not be tried again. But the great flaw in this theory is that the stipulations of this arrangement have been so well kept, as the reported arrival of the hostages and the armed contingent at Meshed has been in many ways confirmed. For more than twelve months the Khorasan frontier has been tranquil, and for the same period Persian troops have been in undisturbed possession of Sarakhs, only fifty miles from Merv. In its essence this arrangement differs from all previous understandings between the Tekes and the Persians, in that it is an accomplished fact and not a mere delusion created by some border official for his own purposes. There is no denying the fact that the Tekes have adhered to the letter of their bond, and it is not to the interest of Persia to infringe either the substance or the spirit of what she has promised. The time has not yet come for the Persian Government to show how it regards the new obligations which it has contracted towards its Turcoman subjects, and for the present we need not anticipate the future. The first theory explaining the action of the Tekes being untenable it only remains to consider the second, which would assume the Turcomans were actuated by some of those motives which are known to influence the majority of mortals.

The harvest in Central Asia during the year 1877 was a bad one, and it promised to be still worse in 1878. The Turcomans who derived their principal supplies from Bokhara underwent considerable deprivation during the former year, and their anticipation of what was to happen in the forthcoming one was far from being hopeful. Such was the story which found favour in Bokhara. There is some reason to believe that the Russians who have recently established themselves more unequivocally at Charjui—the halfway house to Turcomania—had something to do with the stoppage of supplies; and in Khiva also, whence the Tekes derived much of what they required, the Russians have been more vigilant in their efforts at paralysing the strength of the Turcomans while the army from the Caspian was dealing a more direct blow against them. It is doubtful whether the Teke country can support its inhabitants, but considering the wealth and fertility of the Murghab valley it would seem as if they could disregard the cutting-off of their source of supply to the north. For that reason it is probable that there were other causes at work than those which were accepted in Turkestan as the reason for the Tekes becoming reconciled with the Persians.

It is most probable that the advance of General Lomakine to Kizil Arvat and Bourma in the summer of 1877, and the several defeats which he inflicted upon the Akhals, caused great apprehension among the Tekes themselves. That alarm would not be allayed by the subsequent retreat of Lomakine, when the Akhals appear to have harassed his retreating column very much, for the Tekes would well know that the Russians would return and in greater force. The Akhals could but very imperfectly ward off the blow which Lomakine was evidently preparing for by frequent visits to Tiflis, and if they were unable to fulfil their part the brunt of the fray would devolve upon the Tekes. In the winter of 1877 the return of Lomakine in the coming spring was clearly foreseen by the Merv chieftains, and it behoved them to decide what policy they would adopt in their own defence. To them it was evident that when the Russians returned it would be with the full determination to establish themselves at Kizil Arvat, if not in some more advanced position in the Akhal country.

Brought face to face with so serious a danger, their old antipathy for the Persian became a matter of secondary importance, and the loss of their old marauding privileges a thing of little moment. There was the possibility of the Persian Government combining with the Russian in revenge for past injuries, when the collapse of the Turcoman power must have been not only complete but immediate. The Tekes were brought face to face with a double danger, from Russian hostility and from Persian long-standing indignation. It was resolved in the council of the chiefs to avert the latter by a timely surrender. The ruse, for such it was, was successful. The Persian Government was delighted with the sudden reformation of the Tekes, and hastily extended that formal protection over the Turcomans as its subjects to which attention has already been called. It is probable that when the Shah welcomed back his long-wandering subjects he did not consider the wide-reaching consequences of his recognition of the Teke country as being a portion of Persia. When that arrangement was concluded it is doubtful whether there was as clear a view at Teheran of the importance of the Russian advance from Krasnovodsk as there was at Merv. The Persian Government saw but the fact that the Tekes wished to come to terms, and were willing to give the long-coveted hold upon Merv, and it did not delay its acceptance of the proposals so far as to inquire into the motives which actuated the Tekes in their unprecedented compliance with Persian desires.

Since Lomakine has re-appeared, and in greater force, north of the Attock, and perhaps more particularly since the erection of a fortification at the place known as Chat, situated at the junction of the Sumbur and Atrek rivers, it is conceivable that a different view of the transaction is beginning to obtain at

Teheran, where the new obligations incurred by Persia towards the Turcomans cannot be altogether ignored. How Persia will consider herself bound to act in the event of the Russian troops advancing on Khelat-i-Nadiri is a very interesting question, but it cannot be answered with any great confidence. The actual acquisition of Sarakhs, the nominal authority to be exercised at Merv, have both given Persia as much as she can reasonably expect to secure from the Turcomans; and in that quarter no defensive and offensive alliance with Russia could give her more. Persia, having nothing to hope, and everything to fear, from Russia in Turcomania, must be loth to assist Lomakine in any movement against Merv, which is now, technically at least, a Persian city. Sir Henry Rawlinson has declared, in a paper on the road to Merv, lately read before the Royal Geographical Society, that, with Persia hostile, an advance of a Russian army from the south-east shores of the Caspian upon Merv would be an impossibility; and unless Russian statesmen can dazzle the eyes of the Shah's ministers by some more seductive picture, it would appear that there is every reason for supposing that Persia will not regard the development of Lomakine's movement with anything but the greatest dislike. If such be the prevailing sentiment in Teheran, we may look for some interesting situations in the future stages of this question, and we may possibly have some new versions of the meaning of Persian citizenship.

Without following this subject at greater length at the present moment, it will be instructive to remember that both England and Russia are bound by treaty to respect the integrity of Persia; and that technically, and now actually, the Teke country as far as Merv is a portion of the province of Khorasan. This is no new claim invented yesterday, but one of established historical veracity; and the southern Turcomans—the Tekes more especially—are Persian subjects by position and association. The question then arises, Are not the guaranteeing Powers restrained against any aggressive act against these Persian subjects by the terms of the treaty? Is it compatible with past stipulations that fresh conquests should be snatched from the Tekes, who are now *de facto* subjects of the Shah? These are very important questions, which require an authoritative answer. Hitherto our Foreign Secretaries have raised objections to Russia's movements in Kara Kum, because they threatened the integrity of Merv, a question of vital importance to this country; but now it appears that these same operations are directed against Persian territory and subjects, both of which the St. Petersburg Government is bound to respect. Nor is this view of the Turcomans being Persian subjects far-fetched, for such they are by all practical ties, and in that fact the only hope for a continuance of their independence remains. Whatever doubt, too, there may be of the whole Teke country having become an integral part of the Persian dominions, there can be no question of the town of Sarakhs having become so, and of all places, before the capture of Merv, Sarakhs is the most important in this region. Therefore a Russian advance on Sarakhs would certainly be an infringement of Persian territory, and, as a strict matter of fact, any move beyond the Akhal fort at Anef would be in the same category, and should be firmly resisted with all the diplomatic force at our disposal. If persisted in, it should be held to be an hostile act, and as such to be met. The importance of Sarakhs, on the high road from Meshed to Merv, Charjui, and Bokhara, is, as Sir Henry Rawlinson has said, that it is only by it that an advance could be made on Merv from the west. There is no information of any road existing from Abiverd through the Tejend swamp to Merv, and consequently an army coming from Kizil Arvat would have to occupy Sarakhs in the first place.

The arrangement between the Tekes and the Shah has therefore been so far pregnant with beneficial results, that it has pushed Persian territory forward so as to intervene between the Russian forces north of the Attock and the oasis of Merv. An opportunity is thus afforded this country of achieving a very material advantage by strengthening the ties which have been established between the Persians and the Turcomans. By extending the Persian frontier up to the old limits of Khorasan, that is to say, by including the country from Ashkabad to Merv, and by enforcing existing treaties, we can erect in the path of Lomakine an obstacle which he dare not encounter unless he be prepared to undertake that great war which, however inevitable in the end, Russia is at present so unfit to wage. The view that has just been taken of this transaction is, we believe, the most probable one, but we must not ignore the Machiavellian designs which are by some considered to be at the root of this proceeding.

The first view is that Persia has been acting throughout in collusion with Russia, and that the Turcomans have taken service under the Shah in order to share in some great enterprise in Western Afghanistan. Bribery has made the Turcomans complacent, and the promise of Herat has won over the Shah. Of this tripartite arrangement none of the parties would obtain any permanent benefit save Russia, and it would be wronging the astuteness of the Persian, or even of the Turcoman, to suppose that they are so shallow as not to perceive this as clearly as we do. The second view is that although Russia had nothing to do with the negotiations between Persia and the Tekes, yet, now that they have been consummated, she has striven, and, according to these, successfully, to turn the result to her personal advantage. According to this view there is the same tripartite arrangement, made for the same ends and between the same parties.

Both these views are fanciful, and give Russia a credit for superhuman astuteness to which she is by no means entitled. The probable state of the case is that Persia, without being downright hostile, is watchful and suspicious of Russia's designs—perhaps also nervous at the progress of events on the Atrek and round Kizil Arvat; that the Turcomans are fairly alarmed at the danger of their position, and anxiously regarding the attitude of both Persia and this country

—and it is just possible that, in the event of the former refusing to perform its duties, and of the latter remaining passive, they may throw up the sponge and come to terms with Lomakine. The Russians themselves are hampered by some of the doubts that must beset them when on the point of attempting another great enterprise in Central Asia. In the meanwhile they are gathering their strength to a point, so that when the blow has to be struck it may be dealt rapidly and without hesitation. On the action of Persia the whole affair depends. The Shah can inspire the Turcomans with the necessary courage, and he can provide them with most of their wants. He can, by withholding supplies, and by giving *carte blanche* to the Kurd borderers, seriously delay the march of a Russian army beyond Kizil Arvat. But of his intention to play this bold part there is no evidence. His strict neutrality is probably the most the Tekes can count upon.

One of the principal reasons for regarding the Turcomans as among the best material for cavalry in the world is that they possess an abundant supply of the most excellent horses. They are mounted men at the present moment, and as riders have few equals and no superiors. In the tactics pursued by irregular cavalry they are already adepts, and little would be left to be done by the drill-sergeant. The weak point —and for irregular warfare it is their only weak point —is their weapons. Their most desperate onset—and those who have seen a Turcoman charge say that it is delivered in the most admirable manner—breaks before the volleys of rapidly-repeating rifles which deal destruction into their ranks hundreds of yards before their own wretched weapons can have any effect. They have striven, not always with ill-success, to make up for this inferiority by having recourse to stratagem, and by selecting the night-time as the season for their attack. But for the purposes of defensive warfare, such as the defence of Merv, they are unfortunately without the necessary means. They have no artillery, and their own personal weapons are antiquated and useless for modern warfare. Their valour and the excellence of their horses can only very imperfectly supply those wants. But the good qualities of the Turcoman horses undoubtedly facilitate the task of converting these tribes into the most formidable mounted force in Central Asia.

The Turcoman horse is not less an object of affection to his master than the Arab is to his. When it has been decided to carry out a raid into Persia, the Turcoman puts his horse through a regular course of training, of which the following is a description. For thirty days before the time appointed for the start the animal is exercised daily, part of that exercise being to gallop at full speed for half an hour. Some hours after he is brought in he is fed, his food consisting of six pounds of hay, or clover-hay, and about three pounds of barley or one-half the usual allowance of corn. During this period as little water as possible is given to the horse. Sometimes this period is shorter than the time specified, particularly if the animal appears to be in the necessary hard condition. But the preparatory course of training does not stop here, although the start for the scene of the proposed foray, or *chapaoul*, is then made. Each Turcoman takes with him an inferior horse called *yaboo*, which he himself rides until he reaches the place of action. It then serves to carry back the plunder. The charger, as it may be termed, follows bare-backed and without bridle his master, and the advance is graduated so that the daily march shall not be excessive. During this later stage, which lasts from the time of starting until the arrival at the scene where it is proposed to assail the Persian village, the horse's food is changed to four pounds and a quarter of barley flour, two pounds of maize flour, and two pounds of raw sheep's-tail fat chopped very fine. These are well mixed and kneaded together, and given to the horse in the form of a ball. While taking this no hay is given to him, and this food is much liked by the horse. After four days of this food he is considered to be in prime condition, and capable not only of attaining the greatest speed but also of sustaining the most protracted fatigue. Then the *yaboo* is discarded and left in the rear, while the Turcoman on his charger goes forward to carry out the design which has occasioned the whole enterprise. It is said that when in this high state of training the Turcoman horse can perform a daily journey of one hundred miles, and continue the same degree of sustained speed for several days. There is no valid reason for doubting this statement, and the performance of this almost unequalled feat rests upon testimony of the most unequivocal kind.

The grand secret of the treatment of their horses by the Turcomans is undoubtedly to be found in the fact that they most carefully prevent their taking any green food. The character of the soil of Kara Kum is peculiarly favourable to the practice of this sound theory, for it produces only during the spring anything green at all. During that period the Turcomans are always quiescent; but in the month of August, and sometimes before, the horse is put upon his regular allowance of dry food, viz. seven pounds of barley mixed with dry chopped straw, lucerne, and clover hay. This treatment undoubtedly tends to give the horse a stamina and higher temperature than any other horse of which we know, not excepting the Arab.

The horse is also treated by these people with quite as much sympathy and affection as he is in Arabia. He is never ill-treated, and any Turcoman who attempted to ill-use him would be visited with the scorn of all men. The feeling is clearly traceable to the companionship which exists between the master and his horse from the time when the latter was a foal; and as the Turcoman's safety often depends exclusively upon the good qualities of his charger, it is intelligible that that affection should become stronger with age instead of weaker.

The Turcoman horse is no doubt a cross-breed between some indigenous animal and the Arab. At various known periods it has been strengthened by a fresh importation of Arab blood; such was the case when Timour distributed more than four thousand mares amongst the tribes, and again when Nadir gave

six hundred to the Tekes, of whom his own clan of
Affshar was an off-shoot. But it probably owes its
innate excellence to the more remote period when
the Arab conquerors advanced into Persia and Turcomania. Be that as it may, however, there can be no
question that in personal appearance it is much inferior
to the pure Arab, although in its useful qualities,
doubtless attributable alone to the method of treatment
adopted by its masters, it equals its rival.* The neck,
which is long and straight, is proudly curved and
slender, but the head is decidedly too long to be in
just proportion. The chest is also too narrow to please
an English eye, and the legs are long and apparently
ill-adapted for carrying the exceptionally big body at
any high degree of speed. The task that this animal
accomplishes falsifies its appearance, and its merits and
fame rest on what it has done. There are, however,
degrees of excellence among even the horses of the
Turcoman tribes. Those of the Tekes, and particularly
of the Akhal Tekes, are considered to be the best;
perhaps this is to be attributed to the present of Nadir
Shah. Then come those of the Salor and Erszari,
then the Yomults—whose political importance has now
grown so much less—then the Goklans, and lastly the
Sarik. Much, however, of the influence of the Salor
and Sarik tribes has become merged in the Tekes, and
it is possible that when the former lost Merv they were
also deprived of many of their belongings, particularly

* *See* Ferrier's "Caravan Journeys," and the "Travels of Sir
Alexander Burnes."

of their horses. Among the Turcomans the Tekes possess confessedly the best. The Usbegs of Afghan Turkestan have also a horse which, although smaller than the regular Turcoman, possesses great qualities of endurance and speed.

A useful horse may be purchased from the Turcomans for as small a sum as thirty pounds, and a mediocre horse will now and then be parted with for five times that sum. The best breed of all is never sold, and very rarely do the Persians succeed in capturing one. When they do, it is always reserved for the Shah's stable. While the Turcoman horse is better cared for, more fully appreciated, and more thoroughly developed than any European horse, in one point he suffers from the ignorance of his owners, and that is in medical treatment. As M. Ferrier says, "custom takes the place of science," and when coping with disease custom is a very inefficient guide. The common diseases are similar to those from which English and other horses suffer, glanders, wind galls, etc. The Turcomans have, however, a strange plan of dealing with any young animal which suffers from loss of appetite. They make an incision in its nose and remove a kind of cartilage which grows inside. There is also a terrible disease called by the Persians *nakhoshi yaman*—the wicked disease—which is always incurable and generally fatal in a few hours. It appears to be similar to hydrophobia, but its exact nature is not as yet known.

As so much has been said in this chapter in favour of the Turcomans, it would be wrong to pass by in silence the bad point in their character, and by some it will be considered to more than out-balance all the other high and valuable qualities which they possess. The force of circumstance, the absence of any recognised authority, have made the Turcoman a robber and a depredator. He is the bandit *par excellence* of Turkestan. He is the slave-hunter of the steppes, the man who drags the wearied captive four hundred miles at his saddle-bow to the marts of Khiva, who knows no pity for the sufferings of the Persian, and who keenly seeks to intercept those captives who may have redeemed their liberty and who strive to regain their native village in Khorasan. The tales which have been told of the cruelty of the Turcoman rest upon no hearsay evidence. It has been testified to over and over again by the most circumstantial of travellers. Burnes, Ferrier, Shakespear, Abbott, Vambery, and numerous others all agree on this point. The panegyrist cannot, and if he is prudent will not, attempt to gainsay the fact that the Turcoman is at present a man-hunter of the most remorseless type. His cruelties to the Persians have been narrated over and over again, and they are as horrible as perhaps they well can be.

The reader may make what allowance he may feel disposed to grant for this evil propensity, but he must remember that the Turcomans are but exhibiting one of those features of human life which are to be found at some stage or other in the history of all people. There is no reason for supposing that the Turcomans are irreclaimable. Some of them have been reclaimed, such as the Goklans and the Chaudors. Others, such as the Yomults and the Erszari, may be considered to be on the road to reclamation. In each case the improvement is clearly traceable to the fact that a more settled mode of livelihood has been placed at their disposal. The Teke has still to live by plunder, and consequently retains longer than his neighbours those qualities in which all Turcomans were much on a par in the last century. But, if we are to credit the stories told by the latest travellers, the Teke is sickening of his occupation. Brought face to face with a great danger, he finds that his mode of livelihood alienates not only the sympathy of Persia but also the friendly feeling which some British officers have very wisely striven to create in this country.

From Persia, the weak and destitute power, what aid can the Turcoman expect? Yet such as that aid is, it is the only source of comfort to the Teke. It will not enable him to cope boldly with Russia, but it may at the worst afford for the relics of his nationality a place whither they may flee. With that object the Teke clan has, as has been seen, surrendered Sarakhs to Persia, and given hostages for future good behaviour; that is to say, it has voluntarily sacrificed its old career in Khorasan. By a supreme effort it has taken a step in the direction of self-reclamation, when the object to be attained cannot be said to be of the highest importance. We may argue from this known fact what the Turcomans would be prepared to concede as the equivalent for moral and material support from this country, which possesses the means and the power either to make Turcomania a very valuable dependency of a reinvigorated Persia, or an autonomous and respectable community. All nations reach a point in their career when they will abandon the evil customs and practices that obtain amongst them if they are only fairly shown the way by some superior race. The Turcomans have apparently reached that stage, and upon this country more than any other devolves the duty and the responsibility of showing them the broad, straight road, by following which they must find increased prosperity and greater security.

Nothing points more clearly to this conclusion than the confidential report of Captain Napier made in the year 1876. That officer, who has been in Khorasan on several occasions during the last six years, collected the most important information and the most interesting details that we possess concerning the Tekes; and to his efforts it is to a great extent due that a more hopeful view has obtained in this country of the possibility of reclaiming the Tekes. The following passage taken from this report deserves close consideration, for the facts mentioned in it clearly go to prove that the Turcoman is far from being so steeped in barbarism and cruelty as a reference to his marauding characteristics alone would imply. "The Turcoman nomad is not by any means the mere plundering savage that his Persian neighbour paints him. From what I have seen and heard, I would describe the average Turcoman as exceedingly intelligent, *shrewd, and alive to his own interests.* Accustomed from childhood to a free, roving life, anything like restraint would be at first irksome to him, but he does not appear to be incapable of discipline. The Turcoman of Merv is also now fully alive to the advantages he enjoys in the possession of one of the most fertile tracts in the world, and a guarantee of its undisturbed possession would be one of the strongest inducements that could be held out to him. He is already in some degree changing his habits, and there is every indication of the possibility of his settling down in course of time, of his own impulse, to peaceful occupations. Two large sections of the race, the Arsari and the Goklan, have already done so, and the character of the Teke cannot be radically different."

This favourable opinion is formed by a man who has been brought much into contact with them, and although the evidence may not be free from the suspicion of personal sympathy with the Turcomans, it is of the highest importance, inasmuch as it must tend to undeceive those who believe that the Teke will oppose Russia on his own resources alone. The Teke is "shrewd and alive to his own interests," and also "to the advantages he enjoys in the possession of one of the most fertile tracts in the world." Unless we are alive, then, to our interests, and while the opportunity is in our hands proceed to bind the Turcoman in a firm alliance with us, we shall probably discover that the Teke may prove his shrewdness and the perception of his own interests by coming to terms with Russia. In this nineteenth century even the Teke Turcomans are not paladins of romance.

But of all living authorities on the subject, none

deserves to rank higher than Captain, or Major he is now called, Francis Butler, of the 9th Regiment. This officer, in the spring of the year 1876, passed his leave in exploring the valley of the Atrek. He carried on his investigations in an unostentatious manner, and, publishing no narrative of his journey, received small notice, and less credit, for his very gallant and useful undertaking. But for one circumstance it is probable that nothing more would have been heard of this affair. For reasons that have not been divulged, but possibly on account of his ignorance of Persian, Captain Butler travelled on this occasion in the disguise of a Chinaman. Travelling on the borders of civilised life, in the neighbourhood of the marauding Teke and the scarcely-more-to-be-trusted Kurd, the English officer found security in the dress of a subject from far Cathay. So far as we know, Captain Butler was permitted to go where he liked, and without molestation. To us we admit this fact is most significant, showing not only the wide influence of China, but also the great difference there is between Asiatic life and our own. An Englishman would scarcely care to speculate on what Captain Butler's reception would have been had he chosen the same disguise for a visit to the Potteries. To this circumstance may indubitably be traced the attention which Captain Butler's first journey to the Atrek received at head-quarters in India.

The following year, when the relations between England and Russia were becoming strained over the development of the Eastern Question, Captain Butler received instructions to repeat his journey to the

Turcoman country—this time in the proclaimed character of a British officer. During this later journey he appears to have entered into more circumstantial negotiations with the Tekes; making the Persian frontier town of Kooshan his base, he explored the passes of the Kuren Dagh, which he found passable for artillery, and resided for some time among the Turcomans themselves at the village of Feruza. In these later explorations he was accompanied by a young Englishman, Mr. Henry Hammond. Captain Butler more than confirms what Captain Napier has said about the possibility of greatly improving the physical condition of the Tekes, and from his interviews with their chiefs he has arrived at the decided opinion that the Tekes are most anxious to become our subjects. Of the difficulties and dangers encountered by this gallant officer during his later journey we know little, but the following incident will suffice to show that they deserve the epithet of hair-breadth.

Early on the day following his arrival at a village beyond Kooshan, the Persians ordered a body of sixty soldiers into the fort, where they deprived Captain Butler and his companion of their arms and luggage; while on the morning following this the governor of the place, with some forty men, took them to a spot in the glen, and, after separating them, ordered Captain Butler to dismount, as he was about to be shot. With this request he refused to comply, adding that, if he were to be shot, he would give the signal to fire by taking off his hat. The governor thereupon cocked and presented his gun, but he put it down in astonishment when the Captain took off his hat, and in admiration of his courage asked him to be their chief. The governor was subsequently flogged and dismissed from his post.

During Captain Butler's absence from India on Government service, the Eastern Question reached so acute a stage that Kaufmann openly broke ground in Cabul, and war between England and Russia was imminent. At that crisis much was expected to result from Butler's successful mission among the Turcomans. For a brief space during the summer of 1878 he stood a good chance of finding himself a lion on his return either to England or India. But before he got back the Eastern Question once more slumbered. The advantages of an alliance with the Turcomans sank into the back-ground, and Captain Butler's activity amongst them, from which so much was at one time expected, became absolutely a source of annoyance and inconvenience to our Foreign Office.

The Russian Government was as keenly alive as it could be to the dangers that might arise from the activity of English officers among the Turcoman tribes. Captain Butler's movements were followed with close attention; and at last, early in July, when the peace of the world was being placed upon a new and a firmer basis at Berlin, M. de Giers felt strong enough to call the attention of Lord A. Loftus to the acts of this English officer. In a despatch, dated the 3rd of July, 1878, to the Marquis of Salisbury, Lord A. Loftus says :—

"M. de Giers, the head of the Russian Foreign

Office, admitted that he had sent M. Bakouline, the Russian Consul at Astrabad, to Meshed, to watch the movements of Captains Butler and Napier, who were reported to be inciting the Turcoman tribes to hostilities against Russia. I (Lord A. Loftus) stated to M. Giers that Captain Butler was a mere traveller on his own account, and no agent of Her Majesty's Government, and that urgent orders had been sent to him by the Commander-in-Chief in India to return forthwith to his military duties. M. de Giers, who appeared to be well informed both in regard to Captain Butler and Captain Napier, stated that he was aware that Captain Butler had been recalled, but that, nevertheless, he had refused to obey the orders he had received, and was persisting in his intention to visit the Akhal tribes. He referred even to the letter which Captain Butler had addressed to certain Turcoman chiefs, of which His Excellency had evidently received copies."

This complaint on the part of M. de Giers was to some extent intended as a reply to the inquiries our Government had been making as to General Lomakine's movements, and the remonstrances which, on that information, Lord A. Loftus had addressed to the Russian Government.

Upon his return to Kurrachee, Captain Butler was ordered to join his regiment at once, and, without receiving any acknowledgment for his services, this officer has been sent back to regimental duty, when he possesses information, such as no other man possesses, of one of the most important phases of the Central

Asian Question. It cannot be supposed that this treatment is to be more than temporary—that is to say, until the Indian Government can find some other service for this most resolute and courageous officer to perform for the benefit of his country. Should it be otherwise, the Indian authorities would have committed an act of ingratitude which could only be compared to that evinced by Russia towards Vickovitch forty years ago. There is considerable indignation in India at the gross neglect shown to Captain Butler, as the following passage from a leading Indian journal clearly indicates. It is quoted here, although it is to be hoped and expected that before these lines are in the hands of the reader the injustice will have been undone, and the blunder, which is not the least serious matter, repaired. No Government will secure such faithful and useful service as that rendered by Captain Butler, if, at a pinch, it deserts its servants, and repudiates acts which it has encouraged when it was thought some advantage might be derived from them. The passage referred to is from the "Civil and Military Gazette," and is as follows :—

"We regret to hear that the distinguished explorer of the Kuren Dagh has been ordered to rejoin his regiment, under circumstances which appear to himself, and to us, harsh and not creditable to the Government of India, which employed him on a peculiarly delicate and dangerous mission, and now shows a disposition apparently to disavow him.

"Major (?) F. W. H. Butler, of the 9th Regiment, the officer to whom we allude, is one whose services to the

State assuredly deserve public recognition. Employed under the immediate orders of the Governor-General of India, he was sent a year ago to explore the little-known regions lying between the Caspian Sea and the gates of our Empire. Within that year's space he has surveyed some thousands of miles of country hitherto unknown, has brought back admirable maps of districts, which may prove of incalculable value; he has literally carried his life in his hand for months together in regions where the slaughter of an unprotected traveller is regarded rather as a meritorious action; he has undergone trials, fatigue, and exposure which no ordinary man could have survived; and he has returned to India triumphantly successful in the objects for which he was sent, only to be received with marked official disfavour, and to meet, for sole acknowledgment, with a curt order to rejoin his regiment. Not a word of thanks, not an invitation to recount the story of his exertions, not even an offer to reimburse him for the expenses to which he has been put, is tendered to him. What misunderstanding or cause for treatment, on the face of it so unworthy, there may be, we do not know.

"We cannot conceive that Lord Lytton should be capable of behaving to an English officer of Major (?) Butler's merit as a Russian Czar behaved to the gallant Vickovitch on his return to St. Petersburg from Cabul. It is not yet, we hope, an English custom to repay exceptionally gallant services with contemptuous neglect. Even supposing that the very strong convictions gathered by this energetic traveller should be unwelcome to the tepid temper of British statesmen, and supposing his political impressions to be opposed to departmental prejudices, we cannot understand why he should be personally neglected or unrewarded. A step in rank, an indulgence of leave, and a liberal reimbursement for expenses incurred, should have been the least return for his good service. Whereas it would appear that he has met with nothing but a most ungracious and chilling absence of all acknowledgment on all sides, civil and military, and has been even left out of pocket as regards travelling expenses.

"So patent and obvious was the personal risk and peril dared by Major (?) Butler, that the Government actually took from him an undertaking in writing, that he absolved them from all responsibility in case of his death by violence, before he started in obedience to his orders. He has returned after fulfilling them to the letter, and he is not even thanked. There is gross wrong here, which we trust for England's sake may be righted."

CHAPTER X.

THE MERV QUESTION.

MERV, the Margiana Antiocha of the ancients, celebrated in Milton's sonorous lines as

"Margiana to the Hyrcanian cliffs
Of Caucasus, and dark Iberian dales,"

has at all times occupied a foremost place in the annals of Central Asia. It was originally founded — so records say—by Alexander, and became the capital of the kingdom of Margiana, established by Antiochus, one of that prince's generals. When that kingdom fell to pieces it became a portion of the Parthian State, and with the decline of that great people it commenced a downward and constantly changing course until in modern times it became the frontier city of the Suffavean kings of Persia. In those days it was one of the four royal cities of Khorasan, of which the other three were Meshed, Nishapore, and Herat. It had partially recovered from the depression to which it had been reduced by the Mongol conquerors and Tamerlane, and under Persian rule enjoyed all those benefits to which its position on the great trade route to Bokhara and Central Asia entitled it.

From this time until after the death of Nadir, Merv continued to be a Persian possession, when it fell into the hands of Mourad of Bokhara, who carried away the inhabitants to his country, where the descendants of many of them are still to be found. In the present century it has acknowledged some kind of fealty to Khiva, and on one occasion at the least a Persian army has succeeded in wringing from its chiefs the concession of those claims which the Shah has always considered his due. But in the main it has, since the fall of Bokharan power, been independent, and during many years the head-quarters of the Salor tribe. More recently the Tekes have dispossessed the Salor, and are for the time being supreme in Merv, which they now admit that they hold in subjection to the Shah.

The river on which Merv is situated is the Murghab, which, rising in the Hazara district of Afghanistan, flows in a northerly direction into Kara Kum, finally losing itself in a lake some fifty miles north of Merv. Near that town the river is eighty yards across and five feet deep. There are several fords, but the bottom is clayey and full of holes. Much of the river is drawn off from the main channel by canals, which carry the water over the adjoining lands and make them fertile and productive. The banks of the river stand a considerable number of feet above the stream; but this fact, which gives the Murghab an appearance of greater shallowness than it possesses, is due to the large quantity of water which is carried off for the purposes just mentioned. Merv, before the time of the Usbeg invasion under Mourad of Bokhara, derived great advantage from the existence of a dam situated just above the town; but among other ruthless acts of that conqueror, this dam was destroyed, and Merv has never recovered its previous prosperity.

The district to the south of Merv is known as Maroochak, or Marutshag, and this is described as being very unhealthy, probably on account of the marshes which are formed here by the Murghab. There is a proverb current in these parts, Burnes tells us, that "Before God gets intelligence the water of Maroochak has killed the man." Probably this local phrase has been assumed to mean more than it actually does, for as far as our information goes, this district is fairly populated. Both Wolfe and Abbott in their journeys to Merv from Herat make no mention of having passed through any pestilential region, although they both refer to the sandy plain which lies for some distance south of Merv, and in the centre of which that place stands.

The present town of Merv is about twelve miles west of the ancient city, which stood on the banks of a canal called the Aub-i-Merv. When that canal was dammed by the Bokharan conqueror, the neighbouring Turcomans moved their encampment to the brink of the river Murghab itself. Here a permanent bazaar of some hundred mud huts was erected, and round this the Turcomans pitched their camp. A mud fort, in which a governor in the time of the recognition of Khivan authority resided, adds little to the appearance of Merv, which must be singularly mean, considering the greatness of its reputation. It is probable that since the rule of Khiva has given place to a state of independence among the Turcomans, Merv has increased in size, and that the bazaar and permanent buildings are now more numerous than when English officers last visited it. As Abbott says in his almost forgotten "Heraut to Khiva," the position of Merv is so important that it will never be long abandoned, and might with judicious care rapidly rise from the dust into wealth and consequence.

Various opinions have been expressed with regard to the productiveness of the plain of Merv. There is no question that that plain is composed to a great extent of sand, and that but for the Murghab it would be identical with the rest of Kara Kum. But as matters are, the system of irrigation answers its purpose so well that the district of Merv provides for probably one hundred thousand Turcomans. Whenever any recognised authority has been established there a revenue of more than twenty thousand pounds sterling has been derived from it. But the principal importance of Merv is due to its position on a great trade route, and as a strategical base its value is also very apparent. There not only can the merchant lay in the necessary supplies to cross the desert to Charjui, or even to Khiva, but a general could maintain at Merv itself and in the valley of the Murghab a large army—certainly one of fifty thousand men, and probably one of double that strength—during the whole of the year in plenty and ready for immediate action. It would also be able to make a further advance without putting any severe strain on its reserves in Khiva or Bokhara.

It would also be as misleading as it would be unwise to judge of Merv by its present condition under the Turcomans. The existing state of things justifies the belief that only a very slight effort would be necessary to make Merv still more productive than it is, nor would the hope of reclaiming a portion of the desert towards Charjui be Utopian. There is some reason to say that the distance of desert between the Oxus and Merv could be reduced very considerably, and that at the wells at Balghooe, now so limited in their supply, it would be possible to create a very efficient halting-place for a considerable body of men. But the great advantage of Merv is that it is the last piece of fertile soil thrust forth from Khorasan into the desert. It is the extreme limit of a new continent, of the rich and fertile lands of Southern Asia. An enemy established there has his foot firmly planted upon the threshold of those lands. He can there conceive some slight imagining of the greater wealth to be found in the country to the south. He is at the head of the roads to Meshed and Herat. Before him lies an easy route to either of those places, and their occupation is but the prelude to the most alluring of possibilities, and to the summit of earthly ambition.

Having proceeded thus far with the ancient history of Merv, and explained the reasons of its importance, we may turn to the consideration of those later moves in the direction of Merv which General Lomakine made during the year 1878. We have already seen how this later advance was made more imperative by the check which that officer received in the previous year. The winter of 1877-78 was employed by the Governor of Trans-Caspiania in paying a visit to Tiflis, and in making strenuous preparations for the forthcoming campaign, which was to be one of great importance. We have received details of considerable interest from several quarters, principally from our Minister at Teheran, and from the columns of the Russian press. The correspondence on Central Asia presented to Parliament during the winter session of 1878 contains several important translations by Mr. Michell from the "Moscow Gazette," and other journals. Out of these materials it is possible to construct a tolerably clear narrative of Lomakine's movements.

On the eastern shores of the Caspian for operations against the Turcomans Russia has only the two bases, Krasnovodsk and Chikishlar, of which the former is much the more important. In 1877 Lomakine's advance was made from the former place alone; but before that year Markozof had conducted several attacks on the Turcomans in the Atrek region. On one occasion he even crossed the Gurgan into Persia. The river Atrek itself was thoroughly explored as far up its course as Chat. But when a fresh campaign was decided upon for the early part of 1878 Russia had not advanced her position in the Atrek region beyond the Caspian shore. The plan of campaign was that a double advance should be made on the Akhal country. While one division advanced from Krasnovodsk on Kizil Arvat, another starting from

Chikishlar was directed to march by the Atrek towards the same place, thus taking the Akhals in flank.

The permanent garrison of Chikishlar was strongly reinforced from Krasnovodsk by a force which marched along the Chikishlar littoral. The reason for this trying land march of three hundred miles, during which the Russians lost many camels, was the bad landing that there is at Chikishlar. The bay which bears that name is a great and shallow piece of water, the depth of which at more than half a mile from the shore is only two feet, and close in on shore it is only one inch. In fine weather steamers stop one mile and a half from shore, and during rough weather at a much greater distance. Passengers and stores are landed in the flat-bottomed boats of the Turcomans; but even these cannot approach nearer than six hundred yards, and for that distance the journey must be performed by wading. It was for this reason that the reinforcements for Chikishlar were sent by land over the steppe from Krasnovodsk.

Following a new road which had never been before used, this army advanced on the Atrek, reaching that river at Baiat Khaji, or Bayat Adji, a place which lies on the left bank of the Atrek, and consequently in Persian territory. The Goklan tribe of Turcomans hold this portion of the Atrek region. The best account of these operations is that contained in the letters of a Russian officer—probably on Lomakine's staff—which originally appeared in the "Moscow Gazette," and which Mr. J. Michell translated (see "Further Correspondence on Central Asia, 1878"), and we give these here *verbatim*. The first letter is dated July 30th (August 11th, N.S.), and is written from Baiat Khaji.

"Early on the morning of the 22nd July (August 3rd, N. S.) we broke up our camp; our detachment advanced under the cover of infantry, Cossacks, Kirghizes, local militia, and some guns. The long line of camels, heavily laden with a large quantity of stores, stretched for a considerable distance. As we receded from the shore, the shells, which covered the ground and made it firmer, gradually disappeared, and the vehicles in the rear sank deeper and deeper into the sand. At the seventh verst the ground, instead of being formed of clean sand, now presented the appearance of a salt marsh petrified by the heat of the sun. Verdure between the low mounds is observed at intervals, and the vegetation itself proves that the soil is capable of cultivation. After proceeding about four versts over these salt marshes, the road again reaches a sand bank, vegetation almost entirely disappears, and the wheels sink into the friable sand. This sand, however, does not extend for a long distance, and a depression is reached, which is surrounded on all sides by low hillocks; the ground becomes firmer, and emits under the horses' hoofs a hollow sound, which would seem to indicate a cavity under the upper crust of the soil, suggesting also the existence of a 'subterranean basin.' All the hollows are covered with a rich vegetation. Plants appear which plainly show the presence of water in the subsoil. A halt was made after a march of four hours along this hollow. It was near 11 o'clock; the heat, scorching rays of the sun, together with the dust and flies, had so exhausted the men that they all threw themselves down on the ground. The poor horses refused the forage, while none of us thought of food; each economised his supply of water, and only moistened his lips and throat. 'Samovars' (tea-urns), however, soon made their appearance, and the unharnessed camels made for the steppe, where they found forage in the shape of the high grass of the steppe. The Cossacks and Kirghizes collect this grass for fuel. No water was here given to the poor horses, as the wells were still a day's march distant. At 5 o'clock in the evening we again started; the heat had decreased, but the flies, which were in myriads, continued to be very troublesome. The steppe over which the road now ran presented a livelier and more animated appearance; salines, with patches of verdure, became here and there visible; the sand was almost everywhere overgrown with grass; numerous camel tracts and roads were noticed; the soil became firmer, so that even the guns moved along easily. About 9 in the evening we reached Murat-Lar locality, where there are no wells, though, judging from the sounds which the earth emits when struck by horses' hoofs, from the surrounding vegetation, and from the temperature of the soil on a sultry day, it may, with safety, be asserted that water is to be found at no great depth.

" Early on the following morning we continued our march, and the horses, having received a bucket of water each, advanced with greater spirits. The farther we proceeded, the more verdant did the vegetation become, hillocks and undulations were now frequent, the sand disappeared, and the soil became firmer and argillaceous. About six versts beyond Murat-Lar, and in close proximity to the road, traces of old melon plantations and cultivated fields are visible. The Djefarbaï Turcomans, who roam in this part of the country, cultivate the ground here every year, and, after gathering their harvests, remove to other camping grounds. At one place I receded somewhat from the road, and observed clear traces of an old encampment, and also of fields cultivated by means of regular irrigation. We reached the wells at about 10 o'clock in the morning, or after a journey of five hours from Murat-Lar locality. The place where the wells are situated is called Karadji-Batyr, and represents several sandy hillocks surrounded for about a verst by friable sand. These hillocks are easily distinguishable by their contrast to the argillaceous and affluvial soil in the immediate vicinity of the wells. There are here at present twenty-seven wells, and probably as great a number abandoned, and each well gives, if properly attended to, excellent clear and cool water, especially when it is covered up and left untouched for several hours. We remained at these wells for nearly a whole day, and it was near 7 A.M. before we started further. The road took a sharp turn to the right, as though leading directly into the heart of the steppe. The traces of artificial irrigation continued for about seven versts, and they then disappeared, reappearing again about four versts beyond, though not in the same regular form as at the wells. ' About twelve versts from the wells we arrived at the gates, as it were, of an enormous wall, which bore a greater resemblance to an artificial structure than to a natural conformation of the soil. Three versts beyond this point the valley of the river Atrek appeared in sight, with the river itself winding in zig-zags between high and verdant banks.

" To the left of the road, and on a high mound, stands a little stone edifice, which is called Bayat-Adji, and forms the tomb of a Mussulman who had performed the pilgrimage to Mecca. This monument gives the name to the whole of the surrounding country. There are no settlements here, but the Atabai Turcomans, who are semi-independent and semi-submissive, roam in the neighbourhood. Beyond the Atrek is the Persian frontier, and an old fortified camp, which served to protect our detachments in 1869 and 1872, stands on the bank of the river.

" 10th (22nd) August.—We were compelled to stay at Bayat-Adji a whole week. I rode for a considerable distance down the course of the Atrek, and, in spite of the excessive heat of the last three months, the banks were everywhere covered with luxuriant vegetation. Large bushes, which sometimes approach the size of small trees, grow between the edge of the river and the high shelving banks. Grass grows so abundantly in the valley of the Atrek that thousands of horses might be fed there, and the quality of the grass is very good. About ten versts below Bayat-Adji the banks begin to be boggy. Here a different vegetation presents itself, and with it reeds appear, which, on being brought to the camp by the Turcomans, the horses ate greedily. About forty versts from the mouth of the river in Hasan-Kuli Bay the marshy zone merges into an impassable swamp or 'tundra,' which, from the Russian or right side of the Atrek, is connected with a salt marsh, and from the left, or Persian side, is bordered by steep heights known under the name of the Persian mounds.

"Ascending the Atrek, its very steep banks gradually narrow the basin of the river, and the valley opens out again in the form of small islands in places where the Atrek during its overflow separates into two streams.

"From Bayat-Adji we proceeded up the Atrek to 'Tchat' or 'Tchid,' but the bed of the river is not seen from the road, and the steppe itself presents a picture similar to that on the road from the hills of Kara-Batyr to Bayat-Adji. We continued to advance along an excellent road, which did not, however, run in a straight line, at times approaching nearer to the river and receding from it at other places. On the first day after our departure we traversed twenty versts, and then made a halt. The head of the column had advanced a considerable distance further; the guide having mistaken the road, missed a turning to the Atrek which led to an open space on its banks, where we should have halted. Notwithstanding the fifteen versts that had been uselessly traversed, the column halted about four versts from the Atrek on an open plain, which resembled an enormous terrace. We remained at the foot of this terrace until the following morning. The country here is very picturesque, and masses of thick 'gribinchuk' border the banks, so that at mid-day it is quite shady. This place, at which we halted for a day and night, is called Yatchny-Ulun. On the following day we again struck the old road, and having traversed about twenty versts turned off to the Atrek, and halted until the following morning at Domakh-Olun locality. Domakh-Olun is a very convenient halting-place, and is also somewhat like a terrace, but the descent to it is tedious. The bank is steep to the water on our side, while from the Persian the river is reached by a long wide road. From this place we proceeded for twenty-two versts more and halted at Tchat. The road presented no extraordinary features, and runs close to the Atrek in a tortuous manner. The incline from our side, which comprises the bank of the river, is so full of depressions and holes as to render the cultivation of this bank impossible.

"About ten versts before reaching Tchat the road turned to the left, receding from the Atrek; on the right side large auls, or settlements, are visible at a place called Bairam-Olun (Holiday Ferry), a beautiful river-terrace animated with abundant verdure, but the descents on each side of the stream are narrow and inconvenient. The large auls, the inhabitants of which did not fly from us (though they belonged to the Atabai tribe, who bear us no love), possess large flocks of sheep. Nearly all the shepherds had white asses of an excellent breed. At length we reached Tchat. This is the most repulsive place along the whole Atrek, although, from a strategical point of view, the most important, because it is here that the river Sumbar flows into the Atrek, and the Delta may, if fortified, be converted into an impregnable position. The Sumbar is that dirty stream which, uniting with the waters of the Atrek, makes the latter turbid; the water in the Sumbar is bitter salt, with a mixture of injurious salts, and its narrow stream is of a dirty green colour. We have been already a week at Tchat. Fifty versts higher than Tchat rise two enormous rocks out of the Atrek, forming a sharp delimitation of the geological structure of the country as well as of the river itself. This place is called Su-Sium. Above Su-Sium the water in the Atrek again becomes clear, the bed stony, and the banks covered with a rich vegetation; the grass here grows up to one's waist, and whole copses of oak dot the surface of the country. Wild grapes also grow in abundance. Pheasants are also numerous. Unfortunately the road becomes impassable for camels, and ten versts further on becomes very difficult even for horses. One hundred versts beyond Tchat the course of the Atrek can only be followed on foot, and to make the road practicable three months would at least be required. At the one hundred and eighth verst beyond the ridge of rocks that rise perpendicularly to the Atrek are to be seen ruins of enormous forts, which must have existed at some distant period. Their names were not accurately known. The local inhabitants call them Komnuk-Kala, and on the right side of the Atrek they are called Oklan-Kala. Traces of irrigation are to be seen at this place on all the neighbouring steppes. The bank itself resembles a series of gardens, and the elevated plateau is abundantly covered with grass. It would be possible to depasture any quantity of cattle here, but wildness and desolation reign around.

"For two weeks past the barometer has shown from 35° to 38° Reaumur in the shade. In the sun the temperature far exceeds 40°. In the morning there are only 14°. Rain fell only once for about half an hour in large but few drops. The sky is cloudy only in the morning, and the heat commences at mid-day. The wind, which covers everything with sand, is so violent, especially in the evening, that not unfrequently the tents have been broken. Even inside the tents it is necessary to use lamps for writing at night. The steppe is desolate in appearance from the dust, and the heat, flies, etc., cause no small inconvenience. Life, however, is still possible, even at Tchat."

The second letter is dated August 22nd (September 3rd), and was probably written at Hadjan-Kala.

"In my last letter I informed you that the road along the Atrek, eight versts beyond Su-Sium, proved inconvenient for pack animals, and that it was therefore necessary to abandon the line of the Persian frontier, that is, the course of the Atrek along which we had hitherto proceeded, and to strike a new road. After making the necessary surveys we turned to the left, at a place called Alun-Yak (where there is a ferry across the Atrek, twenty-two versts from Tchat), and proceeded over the high Sugundag chain, after having crossed the bridge which exists between the Atrek and Sumbar. The Sugundag forms, together with these two rivers, a triangle, the smallest angle of which is at the point at which the Atrek receives the Sumbar, and is equal to about 48°, whilst its opposite side, that is, the line of the Sugundag, presents a distance of fifty versts. This line commences at first with a gentle ascent at Alun-Yak, and then rises steeply over an extent of twenty-four versts. At the foot of the most abrupt part of the ascent there are springs of excellent water; these springs are called Kabeli-Katje, and are separated from the steep ascent by a deep precipice. Strangely enough, the water in the springs is completely black, and yet its colour does not affect its taste. The particles of black mud which it holds in suspension are easily precipitated, and the water becomes quite clear. The grasses in the neighbourhood of the springs are very luxuriant, date and pomegranate trees being also found in abundance at this spot. The ascent and descent of the Sugundag, the highest point of which I estimate at two thousand feet, extends over a distance of sixteen versts (ten miles and two-thirds), the descent terminates at the small river Chandyr, which falls into the Sumbar. There is a spring of cold and clear water, containing, however, particles of lime, at the point of junction of the Chandyr with the Sumbar. In spring, it is said that the former stream has a very rapid current, but its appearance, as we observed it in the summer, was not at all imposing.

"At twenty-five versts from Tchat we crossed over

to the left bank of the Sumbar. The country traversed by us along the right bank of this river is of a similar nature to that of the elevated steppe stretching along the Atrek; the chief features are clay, mud, sand, and deep fissures, and hillocks of various shapes, forming narrow, and oftener broad, defiles through which the road trends. There are no considerable elevations. Receding from the Atrek the soil becomes more and more barren, the vegetation scantier, and yellow in appearance, succulent grasses disappear, and prickly shrubs predominate.

"The appearance of the steppe and hillocks is dreary and monotonous; no good water is to be found, that in the Sumbar being bitter and salt to the taste. Our night halt at Har Alun was a very trying one, owing to the scarcity of good water. Commencing from the Chandyr to the point of its fall into the Atrek no drinkable water was found. This can only be explained by the circumstance that both the Chandyr and Sumbar had at this time (August) become dry in many parts of their course, and the remaining water had become impregnated with the saline soil through which these rivers flow.

"At Sharol-Dau, five versts beyond Har Alun, and a verst and a half below the fall of the Chandyr into the Sumbar, we crossed over to the left bank of the Sumbar. After a very difficult passage over the river (the banks being here very high and precipitous), we continued our advance along the left bank of the Sumbar (between the Sumbar and Chandyr), and reached an elevated mountain called Bek-Tepe, belonging to the spurs of the Kurin Dag. The whole distance traversed by us along the bank from the Sharol-Dau and Bek-Tepe is about forty versts; the march was a difficult one, in consequence of the scarcity of water and barren soil. It was only at Bek-Tepe that we again struck the Sumbar; the water here was rather better, though muddy, the bitter saltness of taste having completely disappeared. The course of the Sumbar at this point is more rapid, the volume of water greater, the bed harder, and the evaporation of the river less. Here we again crossed over to the right bank, and proceeded along a bad though deeply-trodden camel's path, and again reached the Sumbar, having receded from it about ten versts in order to strike the head of the defile, which extends between the more elevated spurs of the Kurin Dag, extending perpendicularly in the direction of the Sumbar. This defile, and the locality adjoining the river, is called Ters Akon. Here we finally separated from the Sumbar, and, proceeding through the waterless defiles of the Ters Akon and through the Morgo defile (belonging to the Kaplan Dag range), reached the ruined fort of Hadjan-Kala."

The third and last of these interesting letters was written from Bent-Essent, and bears date September 5 (17).

"Leaving behind us the fortress of Kizil Arvad, where our Cossacks, under Arnoldi, distinguished themselves last year in an unequal combat with the Tekes, we crossed the undetermined though really existing line of frontier between Russian territory and the land inhabited by the Tekes, who recognise no authority over themselves. I consider the extreme point of this line of demarcation to be the fortress of Hadjan-Kala, which is flanked on one side by the Teke fort of Kizil Arvad, and on the other by the Karakala fort; in front, then, is a line of Teke forts, the more important of which are Bami, Buirma, etc.

"The road from the river Sumbar, which we left at Ters Akon, to Hadjan-Kala passes through long defiles formed by the spurs of the Kurin Dag; they are severally known under the names of Dairon, Nishik Sund, Turugai, and Kuvmius. The entrances into these defiles are very narrow, and present the most dangerous places for caravans. The road winds through them along steep ascents and descents, and only two horses can proceed abreast at a time along it. The most dangerous portion of the route terminates at about twelve versts before reaching Hadjan-Kala. It would be neither difficult nor expensive to construct a good road through these defiles; if this were done, the caravans would derive great benefit from it, and the defiles would no longer serve as hiding-places for the marauding Teke bands. Beyond the defiles, in the direction of Hadjan-Kala, the vegetation becomes extremely rich, and wild boar and other game is found in great abundance. In these respects the country is similar to that stretching along the banks of the Atrek.

"In close proximity to Hadjan-Kala stands an old deserted earthwork in the shape of a regular quadrangle, flanked by two conical crenelated towers, about two fathoms in height. The upper platforms of these are protected by a low wall, pierced with apertures for musketry firing. A similar fort, though of smaller dimensions, and with one tower only, is passed at a place three versts before reaching Hadjan-Kala. This kala, or small fort, proved to be a Teke habitation; it was surrounded by cultivated and well-irrigated fields, the water being obtained from a small rivulet which flows through the neighbouring bushes and reeds, and ultimately reaches Hadjan-Kala. Not far from the latter place, and in the middle of the so-called Teke oasis, there is a fine spring, which yields an abundant supply of water, and which forms the source of the rivulet that flows on in the vicinity of the small fort three versts distant from Hadjan-Kala. At this point, from a hill on the right, is obtained a fine view of the Goklan fort of Kara-Kala, and of the surrounding country, which is well cultivated and thickly populated. Ascending a high hill on the left, at Bent-Essent (which likewise stands high), the whole Teke oasis presents itself to the view, dotted with numerous dwellings. On the immediate horizon is seen the fort of Bami, an awkward structure resembling Hadjan-Kala; beyond again appears fort Buirma. The Teke oasis, although producing cotton in some places, cannot be described as a fertile land; small patches of cultivated ground alternate with stretches of brushwood and dry sterile salines."

Up to this date, the middle of last September, the advance of the Chikishlar column had been completely successful, and when the writer of these graphic letters closed his narrative the Russians were on the heights of the Kuren Dagh, looking down on the Akhal country. The events which then followed are by no means clear. A letter from our Minister in Persia, dated the 26th of September, throws some light on the whereabouts of the Russian column at this time, and confirms in one respect the account of the Russian correspondent quoted. He announced that General Lomakine's force was encamped in the vicinity of Kara Kala, and that it was suffering from sickness and want of provisions, whilst there was also great mortality among the camels. It is probable that these causes compelled the Russian general to order a retreat to Chat. On the 14th of October Mr. Thomson telegraphed that the Russians had reached Chat, and that there had been fighting on the road with the Akhals. Chat was then fortified and garrisoned, and Lomakine continued his retreat to Chikishlar. The Akhals appear to have followed him up, and to have inflicted some loss upon him. In consequence of this boldness on the part of the Akhals, he fortified and garrisoned Baiat Khaji, as well as Chat. Later on in the year he returned to Chat with provisions and other necessary stores. But on the 28th of November Lord A. Loftus reported that Lomakine had finally returned to Chikishlar after a two months' campaign in the steppe. From other sources we know that he then proceeded to Tiflis.

The Turcomans appear to have seized the opportunity afforded by the retreat of Lomakine to fortify the position of Khoja or Hadjan Kala, where Mr.

Thomson, on the 29th of October, reported them to be building a fort with a ditch, and with parapets capable of holding guns. It was said that the whole force of the Akhals, with a large contingent of Tekes, was assembled there, and that they had secured as leaders several Afghans of the Jamshedee tribe. The position of Khoja Kala is very strong, and if the Turcomans have anyone among them capable of showing them how to construct earthworks, they can make a good stand there. For reasons already given, it is much to be feared that they themselves do not possess the necessary capacity. But at all events it is at Khoja Kala, and not at any of the Akhal forts in the plain, that these Turcomans appear to have elected to make their chief stand.

The movements of the Chikishlar column are therefore clearly ascertained. It remains only to fix to some extent the operations of the other column, of whose existence the German press first informed us, which advanced on Kizil Arvat from Krasnovodsk. When Lomakine reached the skirts of the Kuren Dagh, as described in the last letter quoted, dated the 17th of September, the Krasnovodsk column had evidently not reached Kizil Arvat, or a junction would have been effected between the two columns. We are therefore compelled to assume that it arrived after Lomakine's force had retreated. The name of the officer commanding this force has not been mentioned, and its actual advance upon Kizil Arvat seems to have been unopposed. Upon the occupation of that place the Akhals appear to have striven to cut off its communications with Krasnovodsk. This, to some extent, they succeeded in doing, as it was reported on good authority that a convoy had been captured, and that the Khoja Shehee tribe of Turcomans, Russian subjects, had been attacked. The advance of the Russian column was, however, unopposed, and it is ascertained that the Russians have not only fortified Kizil Arvat, but also Kizil Tchesme, twenty miles further on. This was probably accomplished early in October, thus leaving ample time for those rumours to have reached us, which were believed in high quarters to be accurate, of the Russians having advanced as far as the important town of Ashkabad. Still more recently we heard that they were coercing the Turcomans of the Tejend swamp, which could only be accomplished from the village of Abiverd, still nearer to Merv and Sarakhs. This later advance, of which we as yet know so little, must have occurred during the month of November. It is probable that if the Russians did advance as far as Ashkabad, it was only a reconnoissance in force, and that, having completed its survey of the road along the Attock, it returned to Kizil Tchesme.

Nothing has been heard of any movement against Khoja Kala from Kizil Arvat, and so long as the Akhals hold this very formidable position in the mountains, it would be hazardous in the extreme for the Russian force to make any further advance towards Abiverd. The Akhals are supposed to be able to bring ten thousand fighting-men into the field, but according to the information current on the Persian frontier twenty-five thousand men were assembled at Khoja Kala. Without accepting this number as correct, it may be admitted that the main fighting-population is collected here, and that consequently the Akhal country has been more or less deserted by its inhabitants. That fact would explain the facility with which the Russians have been able to explore the country as far as the places previously mentioned. There were none left to oppose their advance. More recently still we have heard rumours of a Russian occupation of Guk Tepeh, a place not marked on many maps, which lies a short distance to the north of the Attock road in the desert. This is said to be an admirable strategical position, and destined to become the principal Russian out-post in this quarter.

Since the preceding lines were written the following further information has been received from our Minister at Teheran, and has appeared in "Further Official Correspondence on Central Asia." The following extracts therefrom are far from being as clear as could be wished, but they are the latest information upon the subject (March 1st), although evidently in many cases being the mere rumour of native travellers.

A private letter from Astrabad, dated the 16th September, confirms the general accuracy of the earlier reports. It is as follows:—

"Yesterday a man came in from the Russian camp. He reported that the troops remained three days at Kara Kala, and their provisions running short, they sent to the Goklan tribe to procure some. That tribe, however, made excuses, saying that they had no means of transport. They then applied to the inhabitants of Kara Kala, who are a mixture of Teke and Yomult Turcomans; they also proffered some excuse. Afterwards they despatched one thousand camels to Chikishlar to bring provisions. Noor Verdee Khan, chief of the Teke Turcomans, and the chiefs of Merv and Akhal, have bound themselves to fight. It is also said that thirty persons in the Afghan costume have appeared amongst the Teke tribes; some say they are Afghans, whilst others say they are Englishmen; that two elders of the Teke tribe recently came with two hundred horsemen to the Russian general, but he refused to admit the latter into the camp. The elders then asked the general why he did not allow the horsemen to enter the camp, upon which General Lomakine got angry, and ordered the elders to be arrested, whilst the horsemen returned; the general, however, afterwards released the elders, and made them a present of money. It appears that the Russians afterwards went to Khoja Kala, which is a strong place between Kara Kala and Kizil Arvat, and encamped there. The Teke tribes are mustering in great force. The troops are suffering greatly from the brackish water and unhealthy climate. It is rumoured that General Lomakine has sent word to the Teke tribes that if they allow the Russian flag to be hoisted amongst them, and a garrison to protect it, he would return; but they had replied that as long as they lived they would not allow such a thing, and that they would fight, as the Merv Turcomans and the Afghans were with them also."

The Astrabad Agent sent later intelligence on the 6th of October :—

"Authentic news has been received that the Russian troops were obliged to make a retreat from Khoja Kala. The Teke Turcomans besieged their camp for two days, and at last General Lomakine retreated fighting. The Tekes then went and intercepted the caravan coming with provisions from Krasnovodsk; they carried off the whole of it, consisting of three hundred camels laden with grain. Small garrisons have been left at Chat and Baiat Khaji. The general has returned to Chikishlar with the intention of making a second expedition against the Turcomans. The Daz Davajee tribes have revolted, and the prince governor is only waiting for the arrival of money from Teheran to form another camp at Ak Kala."

A private letter from Astrabad, presumably from the same source as the previous one, dated October 16, 1878, continues the narrative :—

"After General Lomakine returned from Khoja Kala, he came to Chat, and thence went to Baiat Khaji. The Teke horse followed him everywhere, and he retreated fighting until he got to Gumesh Teppeh. He left some men at Chat. The Tekes carried off a caravan of provisions, with the chief of the caravan, as well as two Cossacks. As for the report that seventy of the Turcomans were killed, it is false. Intelligence was received yesterday that a new official had arrived from Russia, with a sum of twelve thousand tomans, who is buying up the Pampas grass at the rate of five or six krans per camel load, and storing it up. They are building a fort at Charkan, and have hoisted the Russian flag there, engaging the Turcomans of that place as servants. They have purchased one hundred Turcoman tents, and are purchasing others. They are also building a fort at Chat. The Merv and Teke Turcomans, accompanied by the Jemsheedee Afghans, have come to Khoja Kala, whence the Russians fled, and are fortifying the place and digging a moat round the fort, under the directions of some Afghans. About twenty-five thousand Teke horse are now assembled here, and they are strengthening all the passes. All the Charva Yomults have removed from those districts through fear of the Teke Turcomans. Some have come to the Gurgan valley, and some have gone to the Atrek. The Tekes are daily increasing in force and numbers. A report was also received that two thousand of them have gone in the direction of Bujnoord to make a raid. Affairs are in a bad state at present."

The Meshed Agent wrote on October 22, stating that he had received a letter from a friend at Sarakhs, to the effect that news had been received from Chehar Jong (Charjui?) that a party of Russian troops had been seen sailing up the Jaxartes, but that it was unknown whether they were going to Afghanistan or elsewhere.

The following telegram was received from Teheran on the 16th of January:—

"It would seem that the Russian detachment at Chat, consisting of six hundred men, is in a critical position. The place is said to be surrounded by the

Akhal Turcomans. They have also attacked Chikishlar, and carried off all the camels collected there from under the guns of the Ashourada squadron sent to protect the place."

As has been said, it is necessary to make a considerable allowance from these various sources of information. At the least, what they report is exaggerated, and in some instances probably wholly false. Yet there is a sub-stratum of fact in them. The last telegram of all is misleading, for Chat had been placed in a position capable of resisting the attack of the Akhals, and was not likely to be in a critical position although surrounded by the Turcomans. It is also clear that Persia has assembled an army at Ak Kala, but that it melts away when money is not forthcoming.

General Lomakine, who, after placing the garrison of Chat in a condition to defend themselves against attack, paid a visit to Tiflis, probably for the purpose of obtaining further instructions, has now, by a still later telegram, arrived at Kizil Arvat from Krasnovodsk, probably with fresh troops. The first undertaking which he will have to perform will be to disperse the Turcomans who have collected at Khoja Kala. The attack will be made up the Sumbur river by a column from Chat, and also from Kizil Arvat. If the Russians make the attack in anything like the force which they are said to possess here, there cannot be two opinions about the result. The Turcomans will be completely overthrown. Of the result of the fight at this place, which will probably come off in the spring, we shall be quickly apprised from Persia, where there is well-founded apprehension at Russia's activity in this quarter, more especially since the Turcomans have given earnest of their desire to be good Persian subjects. The overthrow of the Akhals at Khoja Kala, and the capture of that place, will, it must be remembered, mean the collapse of the Akhal defence. These people have elected to defend a strong position in the Kuren Dagh in preference to retreating upon Merv, and there combining with the Tekes in a stubborn resistance against their foe, upon whose long line of communications they could act with terrible effect. The strategy of the Turcomans should be that of the Parthians, whose country they are defending in this nineteenth century against the inroads of a Western Power, and from whose history, if they were but acquainted with it, the Tekes might derive the most practical advice. The capture of Khoja Kala, and a victory over the Akhals, will not only leave the country up to Abiverd open for an immediate advance, but must influence the policy of Persia in a manner favourable to Russian interests.

In the meanwhile Lomakine is represented to be making every preparation for the forthcoming campaign, on which the fate of the Turcomans, and to some extent of Merv itself, depends. Vast quantities of stores are alleged to have been forwarded to Kizil Arvat, and agents are busy purchasing camels from the Kirghiz far away on the northern steppes. At Uralsk in particular there is reason to say that large purchases have lately been made. These preparations shadow forth a campaign on a much larger scale than any that has as yet taken place, and they point conclusively to some more extended design than an attack upon the Akhal clan. The Russian press is unanimous in declaring that the occupation of Merv has been rendered necessary by the triumphs of this country in Afghanistan, and there can be no doubt that the Russian authorities are disposed to look with a friendly eye upon the suggested expedition against Merv. The continued presence of Colonel Grotenhelm with a body of troops—supposed to be nearly two thousand in all —at Charjui, gives further consistency to these reports, and with the overthrow of the Akhals we shall be on the verge of the acute and final stage of the long-talked-of Merv question.

Sir Henry Rawlinson declared, in a paper read in January before the Royal Geographical Society on the subject of the road to Merv from the Caspian, that an advance on the part of Russian troops in this direction would be easy if Persia were friendly; that it could be done, but with difficulty, if Persia were neutral; but that it would be impossible if Persia were inimical to it. Like everything else that Sir Henry Rawlinson has written upon the Central Asian subject, this paper should be most carefully studied, and by its perusal many idle fears may be removed. It should, however, be remembered, that we can only consider Persia as either friendly or neutral to Russia in this matter. It is out of the question to suppose that Persia would dare, even were she disposed—of which there is no evidence—to manifest hostility or ill-will towards Russia. Persia is completely under her thumb, and both from Trans-Caucasia and the Caspian, Russia has so many ways of coercing her that she dare not adopt even covert hostility on the frontiers of Khorasan. It undoubtedly lies in the power of this country, if Russia will remain quiescent for six months longer, to do something in the direction of strengthening Persia's hand, but at present Persia is helpless. We have it, therefore, on the highest living authority, that with Persia neutral an advance on Merv is possible, and for several reasons it is probable that, though Persia cannot have any sympathy with Russian schemes in Turcomania, she would so far assist General Lomakine's army as to permit supplies to pass through the Kuren Dagh from Kooshan, Bujnoord, and other frontier towns, to it. It would be practically impossible for the Persian authorities to stop that trade, although they certainly might throw obstacles in its way. Therefore Russia would most probably receive all the assistance she could reasonably expect from Persia if she made her advance against Merv during the coming summer, that is while the present conditions obtain.

Sir Henry Rawlinson made one statement which is of the very highest importance. He said there was every reason to believe that an army advancing on Merv would have to follow the recognised road to Sarakhs, and thence on to Merv. A route is marked across the desert to Merv from Artok, but this is probably unavailable for an army. The distance from Artok to Merv is, however, only seventy miles. The Russian army, therefore, advancing from the Caspian would find itself installed in Sarakhs before it had entered Merv. This observation possesses practical significance. It would require considerable boldness on the part of a Russian general to occupy Sarakhs, which is within the recognised Persian frontier, and if Lomakine possesses the necessary audacity, it is safe to assume that he would not hesitate to do more and to go still farther. It will be seen that the temptation to do so would be very great.

The importance of Sarakhs cannot be over-estimated. Its position is extremely happy, enjoying all the trade benefits of Merv, and free from many of the disadvantages which attend that place. In a military sense it is still more important, for it commands the approaches to Herat even more effectually than Merv does. The large fort which stands here only requires a few alterations to be made very strong, and perhaps impregnable, and the Turcomans could be effectually coerced by a strong force garrisoned at Sarakhs. In this respect its advantages are most apparent, for by establishing herself at Sarakhs, and by menacing movements on the Oxus, Russia might succeed in maintaining some temporary arrangement with the Turcomans which would prevent any collision between Lomakine and the main body of the Tekes. It must always be borne in mind that one of the best cards Russia can play in her dealings with the Turcomans is to promise not to occupy Merv. That promise, assisted by the effect produced by the overthrow of the Akhals—if they are, as it appears, resolved to resist to the bitter end— might very possibly secure the object which the Russian diplomatists would have in view. Once for all, it must again be asserted that the Tekes are not as yet bitterly hostile to Russia. They do not love her, because they perceive that she has aggressive purposes towards themselves; and it is because they know that England can have none, that their inclinations point to an alliance with this country, if such were possible. But inclinations will have very little to do with the matter. As the Turcomans expressed the opinion long ago to that intrepid traveller, Dr. Wolfe, they did not care who it was who ruled over them "so long as they received khelats—robes of honour—and tillahs—ducats." That sentence throws a flood of light upon Turcoman nature, and such as it was then there is good reason for saying it still remains.

The Merv question, therefore, assumes this strange aspect, that it is possible that its most critical stage will come when Merv itself still retains a nominal independence. A Russian force at Sarakhs secures the double object that it commands Merv while it menaces Herat. If there be, as is alleged, a way by the Heri Rud, Sarakhs is at the head of the best and shortest road to Herat—the distance being only one hundred and eighty miles, with water procurable throughout the whole journey. After all, then, the Merv question resolves itself into the Herat. The road to Merv is only another way of expressing the road to Herat. The road to Sarakhs is a still more significant form of the same expression. If Herat is the "key of India," there is no less doubt on the point that Merv and Sarakhs are the keys of Herat. They each command the only approaches to that town by the banks of rivers, the one by the Murghab, the other by the Heri Rud, and both contain sufficient supplies to form the base for a considerable army. The plains round Merv sustain a large population; the latter is situated in close proximity to Meshed and the Persian frontier, and water can always be obtained there twenty feet below the surface of the sand. Between Sarakhs and Kizil Arvat there lies a succession of natural fortresses that would be most useful to a general in maintaining his line of communication with the Caspian. Some of these are well known, such as Khelat-i-Nadiri, and Mahomedabad; others are not so frequently mentioned, as Guk Tepeh and Kabuchak.

The importance of the Merv question is therefore to be found exclusively in the fact that it is the preliminary step to an active intervention in the affairs of Herat. We are told that Russia desires to occupy Merv for the purpose of connecting her possessions on the Oxus with the Caspian, but persons who mention this as an excuse for Russia's desire to occupy that place surely forget what a very round-about road it will be from Charjui to Merv, Merv to Sarakhs, and Sarakhs to Krasnovodsk—a road, moreover, which lies for a large portion of the way through desert offering every conceivable hindrance to commerce. It is in vain to try to discover in a Russian occupation of Merv any benefit to general trade other than that between Turkestan and Persia. It will take generations to bring back prosperity to Merv and the neighbourhood; and judging from what Russia has done in Turkestan, there is every reason for saying that the Russian administrators once installed in Merv would trouble their heads very little about the reclamation of the country. The occupation of Merv would be essentially military, and it would only be regarded as a temporary halting-stage on the road to Herat. The occupation of Sarakhs would still more forcibly suggest the same view of things. When considering the Herat question, later on, we may amplify this view of the case; but here we may insist upon the vital importance of the Merv question as the preliminary stage of the still greater one.

With a Russian force at either Sarakhs or Merv, and with Persia and the Herat authorities benevolently disposed, it would be absurd to say that there could be a race for Herat between England and Russia, even though at that moment we should have an army on the Helmund. Not only would Russia be one hundred miles nearer the goal than we, but her advance would be through a friendly country, to assist a people whom nominally we were about to invade and attack. Our march would to some extent be retarded, hers would be facilitated and expedited. We should therefore face this Merv question boldly and without hesitation, for it means more or less the solution of the Herat question as well. It is not a question of a race between the two great powers for the all-important town of Herat. The possession of that town must never be for a single instant a matter of doubt or speculation. So long as England desires to preserve her Indian Empire, Herat must never fall into dubious hands. The capture of Merv or of Sarakhs would most nearly menace it. Our reputation, such as it is in these parts, would still further decline, and our dearest interests would be jeoparded. A Russian army in these places would be the death-knell of the independence of Herat, and to oust a Russian army from that strong position would require, as all military authorities testify, an effort of the greatest magnitude on our part.

Long ago, when his countrymen were lapped in a full but false sense of security, Sir Henry Rawlinson spoke the prophetic words, which then fell mostly upon idle ears, that the day which witnessed the Russians at Merv should find the English at Herat. Since then we have grown wiser, mainly through the indefatigable warnings and wise counsel of Sir Henry Rawlinson, and events have moved so fast in Central Asia and in Afghanistan that something more is now necessary. It is clear that if we permit Russia to occupy Merv we shall not have the option of reaching Herat on the morrow of that event. We must therefore forestall Russia. It is beyond dispute that Russia is aiming at Merv both from Charjui and from the Caspian, and it is equally incontestible that the collapse of the Akhal powers of defence will clear the way for an advance to Sarakhs. The progress of events in the Akhal country must therefore be closely watched, and the instant Lomakine's columns advance on Ashkabad the heads of our regiments must be turned towards Herat. A distinct menace to either Sarakhs or Merv on the part of either Lomakine or Grotenhelm must be followed by the occupation of Herat. It would be sheer folly to trifle with a danger of such vital consequence.

Nor should it be left out of sight that not the least of the advantages that would accrue to this country from the occupation of Herat would be the fact that in face of England strongly placed in that city the Russians would not dare to assail Merv. Not only would the Turcomans voluntarily ally themselves with us when we had garrisoned Herat, the dominant place in all Khorasan; but the exigencies of our position would lead to our forming a close connection with them. From Herat it would be so easy to supply the Tekes with arms that the opportunity would certainly not be thrown away. But from Herat—and this is the great point—we should be able to influence the policy of Persia, and by giving consistency to Persia's carefully concealed apprehension at Russia's designs raise up another bulwark to the ambition of that Power. With the Turcomans' hostility rendered formidable by improved weapons, with Persia distrustful and covertly hostile, protesting and preserving her strict neutrality on the guarantee of the English army at Herat, and with an Anglo-Indian garrison of twenty thousand men in Herat, Russia would not dare to move against Merv, and it is most probable that she would have to withdraw from all the country up to the Caspian sea. This is the bold and practical solution of the Merv question. The danger can now be nipped in the bud by garrisoning Herat, and by taking up a firm position in the council chamber at Teheran. There must be no bullying in our dealings with the Shah, but by a bold act it lies in our power to prove to the mind of that prince that we have resolved that Russia has now reached the farthest limit in her career southward which is compatible with the safety of India. The solution of the Merv question means the solution of the Central Asian Question in its earliest stage. If Russia's policy in Persia be counter-mined, if the Turcomans preserve their independence through our well-timed aid, Lomakine and his superiors will have to turn elsewhere if they still desire to reach the Indus. They will have to abandon their policy of sap and mine, and adopt bolder measures, and a more proclaimed hostility. They will have to crush the resistance of Northern Persia, and assemble their hosts on the shores of the Caspian. They will have to advance, not with fifty thousand men, but with two hundred thousand men, if not still more, and to accept all the risks and enormous outlay of a great war carried on in Khorasan amidst a hostile population. The time necessary for the preparation of such a host as this would alone take years, and until Russia produces a Napoleon it would be practically impossible. Even a superhuman genius would find the task of advancing upon the Indus under the circumstances described one that could only be compared to Napoleon's march on Moscow. The ramparts of Herat have retarded invading armies for months, and engineers could with great ease convert the enormous fortress round Herat into one that should be impregnable. But Herat is only the first, if the most important, of the outer and true defences of India.

Behind it lie Giranch and Ferrah, the Helmund, and the citadel of Candahar. By treating the Merv question as a vital portion of the Central Asian, by regarding the stronghold of the Turcomans as the key to Herat, and as consequently also the key to India, we may achieve the greatest of results. Far away though that speck in the desert may appear from the frontiers of India, its importance is to be gauged by the relation it bears to Herat, to which it is so close. Of the importance of Sarakhs there can be not less doubt, and in some respects the danger there is the more formidable, because the less recognised and the more insidious. The occupation of Herat is for many other reasons necessary, but among the principal must be held the great influence which it will have upon the future of Merv and the action of the Turcomans. The day which witnesses the arrival of British troops in Herat will also behold the retreat of the Russian columns from the vicinity of Merv, provided, of course, that that place had not already been occupied. It is to be hoped that that time is not far distant, for with each day's hesitation on our part Russia's hold on the approaches to Merv becomes more firm, and the defences of that place, which are the half-heartedness of Persia, and the hostility of the Turcomans themselves, less calculated to withstand the forces of General Lomakine. In no quarter is there greater necessity to pursue a bold and far-sighted policy than on the frontiers of Persia and the Turcomans.

297

CHAPTER XI.

BALKH, KUNDUS, AND BADAKSHAN.

IT will not be out of place to say something, before passing on to other subjects, of those khanates which lie north of the Hindoo Koosh, and which are best known as Afghan Turkestan. As a matter of fact, they are now the Afghan provinces in Turkestan, but they have not always been Afghan provinces. Very often, too, the authority of the Cabul ruler has not extended beyond the city of Balkh, and the claims of Bokhara to exercise supremacy over the khanates have been considered to be quite as good as those of Afghanistan. In fact, Balkh has become a bone of contention between these two States, but to exercise suzerainty over Kundus and Badakshan, Bokhara has fewer claims than Cabul. Over Balkh itself, it will be found that history proves their claims to be almost on a par, but independence has been the normal condition of these districts. As the most important of these places, we will consider the history of Balkh first, although it will be difficult to separate them from each other, as they are closely intertwined. Of the early history of Balkh we possess only the vague description of ancient legends. It is said by some to have been founded by Zoroaster; others attribute its magnificence to the great Cyrus; others, again, assert that it was founded by Kaïamur, a prince of the Pishdadian dynasty. But whoever was its actual founder, there can be no doubt that when Alexander visited it Bactra, or Balkh, was a most prosperous city, and when the Chinese traveller, Hwen Thsang, came there in the sixth century it had lost little of its importance. Its great antiquity is proved to some degree by the title which it has obtained from the Persians of *Oumme el Belaud*—the mother of cities. From the Macedonian to the Mongol conqueror, that is through fifteen centuries, is a long stride to make without finding anything of sufficient interest to mention in the life of a State, even though that State be in Central Asia. Yet such is the case with Balkh. When Genghis Khan appeared before the walls of Balkh it still retained much of its old grandeur. But from him it received the most ruthless treatment. Not only was it destroyed, so far as it was possible to destroy it, but its inhabitants were almost annihilated. To some extent it rose from its ashes, but only to meet with an equally hard fate at the hands of Timour. From this second shock Balkh never recovered, but, despite the petty wars of which this region has been the scene ever since, this city still stands forth the undisputed capital of the region lying between the Oxus and the

Hindoo Koosh. Its position is certainly the most favourable, and the neighbourhood is also the most productive in this very considerable tract of territory. It may yet recover its long-departed prosperity.

In the early days of the sixteenth century the Usbegs over-ran the countries between the Syr Darya and the Hindoo Koosh, and established their authority in Balkh and Kundus among other places. Until the time of Nadir Shah the Usbegs ruled without encountering any formidable opposition, but that conqueror turned aside in his advance against India, after he had overthrown the Afghans, and subdued Balkh. Upon his death, in 1747, the authority of Ahmed Khan, who had been made king of the Afghans by a popular vote, was recognised in Balkh without demur, and he appears to have established a garrison and governor there. Kundus and Khulm both acknowledged his supremacy, and even Badakshan was at one time conquered by him, and is said to have sent him tribute. The death of Ahmed was, however, the signal to the chiefs of Kundus and of Khulm to throw off the yoke, and thus commenced the intrigues of these families which ultimately gave them the foremost place in this portion of Turkestan. Ahmed's son Timour sent three armies against the rebellious ruler of Kundus, but, though these were commanded by his best general, Sirdar Jehan Khan, they each failed. When Timour advanced across the Hindoo Koosh to wage war with Bokhara, it was thought that the Kundus chief would at once submit, but he did not. The chief events of that war have already been narrated, and Timour was so glad to be enabled to return to Cabul, that he forgot to enforce his rights over Kundus. The Bokharan ruler, Mourad Shah, speedily began to intrigue in, and to attack these petty States, and in a short time he had practically annexed everything west of Kundus, save the towns of Balkh and Khulm.

In the latter place at this time an independent ruler was beginning to assert his authority. His name was Killich Ali, and under Ahmed Khan he had held the title of Athalik, which in this case may be considered to be equivalent to Vizier. The growing weakness of the Afghan government afforded him his opportunity, and, shortly after the departure of Timour, Killich Ali was a semi-independent ruler in the country from Khulm to Hazrat Imam upon the Oxus. He availed himself of his Afghan title to secure authority over Balkh, and with the Kundus chief he allied himself by marriage. By these means Killich Ali made himself dictator in the countries north of the Hindoo Koosh. His authority was rendered secure by the skilful policy which he pursued towards the Afghan rulers, and although Afghanistan was disturbed by the rival pretensions of the Sudosye princes, he appears to have steered clear through all the difficulties that arose when Zemaun, Mahmoud, and Shuja-ul-Mulk strove to obtain the supreme place. His power was really very formidable, for under his immediate control he had an army of twelve thousand men, mostly cavalry, and from Kundus he could obtain at least five thousand more. He had also that most necessary of all weapons for a prince ruling over such a people as the Usbegs, a settled revenue, which probably amounted in all to thirty thousand pounds. His reputation was very great in all the countries of Central Asia, and travellers declared that in no country were they more exempt from unjust duties, and afforded better protection.

Upon the death of Killich Ali confusion appears to have broken out in Khulm itself and Balkh; and once more Bokharan authority is said to have been asserted in these far-off dependencies. But that reassertion of authority was for a very brief space. We have already mentioned that Killich Ali had allied himself by marriage with the Kundus chief. It is now necessary to turn to that chief, who appears to have acquiesced in the supremacy of, rather than actually submitted to, Killich Ali. Khokan, or Khauldaud, Beg, as he has been indifferently called, chief of the Kataghan branch of the Usbegs, had become the principal ruler in Kundus some time before the close of the last century. Although recognising the claims of Killich Ali, he was probably only biding his time until the occasion should offer for asserting himself in Turkestan. It was towards the east, however, that he first turned his attention, and in 1804 he harried Badakshan, retiring without making any permanent addition to his territory. In 1820 he occupied Balkh, and shortly after this great success he died, leaving to his son Mourad a considerable State, with a large army and a flourishing revenue.

With the accession of Mourad to power a new era commenced in this region, for early in his rule he had firmly established his power as far west as the khanate of Maimenè, and treated on terms of equality with Dost Mahomed, then becoming supreme in Cabul. In 1823 he began a series of expeditions into Badakshan, which resulted in the overthrow of the Mirs of that country, and in the substitution of his authority for that of the native princes. In the year mentioned, a great battle was fought at Taishkan, where the Badakshis, under their chief Miryar Beg, made a gallant stand in defence of their independence. The army on either side consisted of about ten thousand men, but Mourad Beg's superiority in cavalry and artillery gave him the victory. Six years later on Mourad formally annexed Badakshan, whose powers of resistance were crushed on the field of Taishkan, and he installed in Faizabad a governor of his own creation. The later years of his reign witnessed the extension of his authority over Wakhan, and in Shignan, Roshan, and even Hissar, he appears to have asserted his claims to exercise suzerain rights. Thus was the strong Usbeg rule, which had been founded by Khokan Beg in Kundus and extended into Balkh, carried by the talent of that ruler's son into Badakshan; and a consolidated State under the authority of Mourad Beg existed from the border of the Turcoman desert to the Pamir and the sources of the Oxus. For twenty years and more this state of things continued, and when Captain John Wood visited Kundus he was able to say that "countries in former times closed to the traveller may now, with Mourad Beg's protection, be as safely traversed as British India."

This chief possessed a standing army of more than fifteen thousand horsemen, in addition to a local militia which could be called out when emergency required. The Usbeg horse, which is a smaller breed than, but somewhat similar to, the Turcoman, is particularly well adapted for mountain warfare, and this chief owed his foremost position as much to the excellence of his cavalry as to any other circumstance. During the years of Mourad Beg's government Dost Mahomed was steadily extending his authority south of the mountains, but so long as he was absorbed by his relations with the Sikhs and ourselves, so long was he unable to interfere in the progress of affairs in Turkestan. He therefore acquiesced in the suspension of Cabul's sovereign rights. Indeed he had no alternative. Moreover, Mourad Beg had never shown any ill-feeling towards him, and the best of relations possible under the circumstances subsisted between the two States of Kundus and Cabul.

Like so many other Asiatic rulers who have established their authority in their native State and its vicinity by a bold foreign policy of military activity, Mourad's home policy was not free from weakness and crime. His great ambition was to increase the population of his own State of Kundus, and the first use to which he turned his conquests was to carry off from them a certain number of the inhabitants to people his own province. In itself this was a highly laudable desire, but when he depopulated Badakshan in order to people Kundus he committed not only a very violent and unjust, but also a very unwise act, for the Badakshis brought down to the pestiferous atmosphere of Kundus died off as fast as they arrived. There is an old saying in this region, proved true by experience, that "if you wish to die you should go to Kundus." Sir Alexander Burnes had an interview with this redoubtable personage on his journey to Bokhara, and has left the following description of him in his inimitable book of travels. "The chief was a man of tall stature, with harsh Tartar features; his eyes were small to deformity, his forehead broad and frowning, and he wanted the beard which adorns the countenance in most Oriental nations." Burnes does not appear to have formed as favourable an opinion of this ruler as Captain Wood did some years later on; but taken on the whole Mourad Beg seems to have been a wise and astute ruler. His death in 1844 was a loss to all the people north of the Hindoo Koosh.

Much of his authority then passed to another Usbeg chief, Mahomed Ali Khan, Wali of Khulm. Ferrier calls this chief Mahomed Ameen. He had been Wali of Khulm under the Kundus ruler, Mourad Beg, and when the latter died he appears to have succeeded to that supreme position among the Usbegs which had been enjoyed by Killich Ali, of Khulm, before Khokan Beg and his son Mourad. Mourad's own son, Mir Rustem Khan, continued to be Governor of Kundus, recognising, however, in the Khulm chief a superior. Such have been the vicissitudes of fortune among the Usbeg chieftains. For a time Badakshan also remained a vassal province after the death of its conqueror, and its governor was Gendj Ali Beg, son of the Khulm ruler. Probably before the death of Mourad the Ameer of Bokhara had re-asserted his claims over Balkh, but these were never exercised very firmly. Before the year 1846 they had become again shadowy in the extreme, and if there was a nominal Bokharan governor he certainly could do nothing in defiance of the mandates of the ruler of Khulm.

In that year war broke out between Dost Mahomed and the Wali of Khulm, because the latter refused the Ameer permission to march an army through his State against Bokhara, with whom the Ameer had a deadly feud. Dost Mahomed, enraged at the refusal, said that "what was refused to friendship he should take by force." As to have granted this demand would have been to surrender his independence, it is not strange to find that the smaller potentate of Khulm refused the request of his powerful and ambitious neighbour. This was the ostensible cause of the war which then broke out, but Ferrier says that " according to the best-informed persons " the real origin of it was the refusal of Mir Wali to restore a slave of whom Akbar Khan, the Dost's eldest son, had become enamoured. But whatever the origin of this war may have been, it continued for several years in a desultory manner, the Afghan army being commanded by Akhram Khan, one of Dost Mahomed's sons. Later on the Ameer himself took command of his troops and speedily brought the struggle to a termination. In 1850 Balkh and Khulm were occupied and an Afghan governor was installed in the former city. These Afghan successes north of the Hindoo Koosh were extremely distasteful to Bokhara, and both countries raised armies in preparation for a contest. For the time being that danger was staved off, apparently through mutual apprehension. Later on, while the Persian war was in progress and the Afghan people were with difficulty being restrained by their rulers from breaking into the Punjab, the Ameer provided the military ardour of his people with a vent by attacking the khanate of Kundus. Little resistance was encountered there, and Kundus was completely conquered and annexed in the course of the year 1859. This success was followed up by the invasion of Badakshan.

The countries which lie round the upper waters of the Oxus present many features of interest both to the historical and the ethnological observer, and of these Badakshan is the principal. The chiefs of these States lay claim to a descent from Alexander, and certain historians have told us that the claims of the King of Darwaz, in particular, have been admitted to be well founded by his neighbours. We possess such meagre records of the past history of Badakshan that it would be next to impossible to give any account of its native line of Mirs or chiefs. We know, however, that the Emperor Baber established a cousin of his there as ruler, and that this dynasty continued to rule until about the middle of the last century, shortly before Ahmed Khan's general, Shah Wali Khan, occupied it for his master. The Afghans speedily evacuated it, contenting themselves with carying off some relics of great importance, among which was the supposed shirt of Mahomed, which in Mahomedan eyes was a prize of the highest value. At the beginning of the present century it was ruled by a chieftain named Sultan Mahomed, and he possessed a revenue computed at sixty thousand pounds sterling and an armed force of about ten thousand men. He was succeeded by his son Miryar Beg, who was routed, as already described, by Mourad Beg at the battle of Taishkan.

When Dost Mahomed resolved upon invading Badakshan he found that the undertaking had been simplified for him by a revolution in that State. The lawful ruler had been deposed and a younger branch of his family enthroned in his stead. Dost Mahomed resolved to support the rightful cause, and by his aid Mir Jehandir Shah was re-installed on the seat of his ancestors in Faizabad. That prince recognised the Ameer as his liege lord, and paid tribute accordingly. He continued to exercise authority until the year 1867, when he was deposed by Afzul Khan, then ruling in Cabul, in favour of his cousin Mir Mahomed Shah. At this time the tribute money amounted to fifty thousand rupees.

From 1859 until his death in 1867 Faiz Mahomed, one of the sons of the Dost, was governor in Afghan Turkestan, and, after his death in a battle near Bamian, he was succeeded by his nephew Abderrahman, who in his turn was supplanted by his cousin, Shere Ali's son, Ibrahim. These changes in authority north of the Hindoo Koosh reflected the result of the war south of it between Shere Ali and his brothers. Latterly,

Ibrahim, who does not seem to possess any great ability, has exercised his authority by deputy; but the result of all these changes has been that the claims of Bokhara have sunk more and more into the background, and that, so far as our information goes, the various Usbeg ruling families would appear to have disappeared. The Afghans have, however, always employed their power in this region for moderate ends, and have interfered but very slightly with the privileges of the Usbeg people, so that it is quite possible that descendants of the old Usbeg rulers remain. But, politically speaking, Afghan Turkestan forms a province recognising the authority of the Ameer of Cabul, and the residence of Shere Ali for a considerable period near Balkh a few months ago proves that the Afghan power was as strongly consolidated north of the Hindoo Koosh as was assumed during the Granville-Gortchakoff negotiations in 1872. By those diplomatic arrangements it was decided that all the country south of the Oxus was Afghan territory, and consequently beyond the sphere of Russia's action. The clearly-defined barrier of this great river was then sought to be imposed as a check in the path of Russia's progress towards India. This was decided upon not by any uncertain arguments in favour of Bokharan claims over this region from a historical stand-point, but by the incontestable facts that the Duranis had exercised authority therein, with only short periods of independence on the part of some local magnate, and that Shere Ali was *de facto* ruler over all this region.

It is impossible as yet to predict what the future of

this part of Afghanistan will be. The claims of the late Ameer will certainly not be held by Russia to be forfeited if she consider it politic to indulge in sympathy with his successor, should he persist in that policy towards us which ultimately cost Shere Ali his crown. But, in addition, there is the ambition of Abderrahman, who has a strong party in this province, and only requires a sum of money to enforce what he has always considered his lawful claims. Still more perplexing to the Tashkent statesmen is the vanity of Mozaffur Eddin of Bokhara, who sees in the misfortunes of the Barucksyes the very opportunity which he has most desired. The future of Afghan Turkestan is one of the most perplexing questions in the final settlement of the Afghan crisis. On no point is there greater uncertainty, and on none is it permissible for people to entertain more various opinions. History tells us that it has only been when Cabul has been flourishing that the khanates north of the Hindoo Koosh have been closely knit to the central authority; and whatever else may be the result of the Afghan war it may safely be predicted that the Ameer's authority can in future be but feebly supported in his outlying dependencies. So far as the war has yet gone, the English victories have struck a blow at the life of the Barucksye dynasty from which it is doubtful if it can recover. Yet, if this family is to be restored, as appears probable at present, we must face the prospect of witnessing an enfeebled administration retaining nominal possession of places of vital importance to this country. If we fail to take the full measure of the results of the present Afghan war in this respect we may find that our retirement from the State will be the signal for disturbances in Herat and Afghan Turkestan.

Before closing this volume we may say a few words about Wakhan, the small territory lying north of the Hindoo Koosh, between the Chitral country and the Pamir khanate of Shignan. It has at all times been in some kind of subjection to Badakshan, which it touches on the west. Its inhabitants are considered to be of a purer Aryan stock even than the Tajik, and their language is very much akin to Sanscrit or Takri. Their numbers are, however, limited, and the country they hold is barren and inhospitable in the extreme; nevertheless it has, as will be seen, its important functions. In the sixteenth century Baber established a dynasty in Badakshan in the person of a cousin, and that rule continued down to the middle of the last century in this family. Their authority was effaced in the western portion of their State by the inroads of Nadir Shah and Ahmed Khan. About the year 1760 this line became extinct, and a fresh ruling family of Mirs was installed in its place. They likewise ruled in Wakhan and over Shignan, although expelled from Balkh and Kundus, at first by Afghan and at last by Usbeg valour. When Mourad Beg overthrew Miryar Beg, of Badakshan, and annexed his dominions as described, Wakhan passed from a state of subjection to Faizabad to a similar condition under Kundus. Mahomed Rahim Khan, the Mir of Wakhan at the time of Captain Wood's visit, when Wakhan was a

tributary of Mourad Beg, traced his descent from
Alexander, and ruled as a semi-independent prince in
Wakhan, Sirikol, and Sarhadd. His lineage did not
save him from the wrath of the Usbeg ruler, and he
was murdered in the presence of Mourad Beg while
explaining the absence of his tribute money. When
the Usbeg power was overcome by the Afghan, Wakhan so far became Afghan that it retained its old
relations with the Badakshi Mirs, who acknowledged
themselves to be Afghan vassals. That order of
things is still undisturbed. Faizabad pays tribute to
Cabul, and Wakhan bears its own small share of the
levy at the present moment. Such was the state of
things quite recently, and Wakhan is consequently a
dependency of Cabul.

In 1874 the Mir was Futteh Ali Shah, an old man
feeble in health, who has since died and been succeeded by his son Ali Murdan Shah. The reception
given by this ruler and his son to Colonel Gordon and
his party on their return from Kashgar was marked
by the greatest hospitality; and they resided at the
capital of Kila Panja for several days. A very interesting description will be found of this primitive
people in Colonel Gordon's "Roof of the World," and
we need only observe here upon this subject that the
Kirghiz guides told Colonel Gordon that "over the
Pamir, 'the roof of the world,' there are a thousand
roads, and that with a guide you can go in all directions."

The importance of Wakhan is twofold. In the
first place, through it passes the southern route of the

caravan trade between Eastern Turkestan and Western Turkestan and Afghanistan. In the second place, it commands the northern entrance to the Baroghil pass leading from Kashgar to the Chitral valley. For both of these reasons Wakhan is of importance to this country. Regarding it from a purely historical stand-point, Wakhan may be considered to be a dependency of the Afghan Empire, although, ethnologically, it should form one of a confederation of mountain States which should extend from Swat to Karategin. That dream highland feud makes an utter impossibility. In 1872, during the Anglo-Russian negotiations, it may be remembered that considerable confusion was caused by an erroneous definition of the course of the river Oxus in its upper waters, and, had not Sir Henry Rawlinson pointed out the mistake, it is much to be feared that the error would have been passed by unnoticed. Now, as the difference between the two mountain lakes, in which the branches of the Oxus take their origin, is only some forty miles, it would, at a hasty glance, appear that the discrepancy was immaterial; but, when it is stated that the trade route from Yarkand to Balkh lies in that very narrow strip of territory, it will be perceived what importance correct geographical information possessed in the decision of this political question. There are many who consider that this southern route, if properly fostered, could excel the northern route through Kashgar and the Terek pass to the Jaxartes. It is worth while to bear this fact in mind when we come to negotiate with the Chinese in Eastern Turkestan.

But Wakhan, as commanding the northern entrances of the Baroghil and Ishtragh passes, leading into the Chitral valley, only some three hundred and fifty miles by an easy route through Mastuj, Chitral, and Dir, to our frontier north of Peshawur, as shown by the recent explorations of the Mollah, is of more pressing importance still than it may become as the main artery of a great caravan line.

The strategical importance of Wakhan must be readily admitted now that Russia has absorbed Karategin; but should Darwaz and Shignan share the same fate, then our eye would have to be constantly fixed upon the whole northern frontier from Pamir to Merv. Under Mourad Beg, Darwaz was a very prosperous country, and, although its present condition is somewhat obscure, we may assume that, as it has enjoyed a long lease of tranquillity, it maintains something of its old character. It should be remembered that Russia cannot seize Darwaz or Shignan without also taking Karategin—already occupied—Macha, Kulab, and Roshan, the series of small States which intervene between the Oxus and the Alai Tagh range, or a tract of country of great dimensions. From Wakhan, now a border province of the Chinese Empire, to the Turcoman country round Merv, there stretches a broad and clearly defined zone, on which may be written at any point "high road to India." Russia is drawing very near to that zone, if she has not already touched it, and it is idle to doubt that she will very clearly decipher the sign-post, whether her arrival be in the eastern, or the central, or the western portion of that neutral region. Now that the danger is recognised in this country by all parties, England might be considered to be able to cope with whatever emergency there might arise; but it is, nevertheless, very questionable policy to sanction Russian conquests because they do not immediately jeopard our hold upon India. It is true that the Oxus forms an admirable limit to Russian progress, but it by no means follows that it should be made the Russian frontier.

Little need be said of the minor khanates which are to the west of Balkh. These are Andchui, Akche, Shiborgan, Saripul, and Maimene. The principal of these is Maimene. The population is a mixture of Usbeg and Turcoman, and the region is very productive and fairly prosperous. We possess absolutely no authentic account of what has taken place in this quarter of Asia during the last generation—nothing, in fact, since M. Ferrier visited it. All these khanates represent the Afghan possessions in Turkestan, and they have now evidently reached a crisis in their destiny. It is absolutely necessary for the safeguarding of our interests that none of these should pass into the hands either of Russia or of any of her nominees. Too great vigilance cannot be shown in checking the schemes that are already afoot for settling the future of these khanates, and of the province of which they form part.

APPENDIX A.

THE UKASE FOR THE FORMATION OF THE PROVINCE OF
TURKESTAN.

WHEREAS we hold it to be expedient to modify the civil and military organization of the territories bordering on China and the Central Asian khanates which formed portions of the Governments of Orenburg and West Siberia, We ordain by these presents that :

1. A Governor-Generalship be forthwith established in Turkestan, which shall consist of the province of Turkestan, the circle of Tashkend, the districts lying beyond the Syr-Darya, which were occupied by us in the year 1866, and the portion of the province of Semipalatinsk that lies to the south of the Tarbagatai mountain range.

2. The boundaries of the Government of Turkestan shall henceforward be—

(*a.*) With respect to the Government of West Siberia: the ridge of the Tarbagatai mountains, and their offshoots as far as the present frontier line which divides the province of Semipalatinsk from the country inhabited by the Kirghiz of Siberia, shall form the frontier on that side, as far as the lake of Balkash, then extending farther in a curve drawn through the middle of that lake, and equidistant from its shores, and then in a straight line to the river Chu, thence following the course of that river till its confluence with the Syr-Darya.

(b.) With respect to the Government of Orenburg: the frontier line shall be drawn from the middle of the Gulf of Peroffsky in the Sea of Aral, over the Termembes mountain, the place called Terekli, over the Kalmas mountain, the place Muzbill, the Akkum and Chubar-Tubia mountains, the southern point of the sandy desert Myin-Kum, and the place Myin-Bulak, to the confluence of the rivers Saree-Su and Chu.

3. The new government shall be divided into two provinces, one the Syr-Darya, the other Semiretchinsk, and the river Kurogoty will form the boundary line between them.

4. The chief administrative power over the country thus constituted will be entrusted to a Governor-General, and the provinces of the Syr-Darya and the Semiretchinsk to Military Governors; as regards the military administration and the military establishments, the two provinces shall form the military district of Turkestan, and the command of the whole of the troops stationed within the district shall be entrusted to the Governor-General, with the title, "Commander of the Forces of the District;" and the

Military Governors shall command the troops in their own provinces, with the title "Commander of the Forces" in their respective provinces.

5. On the establishment of the provinces of the Syr-Darya and the Semiretchinsk, the civil authorities therein employed shall remain at the disposition and under the control of the respective Military Governors until general regulations for the guidance of the administration of the whole district shall be promulgated.

Dated, July 11 (23 N.S.), *in the year* 1867.

318

APPENDIX B.

RUSSIA'S PROGRAMME IN CENTRAL ASIA.

ONE of Prince Gortchakoff's earliest circulars, dated the 9th (N.S. 21st) of November, 1864, to the British Government, gives so clear an insight into the policy of Russia, more especially when studied by the light of recent events, that it is worth while to bring its principal passages prominently before the English reader.

The following give the pith and substance of this remarkable State Paper :—

" The position of Russia in Central Asia is that of all civilised States which are brought into contact with half-savage, nomad populations, possessing no fixed social organization.

" In such cases it always happens that the more civilised State is forced, in the interest of the security of its frontier and its commercial relations, to exercise a certain ascendancy over those whom their turbulent and unsettled character makes most undesirable neighbours.

"First, there are raids and acts of pillage to be put down. To put a stop to them, the tribes on the frontier have to be reduced to a state of more or less perfect submission. This result once attained, these tribes take to more peaceful habits, but are in their turn exposed to the attacks of the more distant tribes.

"The State is bound to defend them against these depredations, and to punish those who commit them. Hence the necessity of distant, costly, and periodically-recurring expeditions against an enemy whom his social organization makes it impossible to seize. If, the robbers once punished, the expedition is withdrawn, the lesson is soon forgotten; its withdrawal is put down to weakness. It is a peculiarity of Asiatics to respect nothing but visible and palpable force; the moral force of reason and of the interests of civilisation has as yet no hold upon them. The work has then always to be done over again from the beginning.

"In order to put a stop to this state of permanent disorder, fortified posts are established in the midst of these hostile tribes, and an influence is brought to bear upon them which reduces them by degrees to a state of more or less forced submission. But some beyond this second line, other still more distant tribes, come in their turn to threaten the same dangers, and necessitate the same measures of repression. The State thus finds itself forced to choose one of two alternatives—either to give up this endless labour, and to abandon its frontier to perpetual disturbance, rendering all prosperity, all security, all civilisation an impossibility, or, on the other hand, to plunge deeper and deeper into barbarous countries, where the difficulties and expenses increase with every step in advance.

" Such has been the fate of every country which has found itself in a similar position. The United States in America, France in Algeria, Holland in her colonies, England in India—all have been irresistibly forced, less by ambition than by imperious necessity, into this onward march, where the greatest difficulty is to know where to stop.

" Such, too, have been the reasons which have led the Imperial Government to take up at first a position resting on one side on the Syr-Darya, on the other on the lake of Issyk-Kul, and to strengthen these two lines by advanced forts, which, little by little, have crept on into the heart of those distant regions, without, however, succeeding in establishing on the other side of our frontiers that tranquillity which is indispensable for their security.

" The explanation of this unsettled state of things is to be found, first, in the fact that between the extreme points of this double line there is an immense unoccupied space, where all attempts at colonisation or caravan trade are paralysed by the inroads of the robber tribes; and, in the second place, in the perpetual fluctuations of the political condition of those countries where Turkestan and Khokand, sometimes united, sometimes at variance, always at war, either with one another or with Bokhara, presented no chance of settled relations, or of any regular transactions whatever.

" The Imperial Government thus found itself, in spite of all its efforts, in the dilemma we have above alluded to, that is to say, compelled either to permit the continuance of a state of permanent disorder, paralysing to all security and progress, or to condemn itself to costly and distant expeditions leading to no practical result and with the work always to be done anew ; or, lastly, to enter upon the undefined path of conquest and annexation which has given to England the Empire of India, by attempting the subjugation by armed force, one after another, of the small independent States whose habits of pillage and turbulence, and whose perpetual revolts, leave their neighbours neither peace nor repose.

" Neither of these alternative courses was in accordance with the object of our august master's policy, which consists not in extending beyond all reasonable bounds the regions under his sceptre, but in giving a solid basis to his rule, in guaranteeing their security, and in developing their social organization, their commerce, their well-being, and their civilisation.

" Our task was, therefore, to discover a system adapted to the attainment of this threefold object.

" The following principles have, in consequence, been laid down :—

" 1. It has been judged to be indispensable that our two fortified lines, one extending from China to the lake of Issyk-Kul, the other from the sea of Aral, along the Syr-Darya, should be united by fortified points, so that all our posts should be in a position of mutual support, leaving no gap through which the nomad tribes might make their inroads and depredations with impunity.

" 2. It was essential that the line of our advanced forts thus completed should be situated in a country fertile enough not only to insure their supplies, but also to facilitate the regular colonisation, which alone can prepare a future of stability and prosperity for the occupied country by gaining over the neighbouring population to civilised life.

" 3. And lastly. It was urgent to lay down this line definitively, so as to escape the danger of being carried away, as is almost inevitable, by a series of repressive measures and reprisals into an unlimited extension of territory.

" To attain this end, a system had to be established which should depend not only on reason, which may be elastic, but on geographical and political conditions which are fixed and permanent.

" This system was suggested to us by a very simple fact, the result of experience, namely, that the nomad tribes, which can neither be seized nor punished, nor effectually kept in order, are our most inconvenient neighbours; while on the other hand, agricultural and commercial populations attached to the soil, and possessing a more advanced social organization, offer us every chance of gaining neighbours with whom there is a possibility of entering into relations.

" Consequently our frontier line ought to swallow

up the former and stop short at the limit of the latter.

"These three principles supply a clear, natural, and logical explanation of our last military operations in Central Asia. In fact, our original frontier line extending along the Syr-Darya to Fort Peroffsky on one side, and on the other to the lake Issyk-Kul, had the drawback of being almost on the verge of the desert. It was broken by a wide gap between the two extreme points; it did not offer sufficient resources to our troops, and left unsettled tribes over the border, with which any settled arrangement became impossible.

"In spite of our unwillingness to extend our frontier, these motives had been powerful enough to induce the Imperial Government to establish this line between Lake Issyk-Kul and the Syr-Darya by fortifying the town of Tchimkent, lately occupied by us. By the adoption of this line we obtain a double result. In the first place, the country it takes in is fertile, well wooded, and watered by numerous watercourses; it is partly inhabited by various Khirghiz tribes which have already accepted our rule; it consequently offers favourable conditions for colonisation and the supply of provisions to our garrisons. In the second place, it puts us in the immediate neighbourhood of the agricultural and commercial populations of Khokand. We find ourselves in the presence of a more solid and compact, less unsettled, and better organized social state, fixed for us, with geographical precision, the limit up to which we are bound to advance, and at which we must halt, because, while on the one hand any further extension of our rule, meeting, as it would, no longer with unstable communities such as the nomad tribes, but with more regularly constituted States, would entail considerable exertions, and would draw us on from annexation to annexation with unforeseen complications; on the other, with such States for our future neighbours, their backward civilisation and the instability of their political condition do not shut us out from the hope that the day may come when regular relations may, to the advantage of both parties, take the place of the permanent troubles which have up to the present moment paralysed all progress in those countries.

"Such are the interests which inspire the policy of our august master in Central Asia.

" It is needless for me to lay stress upon the interest which Russia evidently has not to increase her territory, and, above all, to avoid raising complications on her frontiers, which can but delay and paralyse her domestic development.

" The programme which I have just traced is in accordance with these views.

" Very frequently of late years the civilisation of these countries, which are her neighbours on the continent of Asia, has been assigned to Russia as her special permission.

" No agent has been found more apt for the progress of civilisation than commercial relations. Their development requires everywhere order and stability, but in Asia it demands a complete transformation of the habits of the people. The first thing to be taught to the population of Asia is that they will gain more in favouring and protecting the caravans trade than in robbing them. These elementary ideas can only be accepted by the public where one exists; that is to say, where there is some organized form of society, and a Government to direct and represent it.

"We are accomplishing the first part of our task in carrying our frontier to the limit where the indispensable conditions are to be found.

"The second we shall accomplish in making every effort henceforward to prove to our neighbouring States, by a system of firmness in the repression of their misdeeds, combined with moderation and justice in the use of our strength, and respect for their independence, that Russia is not their enemy, that she entertains towards them no idea of conquest, and that peaceful and commercial relations with her are more profitable than disorder, pillage, reprisals, and a permanent state of war.

"The Imperial Cabinet, in assuming this task, takes as its guide the interests of Russia. But it believes that at the same time it is promoting the interests of humanity and civilisation. It has a right to expect that the line of conduct it pursues, and the principles which guide it, will meet with a just and candid appreciation.

"(Signed) GORTCHAKOW."

APPENDIX C.

RUSSIA AND KHIVA.

TREATY of Peace between Russia and Khiva, prepared by General Aide-de-Camp Kaufmann, commanding the forces acting against Khiva, and accepted by the Khan of Khiva, Seyyid-Mahomed-Rahim-Bahadur-Khan.

1. Seyyid-Mahomed-Rahim-Bahadur-Khan acknowledges himself to be the humble servant of the Emperor of all the Russias. He renounces the right of maintaining any direct and friendly relations with neighbouring rulers and khans, and of concluding with them commercial or other treaties of any kind whatsoever, and shall not, without the knowledge and permission of the superior Russian authorities in Central Asia, undertake any military operations against such neighbouring countries.

2. The boundary between the Russian and Khivan

territories shall be the Amou Darya from Kukertli down the river as far as the point at which the most westerly branch of the Amou Darya leaves the main stream, and from that point the 'frontier shall pass along such branch as far as its mouth in the Aral sea. Farther, the frontier shall extend along the sea-coast to Cape Urgu, and from thence along the base of the chink (escarpment) of the Ust-Urt, following the so-called ancient bed of the Amou Darya.

3. The whole of the right bank of the Amou Darya, and the lands adjoining thereunto, which have hitherto been considered as belonging to Khiva, shall pass over from the Khan into the possession of Russia, together with the people dwelling and camping thereon. Those parcels of land which are at present the property of the Khan, and of which the usufruct has been given by him to Khivan officers of State, become likewise the property of the Russian Government, free of all claims on the part of the previous owners. The Khan may indemnify them by grants of land on the left bank.

4. In the event of a portion of such right bank being transferred to the possession of the Ameer of Bokhara by the will of His Majesty the Emperor, the Khan of Khiva shall recognise the latter as the lawful possessor of such portion of his former dominions, and engages to renounce all intention of re-establishing his authority therein.

5. Russian steamers, and other Russian vessels, whether belonging to the Government or to private individuals, shall have the free and exclusive right of navigating the Amou Darya river. Khivan and

Bokharan vessels may enjoy the same right, not otherwise than by special permission from the superior Russian authority in Central Asia.

6. Russians shall have the right to construct wharves (landing-places) on the left bank wheresoever the same shall be found necessary and convenient. The Government of the Khan shall be responsible for the safety and security of such wharves. The approval of the localities selected for wharves shall rest with the superior Russian authorities in Central Asia.

7. Independently of such wharves, Russians shall have the right to establish factories on the left bank of the Amou Darya for the purpose of storing and safe-keeping their merchandise. For the purposes of such factories the Government of the Khan shall allot, in the localities which shall have been indicated by the superior Russian authorities in Central Asia, a sufficient quantity of unoccupied land for wharves, and for the construction of storehouses, of buildings for the accommodation of servants of the factories, and of persons transacting business with the factories, and of merchants' offices, as well as for the establishment of domestic farms. Such factories, together with all persons residing thereat and with all goods placed therein, shall be under the immediate protection of the Government of the Khan, which shall be responsible for the safety and security of the same.

8. All the towns and villages, without exception, within the Khanate of Khiva shall henceforward be open to Russian trade. Russian merchants and Russian caravans may freely travel throughout the entire

khanate, and shall enjoy the special protection of the local authorities. The Government of the Khan shall be responsible for the safety of caravans and stores.

9. Russian merchants trading in the khanate shall be free from the payment of customs duties (*zakat*), and of all kinds of dues on trade, in the same manner as the merchants of Khiva have long enjoyed immunity from *zakat* on the route through Kazalinsk, at Orenburg, and at the stations (landing-places) on the Caspian sea.

10. Russian merchants shall have the right of carrying their goods through the Khivan territory to all neighbouring countries free of customs duties (free transit trade).

11. Russian merchants shall, if they desire it, have the right to establish agents (caravan bashis) in Khiva and other towns within the khanate, for the purpose of maintaining communication with the authorities and superintending the regularity of their trade.

12. Russian subjects shall have the right to hold immovable property in Khiva. A land-tax shall be leviable on the same by agreement with the superior Russian authority in Central Asia.

13. Commercial engagements between Russians and Khivans shall be fulfilled inviolably on both sides.

14. The Government of the Khan engages to examine (inquire into), without delay, the complaints and claims of Russian subjects against Khivans, and in case such complaints and claims shall have proved to be well founded, to give immediate satisfaction in respect of the same. In the examination of disputes

(claims) between Russian subjects and Khivans, preference shall be given to Russians in respect to the payment of debts by Khivans.

15. Complaints and claims of Khivans against Russian subjects shall be referred to the nearest Russian authorities for examination and satisfaction, even in the event of such complaints and claims being raised by Russian subjects within the confines of the khanate.

16. The Government of the Khan shall in no case give refuge to emigrants (runaways) from Russia having no permit from Russian authorities, without regard to the nationality of such individuals. Should any Russian subjects, being criminals, seek concealment within the boundaries of Khiva, in order to avoid judicial pursuit, the Government of the Khan engages to capture such persons, and to surrender them to the nearest Russian authorities.

17. The proclamation made by Seyyid-Mahomed-Rahim-Bahadur-Khan on the 12th (24th) of July last respecting the liberation of all slaves in the khanate, and the abolition in perpetuity of slavery and of trade in men, shall remain in full force, and the Government of the Khan engages to employ all the means in its power in order to watch over the strict and conscientious prosecution of this matter.

18. A fine is inflicted on the Khanate of Khiva to the extent of two million two hundred thousand roubles, in order to cover the expenses incurred by the Russian Exchequer in the prosecution of the late war, which was provoked by the Government of the Khan and by the Khivan people. Since, owing to the

insufficiency of money in the country, and particularly in the hands of the Government, the Khivan Government is unable to pay the above sum within a short time, the Khivan Government shāll, in consideration of such difficulty, have the right of paying the said fine by instalments, with the addition of interest thereon at the rate of five per cent. per annum, on condition that, during the first two years, one hundred thousand roubles shall be annually paid into the Russian Exchequer, one hundred and twenty-five thousand roubles per annum during the two ensuing years, and, after that, one hundred and seventy-five thousand roubles per annum during the succeeding two years, and in the year 1881, that is to say, after the expiration of eight years, the sum of two hundred thousand roubles shall be paid; and, lastly, a sum of not less than two hundred thousand roubles per annum shall be paid until the final settlement of the claim. The instalments may be paid both in Russian bank-notes and in the current coin of Khiva, at the pleasure of the Government of the Khan. The first instalment shall be paid on the 1st (13th) of December 1873. On account of this instalment the Khan shall have the right to levy a tax for the current year from the population on the right bank, according to the assessment hitherto in force. This collection shall be terminated by the 1st (13th) of December, by agreement between the Khan's collectors and the local Russian authorities.

Subsequent instalments shall be paid in by the 1st (13th) of November of each year, until the entire fine, with interest thereon, shall have been paid off. After the expiration of nineteen years, that is to say, by the 1st (13th) of November 1892, after the payment of two hundred thousand roubles for the year 1892, the sum of seventy thousand and fifty-four roubles will still be due by the Government of the Khan, and, by the 1st (13th) of November 1893, the last instalment of seventy-three thousand five hundred and fifty-seven roubles shall be paid. Should the Government of the Khan desire to shorten the term of payment, and thus to reduce the amount of accruing interest, it shall have the right to pay larger annual instalments. These conditions have been fixed and accepted for exact execution and constant guidance on the one part by General Aide-de-Camp Kaufmann, Governor-General of Turkestan, and on the other part by Seyyid-Mahomed-Rahim-Bahadur-Khan, Ruler of Khiva, in the garden of Hendemian (the camp of the Russian troops at the city of Khiva), on the 12th (24th) day of August 1873 (on the first day of the month Radjab, in the year 1290). The original treaty was signed and sealed by General Aide-de-Camp Kaufmann, Governor-General of Turkestan, and by Seyyid-Mahomed-Rahim-Bahadur-Khan.

APPENDIX D.

RUSSIA AND BOKHARA.

TREATY concluded between General Aide-de-Camp Kaufmann, Governor-General of Turkestan, and Seyyid-Mozaffur, Ameer of Bokhara.

ART. 1.—The line of frontier between the dominions of His Imperial Majesty the Emperor of all the Russias and those of His Eminence the Ameer of Bokhara remains unaltered. All the Khivan territory on the right bank of the Amou Darya being now annexed to the Russian dominions, the former frontier separating the possessions of the Ameer of Bokhara from the Khanate of Khiva, and stretching on the west from the locality called Khalata towards Gugertli, "Togai," on the right bank of Amou, is abolished. The territory situated between the former Bokharo-Khivan frontier, the right bank of the Amou Darya from Gugertli to Meshekly, "Togai" inclusive, and the line passing from Meshekly to the point of junction of the former Bokharo-Khivan frontier, with the frontier of the Russian Empire, are annexed to the dominions of the Ameer of Bokhara.

ART. 2.—The right bank of the Amou Darya being detached from the Khanate of Khiva, all the caravan routes leading from Bokhara to the north into the Russian dominions traverse henceforth exclusively lands belonging to Bokhara and Russia. The Governments of Russia and Bokhara, each within its own limits, shall both watch over the security of the march of caravans and of the transit trade.

ART. 3.—Russian steamers and other Russian Government vessels, as well as vessels belonging to private individuals, shall have the right of free navigation on that portion of the Amou Darya which belongs to the Ameer of Bokhara.

ART. 4.—Russians shall have the right to establish wharves (landing-places) and storehouses for merchandise in such places on the Bokharan banks of the Amou Darya as may be judged necessary and convenient for that purpose. The Government of Bokhara shall undertake to watch over the safety and security of the said wharves and storehouses. The ratification of the selection of localities for the establishment of wharves shall rest with the superior Russian authorities in Central Asia.

ART. 5.—All the towns and villages of the Khanate of Bokhara shall be open to Russian trade. Russian traders and Russian caravans shall freely pass through all parts of the khanate and shall enjoy the special protection of the local authorities. The Bokharan Government shall be responsible for the security of Russian caravans within the confines of the Khanate of Bokhara.

ART. 6.—All merchandise belonging to Russian traders, whether transported from the Russian possessions into Bokhara or from Bokhara to Russia, shall, without exception, be liable to a tax of two and a half per cent. *ad valorem*, in the same way as a duty of one-fortieth is charged on merchandise in the Turkestan province. Besides this *zakat* no other supplementary tax shall be imposed.

ART. 7.—Russian traders shall have the right to transport their merchandise through Bokhara to all neighbouring countries free of duty.

ART. 8.—Russian traders shall be allowed to establish caravanserais for the storage of their merchandise in all Bokharan towns in which they may consider it necessary to do so. Bokharan traders shall enjoy the same privilege in the towns of the Turkestan province.

ART. 9.—Russian traders shall have the right to have commercial agents in all the towns of Bokhara, whose business it shall be to watch over the regular course of trade and over the legal imposition of customs dues, and who shall also be authorised to enter into communication with the local authorities. Bokharan traders shall enjoy the same privilege in the towns of the Turkestan province.

ART. 10.—Engagements of trade between Russians and Bokharans shall be held sacred and inviolable on both sides. The Bokharan Government shall promise to keep watch over the honest fulfilment of all trading engagements, as also over the conscientious conduct of trading affairs generally.

ART. 11.—Russian subjects shall equally with the subjects of Bokhara have the right to occupy themselves in the Bokharan dominions with the various trades and crafts which are allowed under the *Shahrigate* in exactly the same way as Bokharan subjects are permitted in the Russian dominions to follow those occupations which are sanctioned by the laws of Russia.

ART. 12.—Russian subjects shall have the right to possess immovable property in the khanate, *i.e.* to acquire by purchase gardens and cultivable lands. Such property shall be liable to a land-tax on an equality with properties of Bokharan subjects. The same right shall be enjoyed by Bokharan subjects within the limits of the Russian Empire.

ART. 13.—Russian subjects shall enter the Bokharan dominions with permits, issued by the Russian authorities, for crossing the frontier; they shall have the right of free passage throughout the entire khanate, and they shall enjoy the special protection of the Bokharan authorities.

ART. 14.—The Government of Bokhara shall in no case admit into its country any emigrants from Russia, whatever may be their nationality, who are not provided with permits from Russian authorities. If a criminal, being a Russian subject, seeks refuge within the confines of Bokhara from the pursuit of the law, the same shall be arrested and delivered over to the nearest Russian authorities.

ART. 15.—In order to hold direct and uninterrupted relations with the superior Russian authorities in Central Asia, the Ameer of Bokhara shall select from among those around him a person of 'confidence whom he shall establish at Tashkend as his Envoy Plenipotentiary. Such Envoy shall reside at Tashkend in a house belonging to the Ameer, and at the expense of the latter.

ART. 16.—The Russian Government may in like manner have a permanent representative in Bokhara who shall be near the person of His Eminence the Ameer. The Russian Plenipotentiary in Bokhara, as in the case of the Ameer's Plenipotentiary in Tashkend, shall reside in a house belonging to the Russian Government, and at the expense of the latter.

ART. 17.—In deference to the Emperor of all the Russias, and for the greater glory of His Imperial Majesty, His Eminence the Ameer Seyyid Mozaffur has resolved that henceforth and for ever the shameful trade in men which is so contrary to the laws of humanity, shall be abolished within the limits of Bokhara. In conformity with this resolution, Seyyid Mozaffur shall immediately send to all his beks the strictest orders to that effect. Besides the order abolishing the slave trade, commands shall be sent to all the frontier towns of Bokhara to which slaves are brought for sale from neighbouring countries, to the effect that in case slaves should be brought to such places, notwithstanding the orders of the Ameer, the same should be taken from their owners and immediately liberated.

Art. 18.—His Eminence Seyyid Mozaffur, being sincerely desirous of developing and strengthening the friendly and neighbourly relations which have subsisted for five years to the benefit of Bokhara, shall be guided by the seventeen Articles composing the Treaty of Friendship between Russia and Bokhara. This treaty shall be written in duplicate, each copy being written in the two languages, one in the Russian and the other in the Turkish language. In token of the confirmation of treaty, and of its acceptance as a guide to himself and to his successors, the Ameer Seyyid Mozaffur has attached his seal. In Shaar, the 28th day of September (O.S.), 1873, in the month Shagban, 19th day, 1290.

APPENDIX E.

First Treaty between England and Dost Mahomed of Cabul.

TREATY between the British Government and His Highness Ameer Dost Mahomed Khan, Walee of Cabul, and of those countries of Afghanistan now in his possession, concluded on the part of the British Government by John Lawrence, Esquire, Chief Commissioner of the Punjab, in virtue of full powers vested in him by the Most Noble James Andrew, Marquis of Dalhousie, K.T., etc., Governor-General of India; and on the part of the Ameer of Cabul, Dost Mahomed Khan, by Sirdar Gholam Hyder Khan, in virtue of full authority granted to him by His Highness.

ART. 1.—Between the Honourable East India Company and His Highness Ameer Dost Mahomed Khan, Walee of Cabul, and of those countries now in his possession, and the heirs of the said Ameer, there shall be perpetual peace and friendship.

ART. 2.—The Honourable East India Company engages to respect those territories of Afghanistan now in His Highness's possession, and never to interfere therein.

ART. 3.—His Highness Ameer Dost Mahomed Khan, Walee of Cabul, and of those countries of Afghanistan now in his possession, engages, on his own part and on the part of his heirs, to respect the territories of the Honourable East India Company, and never to interfere therein, and to be the friend of the friends and enemy of the enemies of the Honourable East India Company.

> Done at Peshawur, this 30th day of March, 1855, corresponding with the 11th day of Rujjub, 1271 Hijree.
>
> (Signed) JOHN LAWRENCE,
> (Seal.) Chief Commissioner of the Punjab.
>
> GHOLAM HYDER,
> (Seal of Gholam Hyder, heir-apparent.) As the representative of Ameer Dost Mahomed Khan, and in person on his own account as heir-apparent.
>
> Ratified by the Most Noble the Governor-General at Ootakamund, this 1st day of May, 1855.
>
> (Signed) DALHOUSIE.

APPENDIX F.

SECOND TREATY BETWEEN ENGLAND AND DOST MAHOMED OF CABUL.

ARTICLES of Agreement made at Peshawur on the 26th January 1857 (corresponding with Jumadee-ool-Awul 29th, A.H. 1273), between Ameer Dost Mahomed Khan, Ruler of Cabul, and of those countries of Afghanistan now in his possession, on his own part, and Sir John Lawrence, K.C.B., Chief Commissioner of the Punjab, and Lieutenant-Colonel H. B. Edwardes, C.B., Commissioner of Peshawur, on the part of the Honourable East India Company, under the authority of the Right Honourable Charles John Viscount Canning, Governor-General of India in Council.

1. Whereas the Shah of Persia, contrary to his engagement with the British Government, has taken possession of Herat, and has manifested an intention to interfere in the present possessions of Ameer Dost

Mahomed Khan, and there is now war between the British and Persian Governments, therefore the Honourable East India Company, to aid Ameer Dost Mahomed Khan to defend and maintain his present possessions in Balkh, Cabul, and Kandahar against Persia, hereby agrees, out of friendship, to give the said Ameer one lac of Company's rupees monthly during the war with Persia, on the following conditions :

2. The Ameer shall keep his present number of cavalry and artillery, and shall maintain not less than eighteen thousand infantry, of which thirteen thousand shall be regulars, divided into thirteen regiments.

3. The Ameer is to make his own arrangements for receiving the money at the British Treasuries, and conveying it through his own country.

4. British officers, with suitable establishments and orderlies, shall be deputed, at the pleasure of the British Government, to Cabul or Kandahar or Balkh, or all three places, or wherever an Afghan army be assembled to act against the Persians. It will be their duty to see generally that the subsidy granted to the Ameer be devoted to the military purposes for which it is given, and to keep their own Government informed of all affairs. They will have nothing to do with the payment of the troops, or advising the Cabul Government, and they will not interfere in any way in the internal administration of the country. The Ameer will be responsible for their safety and honourable treatment while in his country, and for keeping them acquainted with all military and political matters connected with the war.

5. The Ameer of Cabul shall appoint and maintain a vakil at Peshawur.

6. The subsidy of one lac per mensem shall cease from the date on which peace is made between the British and Persian Governments, or at any previous time, at the will and pleasure of the Governor-General of India.

7. Whenever the subsidy shall cease, the British officers shall be withdrawn from the Ameer's country; but at the pleasure of the British Government a vakil, not a European officer, shall remain at Cabul on the part of the Government, and one at Peshawur on the part of the Government of Cabul.

8. The Ameer shall furnish a sufficient escort for the British officers from the British border when going to the Ameer's country, and to the British border when returning.

9. The subsidy shall commence from 1st January, 1857, and be payable at the British Treasury one month in arrears.

10. The five lacs of rupees which have been already sent to the Ameer (three to Candahar and two to Cabul) will not be counted in this Agreement. They are a free and separate gift from the Honourable East India Company. But the sixth lac, now in the hands of the mahajuns of Cabul, which was sent for another purpose, will be one of the instalments under this Agreement.

11. This Agreement in no way supersedes the Treaty made at Peshawur on 30th March 1855 (corresponding with 11th of Rujjub, 1271), by which the

Ameer of Cabul engaged to be the friend of the friends and the enemy of the enemies of the Honourable East India Company, and the Ameer of Cabul, in the spirit of that Treaty, agrees to communicate to the British Government any overtures he may receive from Persia or the allies of Persia during the war, or while there is friendship between the Cabul and British Governments.

12. In consideration of the friendship existing between the British Government and Ameer Dost Mahomed Khan, the British Government engages to overlook the past hostilities of all the tribes of Afghanistan, and on no account to visit them with punishment.

13. Whereas the Ameer has expressed a wish to have four thousand muskets given him in addition to the four thousand already given, it is agreed that four thousand muskets shall be sent by the British Government to Tull, whence the Ameer's people will convey them with their own carriage.

(Seal.)

(Signed) JOHN LAWRENCE,
Chief Commissioner.

(Signed) HERBERT B. EDWARDES,
Commissioner of the Peshawur Division.

APPENDIX G.

Treaty between Heraclius, Prince of Georgia, and the Empress Catherine of Russia.

Art. 1.—Heraclius, the Prince of Georgia, renounces his dependence upon Persia, and places himself, heirs, and successors, under the protection of the Empress Catherine, her heirs and successors.

Art. 2.—The Empress Catherine grants her protection, and not only guarantees his actual possessions to the Prince of Georgia, but also all those which may become his in future partitions.

Art. 3.—The Prince of Georgia agrees that his heirs shall solicit and receive their investiture from the Empress, her heirs, etc., and that they shall swear to be faithful to the monarchs of Russia.

Art. 4.—The Prince of Georgia agrees that he will have no communication with neighbouring States, except with the advice and knowledge of the Russian general commanding the forces, or the ambassador residing in his country.

ART. 5.—The ambassador whom the Prince of Georgia keeps at the Empress's Court is to have suitable rank.

ART. 6.—Her Majesty the Empress promises, for herself and successors:—First, That she will regard the enemies of Georgia as her enemies; and that, in consequence, the people of that country will be included in any peace concluded with the Ottoman Porte, or any other State. Secondly: That she will maintain the Prince Heraclius and his heirs and posterity on the throne of Georgia; and thirdly, That she will leave wholly and entirely to the Prince of Georgia the internal administration of his country and the imposition of taxes.

ART. 7.—The Prince of Georgia promises, for himself and heirs:—First, To be always ready with his army to serve the Empress of Russia. Secondly: To act in all that concluded, by which that prince, in his own name, and that of his heirs, transferred his allegiance from the Kings of Persia to her and her successors; while she, on the part of herself and heirs, engaged to protect him and his people, and by a specific article she not only guaranteed to this prince all his actual possessions, but promised to extend the same protection to " other territories that might relate to her service with the advice of her commanders; to comply with their requisitions; and to guarantee her subjects against all injustice and oppression." Thirdly:

To consider chiefly in the promotion of officers in his service those who have deserved well of Russia, because on that empire the safety and prosperity of Georgia depends.

Art. 8.—Her Majesty the Empress of Russia consents that the first Archbishop of Georgia shall rank with the metropolitans of the eighth class, taking precedence after the Metropolitan of Tobolsk; and the Empress is to give him the title of a member of "The Most Holy Synod."

Art. 9.—The nobles of Georgia shall, in every part of the Russian Empire, enjoy the same prerogatives and advantages as the nobles of Russia.

Art. 10.—The inhabitants of Georgia to be at liberty to settle in Russia, and to return to their own country. The Georgian prisoners, who are released either by arms or capitulation, to return to their homes on paying what has been disbursed for their ransom or their expenses. The Prince of Georgia promises to act in the same manner towards those Russians who have been made captives by neighbouring States.

Art. 11.—Georgian merchants to pass and repass into Russia at pleasure, and to enjoy equal privileges with Russian merchants, and the Prince of Georgia promises to concert measures with the Russian generals to give more facility to the commerce carried on by Russians in his territories.

Art. 12.—The present convention or treaty to be for ever.

Art. 13.—The Articles of this treaty to be ratified

in six months, or sooner if possible. Executed in the fortress of Georges, the twenty-fourth of July, 1783.

   (Signed) PAUL POTEMKIN, PRINCE IVAN-
         BAGRATION.
       PRINCE GARSEWAN - ISCHAWTS -
         CHAWDSEW.

Recently published. 8vo. 16s. With Map and Appendix.

THE LIFE OF YAKOOB BEG,
ATHALIK GHAZI, AND BADAULET,
AMEER OF KASHGAR.

By DEMETRIUS CHARLES BOULGER,
MEMBER OF THE ROYAL ASIATIC SOCIETY.

OPINIONS OF THE PRESS.

Times, Leading Article, 15th *November* 1878.—"A very interesting and instructive volume."

Times, Review (nearly three columns), 26th *December* 1878.—"Under the title of a 'Life of Yakoob Beg, the late Ameer of Kashgar,' Mr. Boulger has given us a systematic history of the kingdom and people of Kashgar: and it is well that he has done so. . . . The publication of Mr. Boulger's volume is, indeed, most opportune. . . . In Sir Bartle Frere's letter public opinion for the first time found firm ground on which to base a national policy in relation to the Russian advance in Central Asia; and now the publication of Mr. Boulger's exhaustive volume supplies the most detailed information as to the significance of that advance, and the errors we have to avoid in meeting it."

Standard, Review, 25th *December* 1878.—"Mr. Boulger has rendered a service equally to history, the public, and the Government, in writing the book before us. . . . We have only been able to deal with a portion of this able and exhaustive book, but we would earnestly advise all those who take an interest in Central Asian politics to read the work before us from beginning to end. Not a chapter, not even a single page, ought to be omitted."

Daily Telegraph, Leading Article, 7th *November* 1878.—"The answer is furnished by Mr. Boulger, in his remarkable and recently published work on 'Yakoob Beg and Kashgar.' . . . Here, then, we have not merely a dramatic event in contemporary history, but what is virtually the advent of a new force, which Mr. Boulger correctly defines as 'the Chinese factor in the Central Asian Question.'"

Daily News, Review, 26th November 1878.—" Mr. Boulger's ' Life of Yakoob Beg ' appears opportunely at a time when it is desirable that no matters bearing upon the affairs of Central Asia should be misunderstood or imperfectly conceived. . . . While exhibiting something of the biographer's enthusiasm for the military and administrative capacity of his hero, Mr. Boulger is so far from under-rating his enemies, that his guiding purpose is to direct the attention of his countrymen to the singular merits of the Chinese as a military and a governing people."

Morning Post, Review, 13th January 1879.—" Mr. Boulger's work reads with all the fascinating interest of a highly sensational novel. He tells his story admirably, and is throughout most instructive, using his authorities with skill and to the point. 'The Life of Yakoob Beg' is a valuable contribution to our Oriental literature, and will prove almost indispensable to all who wish to master the political questions of the East."

Morning Post, Second Review, 4th February 1879.—" Mr. Boulger is to be commended for the industry he has manifested in tracing out the leading incidents in the career of this able man, and in rendering intelligible to English readers the complicated politics of Central Asia. If he should succeed in his main object, of making the British public understand and appreciate better than they have hitherto done the vitality of Chinese institutions, and the important part which China is taking in the affairs of Central Asia, his work will have a distinct political value."

Globe, Review, 8th January 1879.—" The arrival of the Chinese Envoy at St. Petersburg to discuss the Kulja question will occasion a general desire to become acquainted with the relative position of Russia and China in Central Asia; and no recent book, we believe, will throw better light upon the subject than Mr. Boulger's excellent biography of the late Athalik Ghazi. . . . . For some considerable time to come the volume will, in all probability, remain the standard work of reference on matters connected with Kashgaria and Kulja."

La Republique Française, Leading Article, 5th January 1879.—" Cette entreprise a séduit un Orientaliste Anglais, M. D. C. Boulger, qui publiait, il y a quelques semaines, à Londrès, une Vie de Yakoub-beg, émir de Kashgar, où nous avons rencontré les détails les plus intéressants du monde sur une existence aventureuse et pittoresque comme on ne s'imaginerait pas qu'il put y en avcir encore en plein dix-neuvième siècle. . . . Avec une art consommé, M. Boulger a su mettre en œuvre les renseignements puisés et dans la 'Gazette officielle de Pekin' et dans la 'Gazette du Turkestan;' contrôlant les nouvelles de source Russe par celles de source Chinoise, il nous a fait un tableau vraiment étonnant de la renaissance militaire de l'empire du milieu, que nous n'étions pas accoutumés à envisager sous cet aspect. . . . Il faut lire dans le livre de M. Boulger les détails de cette campagne savamment et brillamment conduite par des généraux Chinois, instruits des manœuvres des armées d'Europe; ce récit montre que la Chine possède les éléments nécessaires à une puissance militaire de premier ordre, et il nous paraît, après la campagne de Kashgarie, que ses Voisins en Asie feront bien de compter sérieusement avec elle."

La Republique Française, Review, 6th February 1879.—" Le tableau que nous fait M. Boulger de l'administration Chinoise en Kashgarie est des plus curieux; c'est une véritable révélation. . . . M. Boulger a eu le talent de réagir contre ces influences envahissantes, et nous lui en adressons nos bien sincères compliments."

Economist, 21st December 1878.—" It is difficult for Englishmen with their modern ideas of the effete character of the Pekin Government to think of the

Chinese as a conquering people; yet no one who reads Mr. Boulger's recent book upon Kashgar can doubt that the instinct of conquest still exists among them in an active form."

Saturday Review, 11*th January* 1879.—" Mr. Boulger has made a praiseworthy attempt to treat a subject which lies under peculiar disadvantages. . . . Any book which tends to throw light on the Central Asian problem is entitled to a hearing; and the author deserves credit for research, pains, and general accuracy. . . . We repeat, in conclusion, that the author deserves credit for his compilation, and think that readers may derive pleasure from the laborious career of the principal figure in the book, who, to borrow Mr. Tennyson's diction, rose suddenly through a little arc of heaven, and, without having wandered far, shot quite as suddenly into darkness."

Spectator, 21*st December* 1878.—" This is a valuable book, and one which it would hardly be fair to criticise in the ordinary way. The writer is evidently one of those men who, having taken up an out-of-the-way subject of study, become possessed by it, and gradually accumulate more information than they quite know what to do with. He states the evidence of Chinese ruthlessness as fairly as the evidences of Chinese business-wisdom. But while he greatly admires the latter, he treats the former too much as if the slaughter of all armed males after submission were a regular operation of war. It may be, however, that he thought this style essential to impartiality, as he points out, with cold accuracy, that it was the Chinese cruelty that originally cost them Kashgar. Impartiality, indeed, is his strong point; the very object of his book being to dissolve the great *mythus* with which Englishmen have surrounded his hero."

Academy, 14*th December* 1878.—" The author, after alluding to the revival of the Chinese power as shown in the suppression of the Tae Ping and the Panthay movements, describes with some of the enthusiasm of sympathy the westward advance, steady and resistless, of the great army, disciplined and armed on the latest European model, halting at times to sow and reap the corn needed for its future supplies, and encountering with equal skill and determination the vast distances and other difficulties of the march, and the resistance of the enemy. Mr. Boulger has a high opinion of the administrative skill of the Chinese, and its advantages to the people under their sway. Their administration of Kashgar was certainly, to all appearance, a remarkable instance of liberal treatment of an alien race and creed."

Mayfair, 26*th November* 1878.—" The work of Mr. Boulger forms a complete and interesting volume, which ought to find an honoured place on the shelves of the library of everybody interested in Eastern politics. The situation is therefore much strained, and, to quote from Mr. Boulger, 'there looms in the near distance the prospect of an Anglo-Chinese alliance that must be most beneficial to the peoples of Asia generally.'"

Graphic, 23*rd November* 1878.—" Under the title of 'Yakoob Beg of Kashgar,' Mr. D. C. Boulger tells at much length the story of a man who, more than any celebrity of our time, might have been characterised as a hero born too late. But Mr. Boulger's chief object in this volume is not so much to define the Atalik Ghazi's true place in history, while bringing together all that is known of his career, as to call attention to that third factor in the Central Asian Question, which most of us have hitherto overlooked—the power of China and the Chinese."

Vanity Fair, 16*th November* 1878.—" Most educated Englishmen have heard of Yakoob Beg, but few have any distinct knowledge of his career. For a few years, however, he played a very important part in Central Asian history, and incidentally brought about a state of affairs which may end in a desperate war between China and Russia. Mr. Boulger's book is, therefore, very acceptable."

Allen's Indian Mail, 18th November 1878.—"This would have been a good book at any time, and, perhaps, would have been more valuable if it had been published earlier. It probably tells us as much as (out of Russia) is known about a very important and mysterious country; and in Eastern history and Eastern geography England's backwardness is Russia's opportunity. Mr. Boulger has the rare merit of taking an unexaggerated view of his hero, and he does not, because he thinks him worthy of a biography, think it also necessary to add a single inch to his natural dimensions."

Civil Service Gazette, 4th January 1879.—"In thus briefly noticing the scope of Mr. Boulger's book, we have no hesitation in commending it to our readers, no less for its unaffected style than its solid matter. It is a volume every page of which is replete with information interesting to all, but particularly valuable to Her Majesty's Ministers and Statesmen, to whom the preservation of our Indian Empire is a vital concern."

The London and China Telegraph, 18th November 1878.—"As this evidence of might was caused by the war with Yakoob Beg, a biography of that chief, from his rise to his fall, is replete with interest to the English reader, especially as the work of Mr. Boulger contains a complete account of the campaign which ended so gloriously for the Chinese arms."

Homeward Mail, 18th November 1878.—"Nothing could be more opportune than a book giving precise and accurate information on the history of Central Asian affairs during the present century. Mr. Boulger does this with unusual clearness, and shows, by the excellent arrangement of his material and the care with which each fact is produced, that he possesses a clear and well-ordered mind, and that sound argument leads him to definite conclusions. And the main conclusion at which he arrives is simple, and seems amply warranted by the facts. It is this—that China is a really strong and active Central Asian power, fully determined and well able to maintain her interests in the regions now exciting so much interest, and that in the future she must be taken into account in any settlement or unsettlement of existing affairs."

Edinburgh Scotsman, 16th November 1878.—"The book may be heartily recommended as giving an intelligent, interesting, and carefully written description, drawn from the best sources, of an interesting people and a remarkable career."

Edinburgh Courant, 6th January 1879.—"To anyone wishing to make himself conversant with the pros and cons of the question of the Russian occupation of Kuldja, as at present existing between that nation and China, and the extreme importance which it bears upon the probability or otherwise of Russia taking the field against us in aid of Shere Ali, we would recommend the careful perusal of the last chapter of this work. That he has been successful in exciting the admiration of his readers for the hero there can be no doubt; and if he has done anything to increase our respect for the Chinese as a people earnest and implacable, but as a race to establish cordial relations with whom the highest arts of diplomacy will be required, his book will not have been written in vain."

The Week, 21st December 1878.—"Of Mr. Boulger's labours we would speak respectfully. He has spared no pains to make his work complete, exact, and readable."

The Times of India, 20th January 1879.—"'The Life of Yakoob Beg,' late Ameer of Kashgar, is an important addition to our knowledge of a trans-frontier State, till recently a *terra incognita*. Mr. Boulger's work, moreover, has appeared most opportunely; for at no previous period of the history of British India is information regarding the bulwarks of the Indian Empire likely to excite an equal amount of attention in England. We commend this work to all readers who take an interest in the foreign policy of the Government of India."

www.ingramcontent.com/pod-product-compliance
Lightning Source LLC
Chambersburg PA
CBHW030744250426
43672CB00028B/390